P.G. WODEHOUSE:
A PORTRAIT OF A MASTER

BY THE SAME AUTHOR

A BIBLIOGRAPHY AND READER'S GUIDE TO THE FIRST
EDITIONS OF P. G. WODEHOUSE
RECORDED RAGTIME, *1897–1958*

DAVID A. JASEN

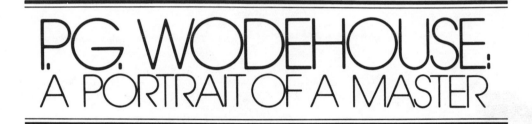

P.G. WODEHOUSE:
A PORTRAIT OF A MASTER

Mason & Lipscomb PUBLISHERS   NEW YORK

ISBN: 0–88405–010–6

Library of Congress Catalog Card Number: 73–84879

Printed in the United States of America

First Printing

Library of Congress Cataloging in Publication Data

Jasen, David A
   P. G. Wodehouse: a portrait of a master.

   Bibliography: p.
   1. Wodehouse, Pelham Grenville, 1881–   —
Biography.
PR6045.O53Z72   823'.9'12[B]   73–84879
ISBN 0–88405–010–6

To my mother and father
Gertrude and Barnet Jasen
with loving gratitude

Contents

List Of Illustrations

The following will be found between pages 74 and 75.

Wodehouse at 21

His parents' wedding picture

Eleanor Wodehouse
Ernest Wodehouse

"Plum" Wodehouse, his mother and brothers

Armine, Peveril and Plum Wodehouse

Plum at age 7

Plum, Armine and Peveril in 1895

Plum at Dulwich, 1898

Cricket team at Dulwich

His first *Saturday Evening Post* appearance

Cover for *Sitting Pretty* score

February 1902 cover of *The Captain*

September 1902 cover of *Punch*

July 1905 cover of *The Strand Magazine*

Title page of *The Pothunters*

Period jackets from Wodehouse's famous books

First to the latest of the Jeeves novels

Wodehouse family group, early twenties

The following will be found between pages 202 and 203.

David Low's caricature of Wodehouse

Party group at Denis Mackail's

Plum at wheel of Ian Hay's car

Ed Wynn, Ethel and P. G. Wodehouse

Lyrics jackets from his great musicals

Ian Hay and Plum

Princess Theatre

Morris Gest, Plum, Guy Bolton, Ray Comstock and Jerome Kern

Saturday Evening Post cover for the World's Fair

Cover for *Redbook's* all star issue, July 1935

Plum and Ethel Wodehouse with E. Phillips and Elsie Oppenheim

Plum and daughter Leonora

Sir Herbert Grierson and Plum at Oxford, 1939

Wodehouse and David Jasen

Preface

P. G. Wodehouse is the funniest writer in the world. Because his prolific writings have spanned nearly three-quarters of this century, and endured the changing scenes of two continents, he is the foremost humorist of the twentieth century.

He is a humorist who has built up a huge following by the use of repetition. It is always a delight to welcome an old friend, for old friends recall happily shared experiences, and this is the sense of intimacy gotten when reading the works of Wodehouse. He took pieces of his childhood, blended with snatches of the quickly altering world of the Edwardians and the early Georgians, and added his own abundantly creative imagination. His plots fit his people, who are consistent not with reality but with themselves and the world of his conception. He attempted to be realistic only in this way and achieved a timelessness in his world which makes his writings universally appealing. His humor depends mainly on exaggeration and understatement, the incongruous, the inappropriate phrase, and the use of the literal interpretation of an idiomatic expression out of context for effect. He developed a new vocabulary, mixing slang along with classical phrases, and fashioning supremely inventive as well as highly diverting hyperboles. He is extremely serious about his work and took tremendous trouble with its construction. He polished his sentences as meticulously as one of his Drones would choose a tie. His only object in writing was purely and simply to amuse.

Wodehouse is a creature of habits and actions peculiar to himself. While he wrote of gregarious people he preferred seclusion. A highly gifted man who is made of hard work and simple tastes, his occupation is work and his hobby is work, a highly convenient and profitable combination. His greatest interest is the phenomena of life and he wrote amusing stories about such phenomena. He is quick to laugh at something funny and delights in reading works by other humorous authors. Because he keeps a large file of clippings from the New York and London daily papers to which he subscribes, he is not only well informed of current events and the intellectual and social movements, but he is also sharply aware of the latest fads and fancies which continue to stimulate his inventive mind. If he was told a story, an incident, or an anecdote, he would give it form and substance in his own inimitable style. However, he rarely tells anecdotes except when he is being interviewed by the press. Like W. W. Jacobs, but unlike two other cricket enthusiasts and fellow humorists (Sir James M. Barrie and A. A. Milne), he is brilliantly funny only on paper.

Wodehouse is a detached spectator who has preferred to observe and write about the life around him rather than to participate in it. He is a great evader of life's problems, shoving all unpleasantness aside and refusing to dwell on it.

The British reserve is nowhere more apparent than in the personality of Mr. Wodehouse, who hides behind the humor so typical of his characters. To conceal his embarrassment and shyness, he withdraws behind this facade, not only to protect himself but to avoid disappointing people. Upon being interviewed, he actually directs the interview, anticipating questions, and telling amusing stories about himself and his wife which are calculated to leave the interviewer, and consequently his readers, with the impression that Wodehouse is his own Bertie Wooster. He likes to be agreeable to everyone and he found that this "Bertie" pose pleased his audience. So the world only knows him as he wishes to be known.

However, what is apparent to all readers is that P. G. Wodehouse is truly kindhearted. This, reflected in his writings as well, is the underlying reason he has remained a constant favorite throughout the world.

David A. Jasen

ACKNOWLEDGMENTS

This book could not have been written without the friendship and active cooperation of Ethel and P. G. Wodehouse who have exhaustively reminisced during extended conversations and supplied valuable diaries, letters, photographs, and assorted memorabilia. The generosity and enthusiastic cooperation of his relatives, friends and admirers, and those having business dealings with Mr. Wodehouse, demonstrate the esteem, respect and affection in which he is held.

Among his relatives, I most heartily thank Helen Wodehouse, Sheran Cazalet, Thelma Cazalet-Keir, Joyce and Patrick Armine Wodehouse, Edward Cazalet, and the late Peter Cazalet.

The following of his loyal friends and admirers graciously submitted to interviews and offered correspondence and pertinent documentation: Guy Bolton, the late Denis Mackail and William Townend, Malcolm Muggeridge, the late George Middleton and McCulloch Christison, R. J. B. Denby, David Magee, and Richard Osborne.

His past and present business associates cooperated fully with unfailing courtesy in rounding out the productive aspects of his professional life: J. D. Grimsdick of Herbert Jenkins Ltd., Peter Schwed of Simon and Schuster, Oliver Swan of Paul R. Reynolds Literary Agency, Henry Morrison then of Scott Meredith Literary Agency, W. P. Watt of A. P. Watt & Son Literary Agency, Bernard Hollowood of *Punch,* and Doubleday and Company.

It is especially pleasing to give thanks to close friends who unselfishly gave of their time and energy to help make this a better book: Lionel Leventhal, Irving Farren, Ellen and Tony Palumbo, Lee Townshend, and Dr. Jack Yocum.

Additional thanks are due Irving Farren for making me so readable by his superb handling of this material as editor.

"He wished to enjoy his mind. He was not given to self-analysis. He would think out his plans, but the originating cause of all his plans had little interest for him. He lived his life by deep impulses into which he never enquired. He rather despised the individuals who were always worrying themselves. His attitude was God's: I am that I am. To wonder why he was what he was hardly occurred to him. And whither he was going did not trouble him more than whence he had come. He constructed no chart, wrote out no annual balance-sheet. He merely knew, felt, that he had work to do and that he was doing it pretty well and was thereby kept continually busy."

Imperial Palace, Arnold Bennett

"I don't have a set of rules guiding me. I just go on living. You don't notice things when you're writing. Just writing one book after another, that's my life."

P. G. Wodehouse

P.G. WODEHOUSE:
A PORTRAIT OF A MASTER

1
1881–1894

Pelham Grenville Wodehouse is not a name that translates easily into Chinese. Indeed, had the Hong Kong newspapers wished to announce to the native population the birth of a baby bearing that name they would have been hard put to it to select appropriate characters from among the several thousand that constitute the language. As it turned out, however, the necessity was avoided by the providential absence from Hong Kong of Mrs. Ernest Wodehouse at more or less the crucial time: "more or less" because the baby, perhaps with some prenatal sympathy for the lot of Chinese newspaper editors, arrived prematurely.

Mrs. Wodehouse had returned to England and was visiting a sister at One Vale Place, Epsom Road, Guildford, Surrey, when she rather unexpectedly gave birth to her third son, Pelham Grenville, on 15th October 1881. The address was typically, unequivocally English—a suitable birthplace, though none could have known it then, for the man who was destined to become the foremost exponent of English humour. Nevertheless, it was in Hong Kong that the child was to spend his infancy when he was taken there to be introduced to his father.

Henry Ernest Wodehouse, who was always known as Ernest, had completed his education at Repton in Derbyshire and then gravitated to Hong Kong by way of the Civil Service in 1867. It was a time when many eager and ambitious young men were turning their eyes to the Colonies, where adventure and opportunity beckoned; and Ernest was no less ready than the next to serve his country in one of its far-flung outposts. That his expectations were realised is evidenced by the fact that he became a magistrate and, in due course, a husband and a father.

There was certainly no shortage of eligible young ladies from among whom the Empire-builders could choose a mate. Many an astute beauty had come to the conclusion that there was little point in dropping a handkerchief or having difficulty with a parasol on some dewy green English lawn when the cream of the young gallants was far removed from the scene. Consequently, handkerchiefs and parasols were hastily packed and shipped off with their owners in the wake of the young men. And perhaps it was thus that

Eleanor Deane, daughter of the Reverend Deane of Bath, came to be in Hong Kong. What is certain is that on 3rd February 1877 she became Mrs. Ernest Wodehouse.

It could be said that Eleanor had done well for herself. Her Mr. Wodehouse had claim to a noble heritage, linked through the unusual spelling of the name—which was pronounced Woodhouse—with the Wodehouses of Norfolk. The family could be traced back as far as Bertram de Wodehouse, a Norfolk knight who had fought with distinction under Edward I in his war against the Scots from 1277 to 1283; and there was a line of direct descent from Lady Mary Boleyn, sister of the ill-fated Anne (from whom the family may well have learned that it was best not to lose one's head in an emergency). A baronetcy was established on 29th June 1611, and an earldom was created in 1866 with the Earl of Kimberley as the head of the family.

The history of the Wodehouse family as it pertains to its most illustrious member, however, commences with Colonel Philip Wodehouse, who was born on 6th August 1788. At the age of twenty-seven, Philip saw active service at the historic battle of Waterloo; and he survived the experience to marry—rather late in life, on 13th June 1832—a Birmingham heiress named Lydia Lee. The union was blessed with five sons, the youngest of whom was born on 14th July 1845 and christened Henry Ernest. Within a year and a half of this addition to the family, on 15th December 1846, Colonel Wodehouse died and his widow took her five children to live at Ham Hill, in Powick, a few miles from Worcester. It was here that Ernest grew up.

What Eleanor Deane's family may have lacked in distinctive lineage in the Wodehouse tradition it more than made up for in size, for Eleanor was the tenth of thirteen children—four boys and nine girls. Her father, John Bathurst Deane, had been educated at Merchant Taylors' School and then found himself in a sort of limbo. Neither he nor his parents could think of an occupation to which he would be suited. It therefore seemed almost inevitable that he should follow in the path of so many like him—well educated but with no special talents—and go into the Church. This accomplished, he married and bought a house, Chyne Court, in Bath, there to propagate the species with remarkable diligence. As a gift, and perhaps as an attempt to direct his energies in other directions, his parents bought him the parish of St. Helen's, Bishopsgate, in London. But he continued to live in Bath and hired a curate to take charge of St. Helen's, which he visited only once a month in order to give a sermon.

Throughout his life, the Reverend Deane drew a stipend of £1000 a year from his parish, despite the fact that during his last fifteen years he was blind and never went near the place.

Of the many Deane children the oldest was Louisa, who practically brought up the rest of them. She was to become one of the young Pelham Grenville's favourite aunts, and would later be the blueprint for Bertie Wooster's kind-hearted Aunt Dahlia. One of her sisters, Mary, was also destined to be the basis for a fictional aunt—but not quite so happily. A professional writer, Mary was something of a tyrant; and her demeanour made an indelible impression on her young nephew that was to manifest itself in Bertie Wooster's unsympathetic Aunt Agatha. The youngest of the Deane girls, Emmaline (affectionately known as Nim), was especially close to her nephew not only in age but also in understanding, for she was a trained artist of no mean ability. Her painting of Cardinal Newman, who was a relative, hangs in the National Portrait Gallery in London.

Eleanor, although self-taught, was also a talented artist. Her excellent water-colours and miniatures were so highly thought of that, in 1885, Sir Isaac Pitman commissioned her to paint his portrait in miniature. All went well until, towards the completion of the work, Sir Isaac started to make what were interpreted as improper advances. This so affronted Eleanor that she refused to give him the finished portrait.

Perhaps it was this artistic streak that influenced Eleanor when it came to naming her children, for she had no taste for the mundane. If Shakespeare's rhetorical "What's in a name?" had been posed to her, she would doubtless have given a quite different answer from the one the Bard provided himself. She might have conceded that a rose by any other name would smell as sweet; but as to whether Juliet would, were she not Juliet called, retain that dear perfection, etc., would have been another matter. A name is something one has to live with, live down, or live up to; and many a parent must have woken suddenly in the dead of night and wondered, in a cold sweat, whether "Marmaduke" or "Clothilda" had in fact been such a good idea. It is certainly open to doubt whether Juliet would have been quite the girl for whom Romeo conceived such a passion had she been named, say, Maud. Events might well have taken an entirely different course; and the world may have had no reason for holding in cherished memory the story of Romeo and Maud. A once-popular American song called *Mr. Franklin D. Roosevelt Jones* contained the line "With that handle how can he go wrong?"—and one cannot help feeling that it was this sentiment, if not expressed in exactly those words, rather than Shakespeare's, that prompted Mrs. Wodehouse. Her children were going to have names to live up to.

The first of Eleanor and Ernest's four sons arrived somewhat ahead of schedule, on 26th September 1877. He was the first English child to be born on the Peak in Hong Kong, and there was a connotation here that could not escape the romantically-minded Eleanor when it came to naming him: Sir Walter Scott's "Peveril of the Peak." So the baby was called Philip Peveril and, not unexpectedly, was thereafter known as Peveril.

For her second son, born in England on 11th May 1879, Eleanor chose the names Ernest Armine—Ernest after his father, and Armine because it was an unusual name that had recurred throughout Wodehouse family history. Naturally, it was the commonplace "Ernest" that was overlooked in favour of "Armine" for popular usage.

The third son's name came ready-made, unusual enough in itself to satisfy even the exacting Eleanor: Pelham Grenville. It was the name of the baby's god-father, Colonel Pelham Grenville von Donop; and one hesitates to suggest that he might have been chosen as godfather for that reason rather than for his popularity in Hong Kong society. As it transpired, however, neither "Pelham" nor "Grenville" was to be heard resounding through the Wodehouse corridors. Almost from the start, the name Pelham was contracted to Plum—and it was as Plum that this particular Wodehouse was to be known to family and friends for ever more.

It was to be eleven years after the coming of Plum that the fourth son was born, on 30th May 1892 in Hong Kong, and perhaps by then inspiration had mellowed: or maybe Eleanor felt that she had reached her zenith with Pelham Grenville and simply could not cap it. Be that as it may, and possibly as a compensatory gesture, the newcomer was given three names—Richard Lancelot Deane. The gap of years that separated him from his brothers may have had something to do with the fact that he was known as Dick.

There was to be no normal family life for the Wodehouse children—surprisingly, perhaps, in view of the extraordinarily large family from which Eleanor came. But both she and Ernest wanted their boys to have a good education and proper English upbringing and were clearly prepared to make the sacrifice of leaving the children in England in order to accomplish this. It meant that parents and children would see each other only once every six or seven years, when Ernest and Eleanor returned on a home-leave from Hong Kong;

and not unnaturally, the boys felt almost like orphans during their all-important formative years. In speaking of these days, Plum has said, "We looked upon mother more like an aunt. She came home very infrequently." For the most part it was boarding-schools, punctuated by holidays during which the youngsters were shunted from relative to relative—never feeling that they really belonged or were wanted; never experiencing the warmth of a home and family of their own.

This way of life began for Plum when he was little more than two years old, after his brief stay in Hong Kong. Eleanor rented a house in Bath, deposited her three sons in it in the charge of a Miss Roper, and went back to Hong Kong. Of Miss Roper—who was apparently not disposed to make use of whatever Christian name or names she owned—Plum has recalled that she was very severe in her manner, making the boys dress formally every day and keeping them spotlessly clean. Her shining hour, as far as he was concerned, was when she saved him from receiving what would have been a particularly vicious clout on the head from his brother Armine, who was then going through a phase of resenting the smallest Wodehouse to the point of near-annihilation. Later, Armine was to become Plum's favourite brother and close friend—both of them being artistic and appreciating and understanding each other's individual dream-world.

In 1886 the Wodehouse parents came to England, when Ernest was made by Queen Victoria a Companion of St. Michael and St. George for his excellent planning and execution of the Chinese section of the Great Exposition. During this visit, it was decided that the three boys should be sent to a Dame school at Croydon, Surrey, where some young cousins had previously received tuition. The school was run by two unmarried sisters, Florrie and Cissie Prince, who lived on the premises with their father. Mr. Prince was apparently "something in the City," for he took himself off to London every day, leaving his daughters to manage their own affairs. There were already two other resident pupils at the school—the brothers Atkinson, whose parents were in India.

Plum remembered feeling very crowded there in a house that seemed small: but surely never as crowded or small as on the day that he and Armine crept into the forbidden drawing room to play. Before they had had time to savour the joys of being "out of bounds," there came the sound of approaching voices and they were forced to seek a hiding place. With one accord, they dived beneath the large plush sofa which dominated the room . . . and only just in time. For into the room came Mr. Scott, a teacher whose voice was unmistakable, in the company of one of the Prince sisters. Inevitably, the pair chose to sit on the sofa—which sagged appreciably under their combined weight and threatened to permanently impress the two small Wodehouses into the flowered carpet beneath them. But the boys stoically accepted what appeared to be their impending doom and remained unmoving, if not entirely unmoved, during what turned out to be a proposal of marriage. It took Mr. Scott, who chose his words carefully, a considerable time to ask whichever Miss Prince it was for her hand; but she, fortunately, was not one to dally over such things and was reasonably prompt in giving him an answer in the affirmative. She then bore him quickly away, perhaps to break the good news to the other Miss Prince before her swain could have second thoughts, and the Wodehouse brothers were able to squirm shakily from beneath the sofa. They were now not disposed to linger in the drawing room, having suddenly lost all desire to play.

The Prince sisters were very religious and inclined to be strict, but Plum recalled that they were always kind to him. He also remembered the ceremony of the daily egg. The system was that each boy was given one boiled egg a week: but each day, the boy whose turn it was to have an egg had to pass it round and share it with the other four. Another golden rule concerned the boys' weekly pocket-money of threepence a head. With this they had to buy a bag of biscuits which, on their walk through Croydon, they had to present to the road-crossing sweeper. The Misses Prince considered that this would show the local people that their pupils were little gentlemen. As a consequence, the little gentlemen—who were frequently hungry—were unable to buy the cakes and sweets that other boys of their age were wont to gorge themselves on. And that was not the only childhood delight of which the children were deprived. Perhaps because Florrie and Cissie were so righteous that they couldn't bring themselves to tell even a white lie, or maybe because they did not believe in hoodwinking youngsters, there was never any mention of Santa Claus in the Prince household. When it came to Christmas presents, there were no illusions about a white-bearded old gentleman in a red cloak, reindeers, or the descent of chimneys. Gifts were to be found in a pillowcase at the foot of each bed, but the boys knew precisely who had put them there.

Plum had other memories of his stay with the Prince family. "Croydon in those days," he recollected, "was almost in the country, and I remember getting into bad trouble for stealing a turnip out of a field. It was looked on as a major crime. Probably that is what has given me the respect for the law which I have always had. I suppose it was a good bringing up, but it certainly did not tend to make one adventurous. I can't remember having done any other naughty thing the whole of the three years I was there. One other thing I remember is how fond I was of the various maids who went through the Prince home. It may have given me my liking for the domestic-servant class."

Despite the fact that by now he and Armine were on the friendliest of terms and that one of the Atkinson brothers, Hughie, had become his bosom pal, Plum preferred to spend much of his time by himself. In his self-imposed solitude he would amuse himself by making up stories which, as soon as he could write, he started to put down on paper. The first was written in 1888, when he was seven years old:

> *About five years ago in a wood*
> *there was a Thrush. who built her nest*
> *in a Poplar tree. and sang so beautifully*
> *that all the worms came up from their*
> *holes and the ants laid down their burd-*
> *ens. and the crickets stopped their mirth.*
> *and moths settled all in a row to hear*
> *her. she sang a song as if she were in*
> *heaven—going up higher and higher*
> *as she sang.*
>
> > *at last the song was done and the*
> *bird came down panting.*
>
> > *Thank you said all the creatures.*
> *Now my story is ended.*
> > > *Pelham G. Wodehouse*

This could be called Plum's "serious" period. The funny stuff was yet to come.

For two weeks every summer the three Wodehouse boys would go to stay at Grandmother Wodehouse's home in Powick. To Plum "it was always the great event of the year." The house, called Ham Hill, stood on a hill overlooking the river Teme, and in its grounds a battle had been fought between the Cavaliers and Roundheads during the Civil War. Plum found these grounds enchanting. "We were left very much to ourselves at Ham Hill," he recalled. "Once a day we were taken in to see our grandmother—a wizened old lady who looked just like a monkey and gave us a kindly audience for about ten minutes. Incidentally, I have always felt how lucky I was not to have been born earlier, as I missed the period during which parents beat their sons unmercifully. My father told me that when he was a boy this kindly grandmother used to whale the tar out of him. . . ." Age had obviously mellowed the old lady; but she was not the only one to give temporary shelter to the boys. "I also spent some of my holidays with Uncle Philip down at Bratton Fleming in Devonshire. You know, they sort of shoved us off on to various uncles for the holidays. I never knew any of them at all. But we were very happy and I had a very happy childhood."

The brothers had been at Croydon for three years when Peveril developed a weak chest. According to Plum, "The best place for a weak chest was supposed to be the Channel Islands, so we were all shipped off to Guernsey. Why Armine and I had to go too I can't imagine, but my parents seemed to like these package deals."

Elizabeth College, Guernsey, was a very small public school catering to no more than one hundred boys. The only place to board was at the headmaster's house, and it was there that the Wodehouse brothers took up residence. As far as Plum was concerned, "Guernsey in those days was a delightful place full of lovely bays; and as far as I can remember, our movements were never restricted and we were allowed to roam where we liked. My recollections are all of wandering about the island and of the awful steamer trips back to England for the holidays. Paddle-wheel steamers, like on the Mississippi—very small and rolling with every wave. It was hell to go back for the holidays at the end of the winter term. . . . We would spend our holidays with various aunts, some of whom I liked but one or two of whom were very formidable Victorian women."

After two years at Elizabeth College, where "life was very pleasant," Plum was designated by his father for a career in the Navy. He was to continue his education at Malvern House, a Navy preparatory school in Kearnsey, Kent, near Dover. This meant that the three brothers would be separated for the first time—Peveril remaining at Elizabeth College on account of his chest, and Armine transferring to Dulwich College in southeast London. Not that scholastic considerations had much to do with the plans for Armine. On one of his rare trips to England, Ernest had happened to pass through the suburb of Dulwich on a train and had been fascinated by the beautifully kept grounds in which the college stood. Armine's removal to those sixty well-tended acres was the logical outcome.

There was a less aesthetic reason for sending Plum to Malvern House. Ernest had allowed himself to be persuaded to do this by Aunt Edith, whose husband, Uncle Gussie, had been in the Navy and now lived in retirement in Dover. As it turned out, however, Malvern House was not a good choice for Plum. All else apart, the fact that his eyesight was less than perfect would have prevented him from passing the Naval examination. He was therefore not much taken with his studies and, since there were no organised games for the students, was apt to exercise himself by going off on long solitary walks.

During one vacation period, he visited Armine at Dulwich and fell in love with the place on the spot. The impression it made on him was so strong that he begged his father to let him go there.

"Incidentally," Plum was reminded, "my father was very indulgent to us boys, my mother less so. Having seen practically nothing of her until I was fifteen, I met her as virtually a stranger and it was not easy to establish cordial relations. With my father, on the other hand, I was always on very good terms— though never in any sense very close. In those days, parents tended to live a life apart from their children: or it may be that that was just what happened in our family owing to not having grown up together. Looking back, I can see that I was just passed from hand to hand. It was an odd life with no home to go to, but I have always accepted everything that happens to me in a philosophical spirit; and I can't remember ever having been unhappy in those days. My feeling now is that it was very decent of those aunts to put up three small boys for all those years. We can't have added much entertainment to their lives. The only thing you could say for us is that we never gave any trouble."

By this time in Plum's life there was, of course, a fourth small Wodehouse —Richard Lancelot Deane—about to embark on that self-same round of aunts and uncles. But this could have been of little consequence to the boy who was about to enter a phase which would have a lasting effect not only on his life but also on his writings.

2 1894– 1900

Dulwich College was founded by Edward Alleyn, a friend of William Shakespeare, who had attained such eminence in the acting profession that he had been described as "the Roscius of our age." Already owning several theatres and a beer garden, Alleyn became, by purchase, Lord of the Manor of Dulwich on 3rd October 1605. Building on the property was begun in 1613 and completed in 1616; but the college was not formally opened until 13th September 1619, when it was known as The College of God's Gift in Dulwich. In 1858 it wǎs formed into two schools—the Upper and the Lower; and in 1882 the Upper School was named Dulwich College and the Lower School became Alleyn's School.

Plum was twelve-and-a-half years old when, on 2nd May 1894, he walked through the suburb of Dulwich, crossed the park which divides it—losing himself in admiration of the flowers, greenery and ponds which constitute this quiet retreat—and continued for another half mile to enter the gates of what was to be virtually his home for the next six years. If he did not at once feel overawed by a sense of loneliness in these new surroundings thanks to the knowledge that Armine had been here for two years and was still in residence, he was soon to discover that "At a public school you tend to mix only with those of your own age. Even a couple of years make a difference. Armine and I were always good friends, but we became closer in the holidays. . . ."

It was the start of the summer term when Plum arrived and, with Eleanor and Ernest still in Hong Kong, arrangements had been made for him to live with H. V. Doulton, an assistant master at the college whose home was in East Dulwich. Plum derived small comfort from the thought that this was where Armine had first boarded upon his entry to Dulwich College. He felt certain that as an optional extra to the household he would make a poor showing in comparison with his brother. For Armine, though not excelling in athletics, was a very talented pianist who was also possessed of all the social graces. Plum, on the other hand, had great enthusiasm for sports, but was in every other way exceedingly and embarrassingly shy. To make matters worse, Armine and Doulton had apparently hit it off splendidly with each other, whereas Plum found himself ill at ease in Doulton's presence. It was simply a matter of personal idiosyncrasy. As Plum has said in talking of Armine, "There was never any feeling of rivalry between us."

The agony was not to endure for too long, however. Plum remained a day-boy in residence with Doulton only until the beginning of the autumn term, at which time he became a boarder at Ivyholme, one of the school houses.

Boarders at Dulwich College were in the minority, the school in this respect differing from almost all other English public schools. But this was because most of the pupils lived in or near the London area and could easily commute to Dulwich—a situation which robbed the school of some of its glamour and led it to be considered less exalted than places of learning further removed from the metropolis. Raymond Chandler, who was a pupil there at the same time as Plum, said of it in his reminiscences: "I was educated at Dulwich College, an English public school not quite on the level of Eton and Harrow from a social point of view but very good educationally."

Plum's version is: "It was what you would call a middle-class school. We were all the sons of reasonably solvent but certainly not wealthy parents, and we all had to earn our living later on. Compared with Eton, Dulwich would be something like an American State University compared with Harvard or Princeton. Bertie Wooster's parents would never have sent him to Dulwich, but Ukridge could very well have been there. There were four 'sides' at the school —the Classical, the Modern, the Science and the Engineering. The Classical was by far the largest, although the present headmaster of Dulwich tells me that everybody today goes on the Science side and the Classical side has become very small. Some farseeing parents, knowing that their sons would have to go into business later, put them on the Modern side, where they learned French and German and mathematics; but the average parent chose the Classical, where they learned Latin and Greek, presumably with a vague idea that if all went well they would go to Oxford or Cambridge. In my day, to the ordinary parent, education meant Classics. I went automatically on the Classical side and, as it turned out, it was the best form of education I could have had as a writer. But it certainly was not much help to me when at the end of my school career I joined the Hong Kong and Shanghai Bank, for I was utterly incapable of understanding business."

For one uneventful year Plum stayed at Ivyholme, greatly preferring being a boarder because "it offered much more opportunity for making friendships and generally feeling that one was part of the life of the school." The pattern, however, was about to undergo a temporary change.

Shortly before the end of the spring term of 1895, Plum found himself very much in the bosom of a family he'd almost forgotten he had. It came about as a result of Ernest's participating in a walking race in Hong Kong on a blazingly hot day and contracting sunstroke so severely that he had to be prematurely retired from overseas service. Given a pension, he returned to England with Eleanor and baby Dick and took a house in Dulwich in order to be near Armine and Plum. And so Plum became a day-boy again, living in the first real home he had ever known and trying to get acquainted with his parents and youngest brother.

It must have been a peculiar experience for all concerned—except, possibly, baby Dick—but certainly not least for the parents. Here were Eleanor and Ernest, somewhat late in the day, having to play the part of full-time parents to a couple of youngsters who were already set in the ways in which their personalities and characters would develop; and the boys, of course, with little practical experience to go on, had to acclimatise themselves to family life. But on the whole, it worked well enough—although Plum found no reason to amend his earlier impressions of his mother with regard to her forbidding appearance and general strictness. His father, however, more than made up for that.

If Ernest was considered a man to look up to, it was not merely because he was over six feet tall. With eyes of an extraordinary blue and a great sense of humour, he dispensed a natural charm that was disarming. And Plum had inherited much from him. Keeping physically fit was of vast importance to Ernest, and he encouraged the boys towards an athletic life—not that Plum needed any urging—by rewarding them financially for every success in any of the sports. He was also a golf addict, and he delighted in taking long walks—a passion which Plum had always had.

But what impressed Plum most profoundly during this period was the loyalty and devotion that existed between his parents. It was apt to show itself in many ways, some of them amusing; but it was there for all to see, and Plum saw and approved. There was the matter of Eleanor's birthday, for instance. Ernest, it transpired, was ever at a loss to know what to buy for his wife to celebrate such an occasion. It had therefore become obligatory for Eleanor to let her wishes be known in the form of strong hints for several weeks before the event; and at this particular time she was making frequent reference to a pair of shoes she had seen in a local shop window. Ernest got the message, of course, but was daunted by the thought of actually having to make the purchase. He had become proficient in the acquisition of chocolates, perfumes and the like; but shoes were an unexpected departure for which he was totally unprepared. Finally, in desperation as the day approached, he gave Eleanor the money to buy them herself. Not at all put out, she did just that on the eve of her birthday, returned home, wrapped the shoes in gift paper and handed the package to Ernest. He, without a word, took it up to their bedroom and carefully hid it. On the following morning, after Eleanor had eaten her birthday breakfast in bed, Ernest presented her with the gift. In an excess of pleasure and curiosity, Eleanor couldn't wait to push aside the breakfast tray and unwrap the package. Her joy at disclosing the shoes she had so much wanted and then discovering that the fit was perfect was unbounded. And Ernest was naturally gratified that he had chosen such a lovely surprise.

This interesting insight that Plum was given into family life was to be of relatively short duration. Towards the end of the school year, Eleanor and Ernest began to think of moving away from Dulwich. Perhaps they felt that they had had their fling at parenthood and, while it was jolly nice, there was no point in overdoing the thing. Or they may simply have felt the need for, as they put it, a nice quiet home in the country. But whatever the motivating factor, the search was on.

Among the many places they visited was Stableford in Shropshire, where they looked over a number of houses. At the last one on their list, Ernest disappeared after a peremptory look and left Eleanor to continue her detailed inspection of the property. By the time he returned to collect her for their homeward journey, Eleanor had come to the conclusion that this was the least desirable of all the houses they had visited.

"Thank goodness we've seen the last of that house," she said to Ernest as they walked away from it.

Ernest stopped in his tracks, and he may have paled a fraction. "Oh, no!" he responded. "I've just taken a lease on it for six years. . . ."

One hesitates to imagine how much more than normally forbidding Eleanor's aspect must have become at this pronouncement. Loyalty and devotion could rarely have been put to such a severe test. That they did indeed triumph was to be all to the eventual good: for it was here at Stableford that Plum's love affair with the Shropshire countryside was to begin. And it was here, too, that he was to cultivate his love of animals with the family's first pet dog—a mongrel named Bob (no hint of Eleanor's fine imagination in that christening). During the remaining summer holidays of his school life, Plum was to happily absorb the atmosphere of Shropshire; and he would never be without a few dogs or cats to his credit.

With the family established at Stableford, he became a school boarder again. This time—from the commencement of the autumn term of 1896— he stayed at Elm Lawn, whose housemaster was T. G. Treadgold. It was Treadgold's custom to give a beginning-of-term supper to his older pupils and prefects, and Plum was of an age to be among those present. Not noted for his scintillating wit or conversational prowess at social gatherings, the usually retiring Plum nevertheless felt it incumbent upon himself to contribute something to the general convivial chit-chat, and he gave the matter considerable thought as the babble of young voices filled the room. What could he possibly say that would seem apposite in these surroundings? And then it came to him in a blinding flash. It had been common knowledge throughout the school that during the last term a penetrating and unpleasant odour had been known to pervade Elm Lawn due to faulty drains. True, there was no actual evidence of it at this moment; and no one had made any reference to it. But that was just the point. Surely some tasteful allusion would not only be topical but would also indicate that young Wodehouse was of a more sensitive nature than the thickheaded clods who were chattering noisily of trivialities. His moment came when there was one of those lulls that occur during even the most animated of get-togethers. In the brief near-silence, he addressed himself to his new house-master with unaccustomed clarity: "Isn't there rather a peculiar smell, sir?"

Treadgold's reaction was, to say the least, unexpected. Turning on Plum with a sour look, he said tightly, "Get out of my sight, Wodehouse!" He didn't bother to explain what was apparently common knowledge to all the others —that during the holidays he had spent £200 on having the plumbing repaired and that the air around Elm Lawn was now as sweet as anywhere within the college precincts.

This abortive attempt to establish himself as a social asset without whom no party would be complete did not blight Plum's scholastic career. Indeed, he was about to embark on a period of intensive studying and cramming in order to try for a scholarship to Oxford in 1897. Four such scholarships, or Exhibitions, were given each year to promising Junior and Senior Fellows. Plum's tutor for this specialised period was the same Mr. Doulton with whom he had boarded on first arriving at Dulwich, and their combined efforts were rewarded when it was announced that Plum had been awarded a scholarship for that year. But hopes of further education at Oxford were not to be fulfilled.

The fact that Armine had already won a similar scholarship and was due to go to Oxford on the completion of his education at Dulwich should have made Plum's success the source of double rejoicing: but in fact it presented the family with an impasse. Ernest's retirement pension, in the region of £900 a year, was at that time adequate for a comfortable but not extravagant way of life. The grants that went with the scholarships won by the boys would not be sufficiently large to enable them to attend Oxford without substantial additional financial aid from him, and he simply could not afford to support both of them. Inevitably, as the younger of the two, it was Plum who had to forego his opportunity. It was decided that when he left Dulwich he would have to enter the world of commerce.

Consequently, and as might have been expected, Plum's academic endeavours began to slacken. Studying seemed pointless when there was no goal to be achieved. Instead, he preferred to spend his time reading for pleasure and writing a series of verses parodying Greek tragedies, in which he substituted friends and teachers for the citizens of Athens. He also wrote for the school magazine, *The Alleynian,* and became even more active in boxing, cricket and Rugby football. His worsening eyesight, however, eventually forced him to give up boxing entirely, and also began to bother him on the cricket field.

Talking of this period when sports were supreme, Plum explained, "We were a great all-round school in those days. In my last year, the captain of football and three of the team got university scholarships, and another member passed into Sandhurst in the first three. The brainless athlete was quite a rarity. We might commit mayhem on the football field, but after the game was over we trotted off to our houses and wrote Latin verse. . . . Proficiency at cricket and football were rewarded with caps. If you looked promising, you were given your third cap—that is, you became a member of the third cricket eleven or the third Rugby football fifteen. Next year you probably got your second; and the year after that, if the captain saw eye to eye with you about your merits, you played for the school and got your first. I was in the school cricket team two years and in the school football team one. I was a forward—what corresponds to the line in American football—and was very heavy for a school footballer, weighing around a hundred and seventy pounds. At cricket I was a fast bowler—the equivalent of a baseball pitcher. We had a great team my year, not losing a school match."

For the two school years from 1897 to 1899 Plum was in the second Rugby team, failing to get his first cap for the second year solely because Armine was already in the first fifteen and the captain seemed to think that one Wodehouse in the school team was a fair ration. In 1898 he was given his third cap in cricket; and for the year 1899 to 1900, with Armine now at Oxford, he was selected for the first teams in Rugby and cricket and was also appointed one of the five editors of *The Alleynian.*

In his first game with the school Rugby team, a nervous Plum, with the ball under his arm, raced, dodged and fought his way through the opposing side until, in order to score a try, he had nothing to do but run on and put the ball down behind the line. It was simplicity itself; he couldn't fail. And the school was yelling him on in this moment of triumph. But instead of continuing on his unrestricted way, he quite inexplicably decided to take a drop-kick . . . and missed the posts by twenty yards!

Subsequent appearances on the field must have been more promising if less spectacular, for the yearly evaluation of the first Rugby and cricket teams by their captains which appeared in the school records said of Plum:

> Rugby: *A heavy forward. Has improved greatly, but is still inclined to slack in the scrum. Always up to take a pass. Good with his feet. Still too much inclined to tackle high.* Cricket: *A fast right-hand bowler with a good swing, though he does not use his head enough. As a bat he was very much improved and he gets extraordinarily well to the pitch of the ball. Has wonderfully improved in the field, though rather hampered by his sight.*

In direct contrast to his achievements in sports and on the magazine, Plum's academic record for this period is best glossed over. In the Classical Sixth Form exams for the summer term of 1899 he came twenty-fourth, the significance of this being not fully apparent until it is pointed out that there were only twenty-five in the class. But by the summer of the following year— his last at Dulwich—he had improved to the extent of coming thirteenth.

Be that as it may, he was in good company in the Classical Sixth. From among his classmates came Sir Edward J. Harding, who was High Commissioner for the United Kingdom in the Union of South Africa from 1939 to 1941; Sir John T. Sheppard, who was Provost of King's College, Cambridge, from 1933 to 1954; J. R. Darbyshire, who was Archbishop of Capetown from 1938 to 1948; and Sir Hilary Jenkinson, who was Deputy Keeper of Public Records from 1947 to 1954. Sir Ernest Shackleton, the renowned explorer, and writers A. E. W. Mason and C. S. Forester, as well as Raymond Chandler, were also educated at Dulwich.

From the time Plum entered the Classical Sixth in 1898—then under an excellent master, P. Hope—until he left the school at the end of the summer term of 1900, he shared a study with William Townend, who was in the form below him. Townend, who became a writer primarily of sea stories, was the only one of Plum's school friends to remain in continual contact with him, maintaining a correspondence that was to end only with Townend's death in 1962. It was Townend who gave Plum the background for the character Ukridge and for *Love Among the Chickens,* in which Ukridge was introduced. He also shared with Plum the authorship of an adventure story for boys, for which they used a combined pseudonym.

In reply to a query about his schooldays with Plum, Townend wrote:

> *We were together in one of the four boarding houses, Elm Lawn, still standing, with its war damage repaired, and now the residence of the Master of Dulwich, the headmaster. Plum and I shared a study at the back of the house: a small room with a sloping roof; though we preferred to work downstairs in what was known as the Senior Common Room—or Senior Study—which had a large table and was unoccupied during the two hours sacred to prep—preparation—each evening when the boys who were not 'house prefects' had to go over to the Great Hall. We were supposed to prepare our lessons for the next day. I don't remember that Plum ever did. He worked, if he worked at all, supremely fast, writing Latin and Greek verses as rapidly as he wrote English. This is my recollection. But certainly the two hours were not filled entirely with work: we talked incessantly, about books and writing. Plum's talk was exhilarating. I had never known such talk. Even at the age of seventeen he could discuss*

lucidly writers of whom I had never heard. I was impressed by his knowledge. He was an omnivorous reader. Some authors were Barry Pain and James Payn, Rudyard Kipling and W. S. Gilbert. But it is impossible to say who were his favourite authors. He liked so many and all kinds. And from the first time I met him, he had decided to write. He never swerved. It was through Plum that I began to have such an admiration for Kipling.

Plum was an established figure in the school, a noted athlete, a fine footballer and cricketer, a boxer: he was a school prefect, in the Classical Sixth, he had a fine voice and sang at the school concerts, he edited the Alleynian: *he was, in fact, one of the most important boys in the school.*

But although Plum was such a well-known figure in the Dulwich precincts and had a great many acquaintances, he remained detached and objective and was not in the least influenced by anyone. He has himself said that "Dulwich was like an American college in that if you're playing football you mix with the people in the football side, and so on. I was pretty friendly with everybody, but I had no very intimate friends."

Controlling the fortunes of the six hundred boys at Dulwich throughout Plum's attendance was the famous headmaster Arthur Herman Gilkes, whose influence was not to be forgotten. In Plum's own words: "Except for Alec Waugh, I seem to be the only author who enjoyed his schooldays. To me, the years between 1894 and 1900 were like heaven. This may have been because we had one of the recognised great headmasters, A. H. Gilkes, who is looked on today as one of England's greatest educators. I came into actual contact with him only in my last two years, but even at that early age I could see how big he was. He was a man with a long white beard who stood six-foot-six in his socks, and he had one of those deep musical voices. I can still remember how he thrilled me when he read us that bit from Carlyle's *Sartor Resartus* which ends 'But I, mine Wether, am above it all'. It was terrific. But he also always scared the pants off me!"

An incident concerning Plum in Gilkes' classroom is related in Richard Usborne's *Wodehouse at Work:*

> *Wodehouse had a schoolboy habit of decorating or, as masters would say, defacing his form text-books with tiny match-stick human figures, page after page. In the Sixth one day Headmaster Gilkes ... asked Wodehouse to lend him his Euripides. Gilkes handed the book back, saying with a shudder: "No, thank you. This book has got a man in it!" This ... made Wodehouse laugh for about a year.*

At the end of the winter term of 1899, Gilkes wrote his impressions of Plum in a report to Eleanor and Ernest: "He is a most impractical boy ... often forgetful; he finds difficulty in the most simple things and asks absurd questions, whereas he can understand the more difficult things. . . . He has the most distorted ideas about wit and humour; he draws over his books in a most distressing way, and writes foolish rhymes in other people's books. One is obliged to like him in spite of his vagaries." In view of the learned headmaster's evaluation of the Wodehouse wit and humour, one cannot help but wistfully wish for the opportunity to see today those "foolish rhymes."

It was during his last term at Dulwich that Plum began to record payments received for literary work in a diary which was eventually to cover his first seven years as a professional writer. The diary commences with the legend:

Money Received for Literary Work
Motto:
"Though never nurtured in the lap
    of luxury, yet, I admonish you,
I am an intellectual chap,

And think of things that would astonish you."
W. S. Gilbert.

For his first story, published in February 1900, the entry reads: "Won 10/6 for a prize contribution to *Public School Magazine,* then under the editorship of P. G. Witson, afterwards Editor of *Fun.* Subject: 'Some Aspects of Game Captaincy.' Paid April 9, 1900." It was a beginning.

But an ending was also in sight. In July 1900 the summer term came to a close, and with it terminated Plum's education at Dulwich. The rest of the summer was to be spent in leisure at Stableford, perhaps already with nostalgic thoughts along the lines recalled here so very many years later:

"You had a fairly good time at school if you were good at games. I had the greatest luck. I always had a good time there. The fashionable thing is to look back and hate your school, but I loved Dulwich...."

3 1900–1902

That summer of 1900, with the drinking-in of the beautiful Shropshire countryside and general air of relaxation, was all too brief. As it began to wane, there arose the question of what was to be done with Plum as far as a livelihood was concerned. If it had been left to him, he would have chosen to stay and immerse himself in "that earthly paradise" while supporting himself by writing. But it was not left to him. This was an age when parents dictated their children's futures, and Ernest was every inch the conventional Victorian father in that respect. His views on what constituted proper gainful employment were limited, and they most certainly didn't include anything as ephemeral and idealistic as writing. He had no objection to Plum writing in his spare time, of course, as long as the boy applied himself to an honest job that would earn him a regular salary and the promise of security as he grew older.

What Ernest finally decided upon as the best of all possible careers for his son was banking. And no sooner was the decision made than he started to do something about it. Using the influence of his Hong Kong connections, he obtained for Plum the position of clerk at the London branch of the Hong Kong and Shanghai Bank at a salary of £80 a year. To supplement this minuscule income, Ernest would make him an allowance of a further £80 a year—

a good deal less than it would have cost him to keep Plum at Oxford.

The head office of the Hong Kong and Shanghai Bank was, predictably, in Hong Kong, and the London branch was really little more than a training ground for young men who would be taking up duties in the Far East. Although heads of departments were on the permanent London staff, a clerk would remain for only two years before being sent out to Siam, as it then was, or Java or China as a branch manager. This, as much as anything else about banking, was dispiriting to Plum. As he has himself put it:

> *I had two reasons for not looking forward to being sent out East—one, that the thought of being a branch manager appalled me, for I knew myself to be incapable of managing a whelk-stall; the other, of course, that I wanted to abandon commerce and earn my living as a writer, and I felt that this could be done only by remaining in London.*
>
> *The cross all young writers have to bear is that, while they know that they are going to be spectacularly successful some day, they find it impossible to convince their nearest and dearest that they will ever amount to a row of beans.*

Having found it impossible to convince *his* nearest and dearest, Plum entered the Lombard Street office of the bank on a fine September morning in 1900 with little enthusiasm for his prospects.

"I have always thought it illustrative of the haphazard methods of education in the nineties of the last century," he remarked in remembering those days, "that I should have been put on the Classical side at Dulwich and taught to write Greek and Latin verse and so on when I was going to wind up in a bank. I had had absolutely no training for commerce, and right through my two years in the bank I never had the slightest inkling of what banking was. I simply could not understand what was going on. Except for that, life in the bank—after the first month or two—was quite pleasant. My fellow clerks were all public school men—from Bedford, Merchant Taylors', Dulwich and other schools where parents could not afford a university career—and the atmosphere was on the informal side. We ran a football and cricket team, of both of which I was a member, and there was a general idea of not taking banking very seriously. I suppose the other fellows had more of a grip on things than I did, but there was none of that grim atmosphere which prevails in the usual London bank, where a clerk in the London office knows that he is going to be in the London office for the rest of his life. Everybody except me was counting the days till he would be able to 'give a Langdon,' which was the term for the party you gave at the Langdon public house when you 'got your orders' and were sent out East."

The bank's training scheme was thorough, giving its young men an insight into every facet of its business by starting them at the bottom and moving them progressively from department to department. It was therefore no reflection on Plum that he was first put to work in the postal department, where he had nothing to do but stamp and dispatch letters. Indeed, the work being of not too technical a nature, he found it well within his scope: and had there been no more to banking than this he might well have made his mark in the world of finance. But all good things come to an end and, in due course, he was transferred to Fixed Deposits. This was to prove more of a challenge—and one to which he wasn't sure he would be able to rise; but just as he felt that he could possibly be on the brink of getting the hang of it, he was moved to Inward Bills and then to Cash. It was during these final stages that he knew he had met his match. The whole scheme revealed itself as being absolutely incomprehensible. That much was crystal clear. He was completely baffled. His own summing up of the situation reads:

> *There were only two things con-*
> *nected with Higher Finance that I really*
> *understood. One was that from now on*
> *all I would be able to afford in the way*
> *of lunch would be a roll and butter and*
> *a cup of coffee, a discovery which, after*
> *the lavish midday meals of school, shook*
> *me to my foundations. The other was*
> *that if I got to the office late three*

> *mornings in a month, I would lose my*
> *Christmas bonus. One of the great sights*
> *in the City in the years 1901–2 was*
> *me rounding into the straight with my*
> *coat-tails flying and just making it across*
> *the threshold while thousands cheered.*
> *It kept me in superb condition, and*
> *gave me a rare appetite for the daily*
> *roll and butter.*

Throughout the period of his employment at the bank, Plum lived alone in a small bed-sitting-room in Markham Square which he described as "horrible lodgings in the Chelsea neighbourhood off the King's Road." Its only advantage was that it was conveniently situated for him to be able to walk, or sometimes run, to work every morning. And when his toil at Lombard Street was over at five o'clock, he would walk back to his room, eat the modest dinner the cost of which was included in his rent, and then settle down to write. There is no mention of new friendships or any kind of social life at this time. As it had been at Dulwich, he was the onlooker rather than the participator—except, of course, when it came to sports—and writing was all-important to him. "I wrote everything in those days," he said, "—verses, short stories, articles for the lowest type of weekly paper, only a very small portion of them ever reaching print."

His main efforts were directed towards the two-year-old *Public School Magazine,* for whom he wrote exclusively about school sports with such articles as "Football at Dulwich" and "School Cricket of 1900," which were published during the latter part of 1900. But in November 1900 he wrote his first humorous article—"Men Who Missed Their Own Weddings"—which was published in *Tit-Bits.*

The *Public School Magazine,* started in 1898 and published by Messrs. Adam and Charles Black, became so popular that George Newnes Limited came out with a rival magazine called *The Captain.* This suited Plum admirably, for he now had "a market for the only sort of work I could do reasonably well—articles and stories about public school life. The *Public School Magazine* paid ten shillings and sixpence for an article and *The Captain* three pounds for a short story; and as I was now getting an occasional guinea from papers like *Tit-Bits* and *Answers,* my savings began to mount."

In 1900, from April to September, *The Captain* ran a serial school story called "Acton's Feud" by Fred Swainson, a popular writer of fiction for boys, and it was this that inspired Plum to try his hand seriously at short stories. He read "Acton's Feud" and thought that, good as it was, he could do better. So although continuing with his light articles, poems, essays on various sports and reporting on the public schools, he began to write stories with a direct appeal to public-school boys. The first of these was called "The Prize Poem," and it was published in the July 1901 issue of the *Public School Magazine*. Said Plum: "Awfully funny how something like that ['Acton's Feud'] gives you a kick-off. I first started writing public school stories because it was the only atmosphere I knew at all."

But he was really to feel that he'd found the secret to success as a regularly published writer when he read J. M. Barrie's novel *When a Man's Single*. The hero of the story was a young man who, like Plum, was endeavouring to become a journalist and who was urged to write to please editors rather than to please himself. Barrie's indirect advice was applied when "I started going in exclusively for the mushy sentiment which, judging from the magazines, was the thing most likely to bring a sparkle into an editor's eye." And it seemed to work. The first of such efforts appeared in the issue of *Answers* dated 26th August 1901, and it was called "When Papa Swore in Hindustani"—a title of which, as he confided to his diary, he did not approve. It had been chosen, he noted, "by them, not mine the loathsome title." Nevertheless, title regardless, the story netted him a record fee of three guineas.

Although the major part of his output was being taken by the *Public School Magazine* and *The Captain,* Plum was now having pieces accepted by *Tit-Bits, Fun, Weekly Telegraph, Sandow's Physical Culture Magazine, Answers, St. James' Gazette* and *To-Day.* In his autobiographical book *Over Seventy,* he asserted that he had also had a story printed in *The Universal and Ludgate Magazine;* but a present-day check revealed no trace of such a story. To refresh his memory, Plum consulted his diary for July 1901 and discovered that "*The Universal and Ludgate Magazine* has accepted a story of mine called 'A Highway Episode' and is paying me a guinea for it. But after they had it six months, a new editor and publisher took on the magazine and rejected my wretched story." A blow, naturally—but not fatal.

During his two years at the bank, Plum had a total of eighty items published—a mere fraction of his actual output since a great deal was rejected. Some idea of the rate at which he could work can be gleaned from his recollection of the time when he had to be absent from the bank for genuine reasons of health: "It was in June 1901 that I got the mumps. That was when I was in my first year at the bank. I went back to my people in Shropshire to have them there. I wrote nineteen short stories in three weeks. I just sent the stories out and they were all returned. They were awful. And to make matters worse, they were all written in longhand. My trouble, as with all beginning authors, was that I did not know how to write. Worse bilge than mine may have been submitted to the editors of London in 1901 and 1902, but I should think it very unlikely."

It was certain, though, that he was undaunted by the mass of rejection slips he was accumulating. Back at the bank, with the mumps a thing of the past, he continued to bombard the editors of London with his articles, poems and short stories.

At about this time, he learned that an ex-Dulwich master was working for *The Globe,* a century-old pink evening newspaper. William Beach-Thomas had given up teaching in favour of journalism, and was now assistant to Harold Begbie, editor of *The Globe's* "By the Way" feature column—the two men running the column between them. On the strength of the Dulwich acquaintanceship, Plum recalled, "I went to see Beach-Thomas to ask if he could get me any work, and he said that he and Begbie often wanted to take a day off and would be glad of somebody who would fill in for them. The payment was ten shillings and sixpence per day." It was an offer that Plum accepted with alacrity, and he eagerly awaited his first call. When it came, on 16th August 1901, he wrote in his diary, "They printed seven of my pars. Good! There is a variable hope of my getting this post permanently. Let the good work go forward!"

It didn't go forward quite as quickly as he might have hoped, however, for his next opportunity to write for the column didn't come until 27th March 1902—when he was asked to work consecutively from that date until 2nd April —and again on the 7th April. To fulfil these engagements he had to absent himself from the bank, which he did "by pleading nonexistent attacks of neuralgia."

In the meantime, he had been putting strenuous effort into the writing of his first serial, "The Pothunters," which was purchased by the *Public School Magazine.* It ran from January to March 1902, at which time Messrs. A. & C. Black decided to discontinue the magazine—but with the promise that they would publish "The Pothunters" as a novel later in the year and pay Plum a ten percent royalty on each copy sold. This was wonderful news which promised an immense step forward to the enthusiastic author; and not unnaturally, he became increasingly impatient with his life at the bank.

Any pretence at acquiring the rudiments of banking had long since been abandoned, and Plum's thoughts were frequently elsewhere during these almost soul-destroying days at his desk. Had the London branch of the Hong Kong and Shanghai Bank been entirely dependent upon his efforts during this period, it would surely have had to close its doors and think of starting up again in some other part of the world. But Plum was the odd man out. His young colleagues gave every appearance of fully understanding and even, incredibly, enjoying what they were doing. He alone, it seemed, was utterly unable to fathom the manifold mysteries that surrounded him.

It may have been thoughts roughly along these lines that filtered his consciousness as he sat one day in idle contemplation of a new ledger that had been placed before him. Its true purpose must have momentarily escaped him as he opened it to its first pristine page and began in absentminded fashion to write a story concerning the celebration of the opening of a new ledger. When reason suddenly returned and he realised what he was doing, he knew at once that to leave the story in the ledger would be to court disaster. Accordingly, he removed the page with consummate skill, but without taking into account that it was numbered.

At this point, the head cashier entered upon the scene in search of a new ledger, and Plum—who could take new ledgers or leave them—was pleased to be able to oblige by handing his over. Within moments, of course, it was discovered that the first page was missing, and the keen-eyed cashier was immediately on the phone to the printer. He had been feuding with this printer for some months and had been awaiting just such concrete evidence of shoddy workmanship. His telephoned comments, spoken in a loud and reverberating voice, were consequently little short of vitriolic.

In no time at all the printer's representative was at the bank and inspecting the offending ledger, shortly to announce that it had quite definitely originally contained the first page and that same must have been removed by a person or persons unknown after delivery to the bank. Was there, he couldn't help wondering, some sort of imbecile on the bank staff? The cashier—a fair-minded man despite the feud—gave the matter careful thought and then said, "Why, yes. Young Wodehouse."

Plum, when sent for and questioned, made a full and frank confession and apologised for his passing aberration. But the irate cashier could not let the desecration of a new ledger pass without giving Plum a severe and blistering tongue-lashing. He left no shadow of doubt that if there was ever to be a Bank Clerk of the Year contest there would be no point in Plum entering for it.

The incident is remembered because it was just about the most dramatic and exciting thing that happened within the Lombard Street edifice during those two years. Summing up his experience in banking, Plum said, "I couldn't follow the thing at all. I didn't know what it was all about. And the prospect of having to go out East and be sub-manager of a branch bank was too much for me."

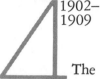

1902–
1909

The head cashier of the Hong Kong and Shanghai Bank might have been less hard on Plum had he known that the despoiler of new ledgers would shortly be departing from the establishment forever. But even Plum would have been unable to spring this heartening news on him at the time. No such prospect seemed even remotely likely when, out of the blue, William Beach-Thomas made him an offer that suddenly opened up an avenue of escape. Beach-Thomas was anxious to find someone to take his place on the "By the Way" column during his annual five-week holiday from *The Globe* and, because of past experience, was giving Plum first refusal. But he had left things rather late and had to have a quick answer.

It is doubtful that Plum's response would have been any different had he been given more time to think it over. What had to be weighed in the balance was his small but steady income from the bank against a very limited period as a full-time journalist at the newspaper's salary of three guineas a week. What price security? He had always wanted to support himself entirely by his writings, and this was the opportunity to find out whether it would work. The relevant entry in his 1902 diary reads: "On September 9th, having to choose between the Globe and the Bank, I chucked the latter and started out on my wild lone as a freelance. This month starts my journalistic career."

Within ten days he was not only a journalist but also an author, for on the 18th September 1902 Messrs. A. & C. Black kept their promise and published *The Pothunters*. A delighted Plum immediately sent a copy of the book to his erstwhile schoolfriend William Townend. In it was a modestly prophetic inscription:

To William Townend
these first fruits of a GENIUS at which the world will (shortly)
be AMAZED (You see if it won't)   from the Author P.G. Wodehouse

Plum had good reason for feeling optimistic that September. It really turned out to be a lucky month for him. Apart from the publication of *The Pothunters,* he was to see one of his articles published in *Punch* for the first time. That was on the 17th September. In addition, two sets of his verses appeared in the *Daily Chronicle,* and an article entitled "London Street Names" was printed in *The Globe* as a feature apart from the "By the Way" column. All of this brought his total earnings for the month to £16.4s.0d.—and since every bit of it had come from his writing, he knew that the literary career he had been so assiduously pursuing was well and truly launched.

If he stopped to think at all, it was only upon the return of Beach-Thomas to *The Globe* after what seemed a particularly brief five weeks.

The prospect now before Plum was of finding another steady job or increasing his literary market value. Having already resolved never again to attempt any work that was not directly connected with writing, his choice was obvious. He simply redoubled his efforts to interest every newspaper and magazine in London in his articles, verses and short stories. And again luck was with him. His work was accepted by *Scraps, Onlooker, Punch, The Captain, Royal, Echo,* the *Evening News, Sportsman, Vanity Fair,* "*V.C.,*" and *Windsor Magazine,* and he still occasionally helped to write "By the Way" when Begbie or Beach-Thomas felt the need of a day off. By the end of December 1902, just under four months into his new career, Plum's writings had earned him £65.6s.7d. and Messrs. A. & C. Black had sold three hundred and ninety-six copies of *The Pothunters.*

While all this had been going on, the Wodehouse parents had apparently had their fill of the Shropshire scene so beloved of Plum, and had removed themselves to the genteel environs of Cheltenham, the Gloucestershire spa where people of modest means were wont to settle in retirement. One could be forgiven for imagining that this new home-base would endear itself to Plum who, socially speaking, was already in a virtual state of retirement. But this was not the case. Visiting them, he discovered that Eleanor and Ernest had carved themselves a niche among people of like interests and found Cheltenham most pleasant. He, on the other hand, thought it "beastly" in comparison with Stableford and was glad to return to London, where he was himself seeking other accommodation.

Early in the new year of 1903, he found what he was looking for and moved to 23 Walpole Street, which was in a more salubrious part of Chelsea. His room was a large bed-sitter at the top of the house, and it was here one cold night that he received a visitor. Herbert W. Westbrook arrived with a letter of introduction from Frank Kendall—a mutual friend whom Plum had known at the bank—to find Plum sitting at a table, a woollen sweater wrapped around his feet, working on a poem for *Punch* by the light of a green-shaded oil lamp. It didn't seem the best time for a would-be writer to ask a professional writer for help, but Plum took the interruption in his stride. Westbrook recalled that "Plum gave me some good advice and, more than that, sincere encouragement."

As a result of that meeting, Plum was invited to stay at Emsworth House—a small preparatory school in the country, at which Westbrook was an assistant master—where the atmosphere would be conducive to writing. The school was situated in the little village of Emsworth, on the border of Hampshire and Sussex, not far from Portsmouth. Plum took up residence there in a room above the school stables. His stay of six months was punctuated by trips to town only when required by *The Globe,* and it was a period that he much enjoyed. The school was run by Baldwin King-Hall, a charming man with whom Plum had great rapport thanks to a shared enthusiasm for cricket. Indeed, although the school cricket pitch was only just about adequate for the pupils, Plum remembered that "We used to play matches against various teams on the ground, though it was really much too small for grown-up cricket."

This rural idyll came to an end in August 1903, when William Beach-Thomas resigned from *The Globe* and Plum inherited his position as assistant to Harold Begbie on "By the Way." As a full-time journalist, Plum's working day started at 10 a.m. and finished at noon—which was less ideal than it sounds. In those two crowded hours, Plum had to scour the morning newspapers for topical items he could use and then write approximately ten amusing paragraphs and a set of verses about them. It was a tough assignment but invaluable to him in training himself to concentrate in the midst of all kinds of chaos in order to meet the deadline.

While coping with the column six days a week, Plum was also churning out verses and short stories and working on a serial—such ceaseless toil no doubt according well with his natural proclivities since it left him little time to worry about a social life. His own observation on that was, "Well, I used to *know* a lot of girls and people" (a distinction that Women's

Lib will probably note) "but I didn't go out very much. I was working too hard. After *The Globe* in the morning, I'd walk back to my lodgings and more or less start work right away, doing short stories and things. I played a certain amount of cricket and I really never wanted anything to do, I was so keen on my work. However, I was always fond of reading anything that came along." But he did feel the occasional need to take a day off from the column, and when that happened he did for Westbrook what Beach-Thomas had done for him by getting his friend, Westbrook, in to work on the "By the Way" feature.

His status as an author was strengthened when, on 11th September 1903, Messrs. A. & C. Black published Plum's second novel about public school life, *A Prefect's Uncle*. Unlike other boys' books of the period, this one was devoid of heavy-handed moralising. More than that, it was the first of his books to contain elements of humour and it introduced the first of what was to become a long line of butlers.

In addition to everything else, Plum was now putting the finishing touches to a new public school serial called "The Gold Bat," for which *The Captain* was paying him £50, the first instalment of which appeared in the October issue. And in November he was to have another book in print—*Tales of St. Austin's*—which was a collection of short stories on public school life which had previously appeared in the *Public School Magazine* and *The Captain*.

One of his rare excursions into the social world at this time was a visit to the Harrow Weald home of Sir William Schwenk Gilbert, king of the Savoy Opera, for Sunday lunch. He had long been an admirer of W. S. Gilbert, and even his natural reserve could not prevent him from accepting this invitation proffered through a mutual friend. As shy and diffident as ever, he was vastly relieved to discover that there were fourteen other guests. It meant, he thought, that he would be able to just sit back quietly and inconspicuously. And indeed, it seemed at first that he could.

As the meal progressed, Sir William began to tell what was clearly intended to be a humorous story. It was one of those very long, deceptively dull tales with a deliberately tedious build-up leading to a dramatic pause before the hilariously funny punch-line. From what Plum could gather, this one concerned the owner of the Drury Lane Theatre, Augustus Harris; but as it dragged on, his attention may have wandered. Had the late Queen Victoria been present, it is doubtful that she would have followed it with anticipatory laughter bubbling on her lips, but Plum was certainly not amused. However, he couldn't ignore the fact that this was the illustrious W. S. Gilbert telling the story and it therefore *had* to be funny. With this in mind, Plum determined not to let his host down. When the dramatic pause before the punch-line came, thinking that the sudden silence meant the story was over, he laughed. "I had a rather distinctive laugh in those days—" he recalled, "something like the last bit of water going down the waste-pipe in a bath. Infectious, I suppose you would call it. The other guests, seeming a little puzzled, as if they had expected something better from the author of *The Mikado,* all laughed politely, and conversation became general. And it was at this juncture that I caught my host's eye. I shall always remember the glare of pure hatred which I saw in it. If you have seen photographs of Gilbert, you will be aware that even when in repose his face was inclined to be formidable and his eye was far from being in repose. His eyes, beneath their beetling brows, seared my very soul."

That Plum had difficulty in showing himself to his best advantage in any gathering where inoffensive people met for pleasant social intercourse is exemplified in his tale of yet another party. This one was held early in January 1904. He had just taken a house called Threepwood, in the village of Emsworth, just down the lane from Emsworth House; and the consequence of his proximity to the school was that his friend Westbrook would always be popping in, often staying the night. On this occasion, Plum had been invited to a formal dinner party at a nearby stately home. Coincidentally, Westbrook, who was in residence, had been invited to a similar party elsewhere and had borrowed Plum's best formal clothes without bothering to tell him. Plum was therefore forced to attend his function in what he called "a primitive suit of soup-and-fish" that had been handed down to him by his Uncle Hugh—a man who stood six feet four inches tall and tipped the scales in the region of two hundred and ten pounds.

"Even as I dressed," Plum mused, "the things seemed roomy. It was not, however, until the fish course that I realised how roomy they were when, glancing down, I suddenly observed the trousers mounting like a rising tide over my shirt-front. I pushed them back, but I knew I was fighting a losing battle. Eventually, when I was helping myself to potatoes and was off my guard, the tide swept up as far as my white tie; and of course, I was absolutely frozen with horror as the rest of the party enjoyed my plight."

It is little wonder that he sought refuge as well as solace in his work.

But even the most prodigious of workers must sometimes take a break, and *The Globe* was not ungenerous to its employees with the five-week holiday it gave annually. If Eleanor and Ernest had not moved, it is possible that Plum might have happily contemplated five weeks in Shropshire. But Cheltenham didn't figure in his holiday plans at all. Instead, his thoughts turned to his long-held dream of visiting America—largely due to his enthusiasm for boxing and a consequent admiration for American boxers; and the more he thought of it the more the dream seemed a possibility. After all, transatlantic travel was not over-expensive and one didn't have to bother about visas and the like. If it took him nine days to make the crossing and another nine days to return, he would have seventeen days in which to see New York City.

There was no further pondering. He booked a passage on the *St. Louis,* travelling second class and sharing a cabin with three other men, and left England for his first trip to the United States on 16th April 1904. He was not without contacts there. Someone he had worked with at the bank, A. Nesbitt Kemp, had gone into business in New York and it was with him and a man named Wigglesworth that Plum went to stay when he arrived on the 25th April. As he remembered it, "They had an apartment—a very cheap sort of place—somewhere very far down on Fifth Avenue."

But there was no disillusionment; the dream was not in vain. New York turned out to be every bit as exciting as he had anticipated and, furthermore, he was to be given a fascinating glimpse of the American boxing scene at first hand.

This came about through a letter of introduction to Norman Thwaites of the *New York World* who, learning of Plum's deep interest in boxing, arranged for him to visit the training camp of Kid McCoy—then preparing for his fight with Philadelphia Jack O'Brien. The outing to the Kid's camp at White Plains, New York, was an unforgettable highlight for Plum, who was thrilled to see the famous American pugilist in training for the world welterweight championship. And he was not slow to appreciate the benefits which might accrue from it when he wrote in his diary, "In New York gathering experience. Worth many guineas in the future, but none for the moment."

He returned to London on the 20th May and very soon thereafter discovered that his prophecy had not been at fault. For his articles about life in New York he was able to command a higher fee, and his finances generally showed a remarkable improvement thanks to the prestige of his trip to America. He had suddenly become regarded as the definitive authority on anything that had to do with the United States, and he could see no reason to modestly deny the truth of this. It might have seemed churlish.

Later, he was to make further use of the experience in the writing of a series of short stories about a young boxer whom he called Kid Brady. But the most immediate effect of the whole adventure was on his importance as a journalist, confirmed by his appointment as editor of "By the Way" when, in August 1904, Harold Begbie resigned from *The Globe* in order to join the *Daily Mail.* As editor of the column, Plum's weekly salary leaped to a princely five guineas; and he was able to give a helping hand to his unpredictable friend Westbrook by introducing him to Sir George Armstrong, owner of *The Globe,* and securing for him the position of assistant on the column.

Within a month of Plum's promotion, in September 1904, Messrs. A. & C. Black published *The Gold Bat.* This was the novel in which Plum introduced Wrykyn, a public school which bore a strong resemblance to Dulwich College. It was an indication of the indelible impression his school had left on him. He never lost interest in its activities, particularly where football and cricket were concerned; and he not only attended as many matches as he could but also reported on them for *The Alleynian.* The overall happiness of his time at Dulwich was constantly reflected in his school stories, in which the younger boys were usually spoiled, scheming and nasty while the boys in the higher classes were virtuous, honest, and well on the way to becoming human beings. But it was not only Dulwich that influenced him. As a source of inspiration, he also drew upon King-Hall's school at Emsworth, where he was a frequent and popular visitor with great opportunities for studying the youngsters. Indeed, he wrote to me, "The scene of an early book of mine called *The Little Nugget* was Emsworth House." Nonetheless, it was a thinly disguised Dulwich around which *The Gold Bat* was centred: and in schoolboy vernacular the book was dedicated "To that Prince of Slackers, Herbert Westbrook"—which was Plum's subtle way of letting Westbrook know that industry was not considered his strong point.

One of the many projects on which Plum had been working at this time was a version of the story of William Tell—a children's book commissioned by his publishers for which colour illustrations had been completed by Philip Dadd as far back as 1900. Now, in November 1904, *William Tell*

Told Again was published. It had been written solely for financial gain and certainly not as a lasting contribution to literature or as a bid for immortal fame, and it is probably just as well that copies are now scarce and very difficult to obtain. If nothing else, the book must have been a sore disappointment to the boys who bought it in expectation of another familiar school story. It remains the only children's book that Plum ever wrote.

Early December of 1904 saw him branching out into yet another field. It began with Owen Hall—a famous musical-comedy actor-playwright (whose real name was James Davis)—asking him to write a lyric for one of the songs to be featured in his new show, *Sergeant Brue,* due to open at the Strand Theatre in London. The thought of this appealed to Plum immensely and he came up with a piece called "Put Me in My Little Cell," to be sung by three "crooks" in the show. Hall paid him five guineas—the equivalent of a week's salary on *The Globe*—and expressed his delight with the lyric. When the show opened, on the 10th December 1904, a Saturday, Plum was in the first-night audience; and he went to see it again on the following Monday night, later recording in his diary: "Encored both times. Audience laughed several times during each verse. This is fame." And if it was fame, he wanted more. The theatre had cast its spell on him, and he was eager to extend his talents in that direction.

Summing up the year in his diary, Plum wrote: "On this, the 13th of December, 1904, time 12 p.m., I set it down that I have *arrived.* Letter from Cosmo Hamilton congratulating me on my work and promising commission to write lyrics for his next piece. I have a lyric in 'Sergeant Brue,' a serial in *The Captain,* 5 books published, I am editing 'By the Way,' *Pearson's* have two stories and two poems of mine, I have finished the 'Kid Brady' stories, and I have a commission to do a weekly poem for *Vanity Fair.*"

As if all this were not enough, he had a new endeavour in mind for 1905. One of his New Year's resolutions was to learn to play the banjo. This sudden thirst for musical accomplishment may have been a direct result of his still-recent introduction to the world of the theatre. Perhaps he had some distant vision of music-hall posters which would proclaim: "PLONKER" WODEHOUSE *Comic lyrics to banjo accompaniment.* But he was quite serious about it and wasted no time in acquiring an instrument, thereafter to practice with rapt concentration at his Emsworth home. What heights he might have scaled as a banjoist will, alas, never be known. There was a fly, so to speak, in the ointment—namely, Westbrook. That worthy was on one of his prolonged stays at Threepwood, which meant that almost anything could happen at any time. What actually did happen was that Westbrook—either because he had no ear for music or because he was temporarily out of ready cash—took advantage of one of Plum's absences from the house to rush the banjo off to an obliging pawnshop. This would not have irked Plum so much had the separation from his instrument been for a specified period. But Westbrook, whether by accident or design, lost the pawn ticket and thus put paid to a possible musical career. For Plum— like a pet-lover whose dog, rhino, marmoset or whatever having passed away hesitates to have another—did not replace the departed banjo.

Perhaps the world is in Westbrook's debt. Time that might have been devoted to the banjo was spent once again in writing. And now Plum wanted to broaden his horizon. He was aware of the limitations of writing public-school stories and was anxious to work himself into the adult market, which meant getting something printed in the *Strand* magazine.

Just as *Punch* was the ultimate goal of the writer of humorous articles, so the *Strand* was that of the short-story writer. The magazine had been launched in the early 1890s by George Newnes Limited, which also published *The Captain,* and had gained popularity mainly because of the Sherlock Holmes stories of Arthur Conan Doyle. Its standards were therefore considered to be very high.

Plum's hope was that the reputation he had earned with his school stories in *The Captain* would stand him in good stead with the editor of the *Strand*. He had won himself a healthy following and was now an established favourite for having broken with the tradition of English school stories by introducing a note of realism. One book critic had said, "Mr. Wodehouse's school stories are hard to surpass. Both boys and masters in these stories show themselves refreshingly human without affectation or priggishness." Could an editor turn a blind eye to an author so acclaimed?

Greenhough Smith, editor of the *Strand,* couldn't. On the strength of Plum's showing in other spheres he accepted the first story submitted to him, called "The Wire-Pullers," and paid fifteen guineas for the privilege. It appeared in the issue for July 1905. But despite the breakthrough, Plum continued to write for *The Captain,* contributing a new serial called "The White Feather"—a sequel to "The Gold Bat"—which commenced in the October 1905 issue and earned him £60. To cap this, the 5th of the same month saw the publication of his latest book, *The Head of Kay's.* The result of this self-imposed hard labour was that his income for the year reached a new high of £500.

If this period was not dotted with memorable social highlights, it is not to be wondered at. Writing is, at the best of times, a lonely occupation. For someone as prolific as Plum, life could have been only little short of monastic: and the calls on his time and talents were increasing. In 1906, the theatre beckoned once again. This time it was Sir Seymour Hicks, actor-manager of the Aldwych Theatre, who required his services. Hicks had borne in mind the success of Plum's lyric in *Sergeant Brue* and now offered him a resident job of writing lyrics and verses for all the Aldwych shows. In his diary for 6th March 1906, Plum recorded: "Regular job at £2 a week, starting with the run of *The Beauty of Bath* (March 19th) to do topical verses etc." Hicks was going to star in *The Beauty of Bath* and particularly wanted a show-stopping comic song with several additional choruses for the expected encores.

Plum took on this task with great delight, for as an official assistant lyric writer he was now given entrée to the special world that existed behind the scenes and in the wings. "On leaving the stage-door," reported Westbrook after the initial heady experience, "Plum was so stunned with joy and excitement that we walked a mile along the Strand without him knowing where he was or whether he was coming or going."

To write the music for *The Beauty of Bath,* Hicks had engaged a young American composer named Jerome Kern, who was already in England to do some work for the famed producer Charles Frohman. Plum's first meeting with Kern took place at the Aldwych Theatre where Kern, in his shirtsleeves, was playing poker with several of the actors. "When I finally managed to free him from the card table and was able to talk with him," Plum recalled, "I became impressed. Here, I thought, was a young man supremely confident of himself—the kind of person who inspires people to seek him out when a job must be done." Between them, the composer and the lyricist came up with a song called "Mr. Chamberlain"—the subject matter being Joseph Chamberlain and his then topical protective tariff policy. And when the show opened at the Aldwych on 19th March 1906, the number proved to be everything that Hicks had hoped for, not only stopping the show but also taking London by storm. Had there been a top-twenty chart in those days it would have led the field.

By now, with the success he'd promised himself assured, Plum was ready to invade the realm of adult literature in volume form. He may not have been consciously aware of it until he received a letter from William Townend which provided him with heaven-sent inspiration. Townend had written at great length of a friend of his who, in partnership with another friend, had started a chicken farm in Devonshire. The man in question had run through an inheritance, quarrelled with a rich aunt, was an inveterate drinker, and habitually sponged on every likely acquaintance. He was, in fact, a character; and so vividly did Townend describe him and his adventures that Plum was moved to put pen to paper, or typewriter key to ribbon. The result was his first humorous book for adults, *Love Among the Chickens,* in which he introduced what was to become his favourite character: Stanley Featherstonehaugh Ukridge (pronounced "Yewkridge").

Ukridge's personality was not entirely drawn from the gentleman with the chicken farm, however. To round out the character, Plum added some of the more eccentric characteristics of his part-time boarder, Herbert West-brook, whose often startling antics were to provide grist for Plum's mill in future stories. Nevertheless, Plum felt indebted to Townend for the impetus he had been given; and he publicly acknowledged this many years later when, in 1920, he revised *Love Among the Chickens.* His dedication in the new edition read: "Sixteen years ago, my William, when we were young and spritely lads; when you were a tricky centre-forward and I a fast bowler; when your head was covered with hair and my list of 'Hobbies' in *Who's Who* included Boxing; I received from you one morning about thirty closely-written foolscap pages giving me the details of your friend ————'s adventures on his Devonshire chicken farm. Round these I wove as funny a plot as I could, but the book stands or falls by the stuff you gave me about 'Ukridge'—the things that actually happened. . . ."

At the time of the original publication, however, he showed his gratitude privately by sending Townend £10 for his help—not that Townend wanted or expected to be rewarded. It was, though, a gesture of extreme generosity on Plum's part since he received only £31.5s.8d. when the book was published by the Newnes organisation in August 1906.

What particularly distinguished *Love Among the Chickens,* from the commercial point of view, was the fact that with it Plum abandoned his practice of selling his work direct to the publishers. For the first time, he was represented by a firm of literary agents—Messrs. James Pinker & Son —to whom he wrote, addressing the letter to Mr. J. B. Pinker:

June 1, 1905.

Dear Sir,

If you should decide to handle my Ms. LOVE AMONG THE CHICK-ENS, which I left with you on Tuesday last, I should be glad if you would try to place it as a serial first. I wrote it with a view to publication in "C. B. Fry's Magazine," but the editor cannot use it.

Yours truly,

P. G. Wodehouse.

Having decided that he ought to try and sell the book to an American publisher too, Plum felt that he could best do this through the good graces of one of his well-placed friends in New York. He therefore "sent the manuscript of *Love Among the Chickens* to Norman Thwaites, with whom I had stayed during my first visit to New York. Pressure of business compelled him to hand it over to a regular agent. He gave it to Baerman. That was the expression he used in writing to me—'I am giving it to A. E. Baerman— and I think Baerman must have taken the word 'giving' literally. Certainly, when the book was published in America by the Circle Publishing Company, it had on its title page, 'Copyright by A. E. Baerman,' and a few years later, when the story was sold for motion pictures, I was obliged to pay him two hundred and fifty dollars to release it.

"He not only sold the book rights but the serial rights at a price which seemed to me fantastic. A thousand dollars it was, and to one who, like myself, had never got above sixty pounds for a serial and whose record royalties for a book were eighteen pounds eleven and fourpence, a thousand dollars was more than merely good. It was great gravy. It made the whole world seem different. A wave of gratitude towards my benefactor swept over me. I felt like a man who has suddenly got in touch with a rich and benevolent uncle.

"There was just one flaw in my happiness. The money seemed a long time coming. In a delightful letter in which he informed me of the sale, Baerman said that a draft would arrive on October 1st. But October came and went. By Christmas I was inclined to restlessness. In March I cabled, and received a reply, 'Letter explaining. Check immediately.' Late April the old restlessness returned, for no explaining letter had arrived. Towards the middle of May he sent me a cheque but didn't sign it.

"My association with Baerman was the making of me. Critics today sometimes say that my work would be improved by being less morbid, but nobody has ever questioned its depth. That depth I owe to A. E. Baerman. (He owes me about two hundred dollars.)"

But even without the money due from Baerman, Plum had managed to accrue a sizeable sum in savings. He was therefore just the chap Sir Seymour Hicks was looking for when that gentleman decided to sell his car, a Darracq, and put the proceeds of the sale towards the cost of a new one. Apart from any other consideration, Hicks thought it was time the up-and-coming author had a car of his own. Plum, who could not resist a good sales talk, confided to his diary, "Bought a motor for £450 from Seymour Hicks (Nov. 17) Lord help me!" His plea to the Almighty was in no way connected with safety on the road. It simply indicated that he had just parted with all the money he had in the world and was only now beginning to realise it.

After a rudimentary and rather hasty driving lesson from Hicks, Plum felt competent to make full use of his latest acquisition by setting out in solitary state for Emsworth. It was a pleasant drive, and he felt happily in control of his destiny as he sat behind the wheel and nosed towards home. He did all the things he was supposed to do, and the car responded perfectly to his directions. Only one incident marred the otherwise flawless performance of man and machine. Just outside Emsworth, Plum drove straight into a hedge. Had the act been intentional, no one could have faulted him. Indeed, even a more accomplished driver might have experienced difficulty in hitting the hedge so fairly and squarely and penetrating to such a depth.

Unhurt and only slightly shaken, Plum found himself not only in a hedge but also in a quandary. Hicks, while trying to impart to his pupil as much knowledge as he could in a comparatively short time, had made no mention of hedges. The matter of driving into them and, more to the point, driving out of them had been entirely neglected. There was nothing to go on. So Plum did what any reasonable man would have done in similar circumstances. Clambering out of the car, he walked to the local railway station and boarded a train for London. He never went back to pick up the car, and he never drove again.

This little mishap in no wise disturbed the amicable relationship that existed between Hicks and Pelham Grenville Wodehouse. On the contrary, when Hicks left the Aldwych Theatre and transferred *The Beauty of Bath* to his own new Hicks Theatre on 27th December 1906, he took Plum with him as chief lyricist. In fact, Plum spent the Christmas season at the home of Sir Seymour and his celebrated actress-wife, Ellaline Terriss. In her auto-biography, Ellaline Terriss told of Plum's various visits and of how he was called "The Hermit" because he hid himself away for hours in a little plan-tation of trees to do his writing. "He always used to make me laugh," she wrote, "—and he still does. Seymour was very fond of him."

During the early part of 1907 Plum remained at Threepwood, hard at work on three major projects. The first of these was a serial called "Junior Jackson," bought by *The Captain* for £70 and commencing in the April issue, followed by another called "The Lost Lambs" in which he introduced a new character—Psmith ("the 'P' is silent as in pshrimp").

"Psmith," explained Plum, "like Ukridge, was to a certain extent drawn from life. A cousin of mine who had been at the public school Winchester with Rupert D'Oyly Carte, the son of the Savoy Opera's D'Oyly Carte, was telling me one day about his eccentricities—how he was very long and lean, immaculately dressed, wore a monocle, and talked kindly but not patronis-ingly to the headmaster. When one of the masters asked him, 'How are you, Carte?', he replied, 'Sir, I get thinnah and thinnah.' It gave me enough to build the character on, and I wrote a boys' story called *Mike* in which he figured largely."

Mike was, in fact, the marrying of two serials into one full-length book —"Junior Jackson" forming the first part and "The Lost Lambs" the second part.

Psmith became one of the most famous of characters to emerge from the pages of *The Captain*. Bored with life at the age of eighteen, he would create excitement and confusion by forcing potentially dramatic situations into reality; and his dialogue and mannerisms while pursuing this aim were the first to bring the Wodehouse comic style truly into focus.

Although *Mike* did not appear until 1909, Frank Swinnerton remem-bered reading the adventures of Psmith in *The Captain* and wrote that "Psmith was one of his (Plum's) earliest attempts at world instruction in pure En-glish," going on to tell how schoolboys of the period denied themselves the common necessities in order to save their pennies to buy *The Captain* "and learn more of a language new and irresistible to them."

To ring the changes while so heavily engaged upon big literary ventures, Plum took time out to write two lyrics for the musical show *The Gay Gordons,* which opened at the Aldwych Theatre in September 1907, thereby earning himself £20.

His second major task at Threepwood was the writing of *The White Feather,* a sequel to *The Gold Bat,* which was published on 9th October 1907. This was to be the last of his books to reflect the influence on him of his years at Dulwich.

On quite a different tack, the third important undertaking was a novel entitled *Not George Washington* in the writing of which he collaborated with Herbert Westbrook. The basic idea for the story was Westbrook's, but the style in which it was presented was entirely Plum's. Using a technique made popular by Wilkie Collins in *The Moonstone*—that of having more than one narrator to tell the tale—Plum let his heroine begin the story, alternating with the accounts of the three other main characters for the remainder of the book.

The plot of *Not George Washington* concerned an author who submitted for publication many different types of material under the names of various nonliterary acquaintances to each of whom he paid a percentage of his earnings for such usage. Here the main theme was carried to an interesting and amusing extreme, but it obviously had its origins in the actual experiences of the two authors. That they did this sort of thing is clearly seen in a short note appearing in Plum's diary for January 1907: "I wrote this (article) under H. Westbrook's name. We divided the gns. Clever work."

Not George Washington was published on 13th October 1907 by Cassell's, which had not previously published any of Plum's work. Sales were small and, as a result, copies of the book are now extremely difficult to come by—which is sad for aficionados not only because it is an immensely entertaining story, but also because of its strong autobiographical overtones. It is impossible not to recognise in the character "James Orlebar Cloyster" Plum himself, and "Julian Eversleigh" is clearly Westbrook.

The collaboration with Westbrook did not stop at *Not George Washington,* though it might have been better if it had. For their next joint venture, they wrote a musical playlet for which the music was composed by the sister of Baldwin King-Hall, owner of Emsworth House. Plum's diary says all that needs to be said about it: "Nov. 11. 'The Bandit's Daughter,' a musical sketch by Herbert Westbrook *and* P. G. Wodehouse, music by Ella

King-Hall, produced at the Bedford Music Hall, Camden Town. A frost!"

To round off the year, Plum parted company with Sir Seymour Hicks on 6th December 1907 to join the Gaiety Theatre as lyricist. His total earnings for the year had amounted to £527.17s.1d., and the recording of it terminated the seven years of the diary's existence.

With the serial "The Lost Lambs" now completed and appearing in *The Captain*, to the delight of its readers, Plum proceeded to amalgamate it with "Junior Jackson" to make his longest and last novel of public school life: but it was not until the following year that *Mike* was published by Messrs. A. & C. Black.

Although Plum and Westbrook were living at Threepwood, they were still writing the "By the Way" column for *The Globe*, which was now under new management. When Plum had started working for the paper it had been owned by the Armstrong family, with Sir George Armstrong as editor-in-chief. But Armstrong had sold the paper to Hildebrand Harmsworth, and his former assistant, Waldon Peacock, was now editor-in-chief. Peacock was not at all in favour of Plum and Westbrook's practice of writing their column at Threepwood and sending the material to the office on the London train. He wanted them working on the premises but had no grounds for insisting on it until, as Plum ruefully remembered, "One day we put it on the train and something went wrong. Peacock didn't get the column on time and this gave him the opportunity of telling us that we must come to the office." The result was that Plum and Westbrook returned to London, where they shared a flat.

It was evident that *The Globe* was not going to remain the paper it had been under Armstrong. Harmsworth was taking an active interest in it, and he had decided ideas of his own with regard to the changing of some features and the publicising of others. High on his list for publicity was "By the Way." "The column itself was an extraordinary affair in England," Plum explained. "You would quote something from the morning paper and then you'd make some little comment on it. It was always the same type of joke. Nobody had altered that formula in all the fifty years of its existence. Hildebrand Harmsworth decided to be a live-wire and a new broom and wanted to jazz everything up. He said we must put out one of those shilling paper-backed books to advertise our column." And so *The Globe By The Way Book: A Literary Quick-Lunch for People Who Have Got Five Minutes to Spare* came into being, summed up succinctly by Plum as "an awful production." It is now the most scarce of all his books.

Like so many other prolific writers, Plum resorted to a variety of pseudonyms as his career progressed. The first of these—if one sets aside the article that had appeared under Westbrook's name in 1907—was an alias that cloaked the identities of himself and William Townend. During the latter part of 1908 they collaborated on a typical blood-and-thunder serial for *Chums,* the weekly illustrated magazine for boys. The story was called "The Luck Stone," and its author purported to be a hitherto unknown Basil Windham.

This work marked a complete departure from Plum's habit of drawing upon his own school experiences. "The Luck Stone" was pure fiction, based entirely upon the imaginings of its joint authors. Richard Usborne, in his excellent *Wodehouse at Work,* suggests that the idea for the story came from Plum's wide reading of similar material—notably Wilkie Collins' *The Moonstone,* Conan Doyle's *The Sign of the Four,* and Anstey's *Baboo Jabberjee.* Says Usborne:

> *He had read* Chums *for years, and knew its needs. It was opencast mining for him to slice out the story off the top of his brain. . . . He had shown, in breezy asides throughout his school novels . . . and elsewhere, that he had read acres of public-school bilge-fiction, had enjoyed it all and knew all the tricks of it. "The Luck Stone" shows that he could now imitate it, too, at the rustle of a cheque.*

This was the only story that Plum ever wrote for *Chums,* and it remained the only one on which he and Townend collaborated. Over the years, they both remembered the partnership with affection and often talked of reviving Basil Windham with other types of stories, but nothing came of it.

By now, Plum was contemplating a second visit to America—not only because New York had captured his imagination but also because of his unfinished business with A. E. Baerman. Before leaving, he was to see the publication of a book he had written for the railway-bookstall trade. It was called *The Swoop,* and it originated in shilling-paperback form on 16th April 1909. The whole thing—all 25,000 words of it—had been written in five days.

Because it was published with such humble and unambitious intent, *The Swoop, or How Clarence Saved England* is now one of the rarest of Wodehouse books: but it is certainly not the least remarkable from the point of view of plot. The story concerns the invasion of England by the Germans and the saving of the nation by a Boy Scout. That the Germans' campaign fails is shown to be partly due to the characteristic refusal of the English to take foreigners seriously, although the country is naturally a little put out because the hostile forces arrive at tea-time. The national preoccupation with cricket also figures largely in this satire.

Although it was never accorded volume status in America, *Vanity Fair* magazine published *The Swoop* in three instalments during 1915. With World War I then raging, its readers may not have appreciated that when the story was written there had been no reason for anyone to suppose that there really would be a large-scale war between England and Germany.

1909–
1914

It was in May 1909 that Plum made his second trip to the United States—principally because, as he remembered it, "A. E. Baerman didn't pay me the money he owed me. . . . I took a single room at the Hotel Earle in Greenwich Village. It was at 103 Waverly Place. Baerman put me on to it. I stayed there whenever I came to America until 1914. There were several other writers also living there: Charlie Sommerville, Joe O'Brien and Charles Neville Burke. One of the fellows put me on to Seth Moyle, who became my next literary agent in New York. I certainly wasn't up to selling a couple of short stories myself. Moyle had got this extraordinary knack of fast-talking an editor into taking a story. But his weakness was that although he could always sell *one* story to any editor he'd also sell a lot of rotten stuff. And so the editor was sort of laying for him the next time. Moyle sold 'The Good Angel' to *Cosmopolitan* for $200 and 'Deep Waters' to *Collier's Weekly* for $300, both in the same morning. Fortunately, those two stories were quite good ones."

The two stories had, in fact, been written in England shortly before this visit to America, and there had been no anticipation of such a quick sale. So sudden was this success, just six days after he had landed, that it rather went to Plum's head. America seemed the place to be. He therefore lost no time in wiring his resignation to *The Globe* and settling in at the Hotel Earle for an indefinite period. To further celebrate his good fortune, he bought himself a second-hand Monarch typewriter and a copy of Bartlett's *Familiar Quotations.* The typewriter was to remain a faithful companion for many years, worn and damaged parts being constantly replaced until no vestige of the original machine was in evidence.

Another quick sale saw the appearance of a short story entitled "Out of School" in the September issue of a pulp magazine called *Ainslee's*—the speedy acceptance of this and the other two stories apparently resulting from the success of the Kid Brady series that Plum had written for the American *Pearson's Magazine* from 1905 to 1907. But a small cloud was to appear in what had promised to be a very blue sky when Plum learned, with some concern, that although *Cosmopolitan* and *Collier's* were paying handsomely for the stories they accepted, they were not prepared to take his work on a regular basis as had *The Captain* and the *Strand* in England. Nevertheless, his earnings had by this time amounted to £1,000, and his continued sales to the *Strand* helped to keep him going. "I wrote for everything in those days," he recalled, "and for anybody who would take anything of mine." There were to be plenty of takers. During this period, from 1909 to 1914, he was to turn out five novels, forty short stories and four plays.

While Plum was concentrating on his writing in 1909, two former collaborators decided to enter into a more permanent partnership. Unaffected by the failure of *The Bandit's Daughter,* one of its authors, Herbert Westbrook, married the composer of its music, Ella King-Hall. Delighted as he was at the union of two close friends, the third ex-collaborator was not moved to any thoughts of romance except insofar as they related to the printed page. For his break away from public school stories was now beginning in earnest, and his genre was clearly the humorous love story.

"The Good Angel," so swiftly bought by *Cosmopolitan,* was in this vein: and it was the first of Plum's stories to feature a comic butler, Keggs. Like some of the other Wodehouse characters, Keggs was to turn up again— but not until Plum had returned to England.

His departure from New York came about early in 1910, when the realisation that his work would not be regularly accepted had fully sunken in. Immediately upon his arrival in England, he took himself off to Emsworth to see Baldwin King-Hall and to buy Threepwood, which he had previously rented. Now empty, it cost him £200; and he furnished it, showing a commendable lack of ostentation, with one bed, one table, one chair, several dogs and, of course, his Monarch typewriter.

No sooner had he settled in than he rejoined *The Globe,* and resumed his partnership with Herbert Westbrook on the "By the Way" column. And with a steady income now assured, he dashed off six short stories before writing the one that reintroduced Keggs. It was first published in America, in *Hampton's Magazine,* under the title "Watch Dog"; but when it appeared in England a month later, in the *Strand,* it had become "Love Me, Love My Dog."

From this time on, Plum wrote his short stories exclusively for the *Strand* as far as publication in England was concerned. His association with the magazine was to endure for a remarkable thirty-four years, although his loyalty was severely tested when Greenhough Smith died and Reeves Shaw became its editor. Shaw was already editor of twenty of Newnes' cheap magazines when he was asked to take on the *Strand* as an additional responsibility. Inevitably, because he couldn't give it the conscientious editorial attention it needed, the magazine suffered to the extent of losing much of its prestige and a sizeable proportion of its readership. But Plum stuck by it, to the eventual benefit of the magazine and himself: for when Shaw was finally replaced, the *Strand* picked up again and regained its position as England's leading magazine.

Apart from the short stories he was writing at Threepwood at this time, Plum also wrote two highly significant novels. The first of these was *Psmith in the City,* of particular interest because the story was based on his two years with the bank and was therefore—being more personally connected with his own experiences than *Not George Washington*—the nearest he had yet come to autobiography. But what may be even more noteworthy is the fact that this novel, with its continuing hero from the second half of *Mike,* bridged the gap between the public school stories and the humorous adult books yet to come. Furthermore, one sees with hindsight that Psmith was a significant link in the evolution of the Blandings Castle saga. *Psmith in the City* was published by Messrs. A. & C. Black in September 1910.

The second important book was *A Gentleman of Leisure,* published in England by Alston Rivers in November 1910 but previously published in

America by W. J. Watt as *The Intrusion of Jimmy.* This was the first humorous story to be set in a stately home in Shropshire, and it featured an amiable but dim peer, the first of a long line of Drones, a tycoon, a formidable aunt, a pretty but foolish girl, and a butler—the standard main ingredients for future Wodehouse novels.

With this work behind him, towards the end of 1910 Plum made a third trip to the United States. And from this time until August 1914 he "sort of shuttled to and fro across the Atlantic." As he explained, "The passage only cost about £10 in those days, and I kept dashing back to England and then to America."

On this particular visit he was contacted by producer William A. Brady, who had read *A Gentleman of Leisure* and decided that it would make a good play. Brady's suggestion was that playwright John Stapleton should dramatise the novel with Plum's assistance as to detail—a project that Plum, with his love of the theatre, was only too willing to go along with. In due course, the work having gone apace and there being nothing further he could do as Stapleton gave the play its final polish, he left for England in company with Brady.

Arriving in London on the 21st June 1911, the eve of King George V's coronation, Plum dined with Herbert Westbrook at the Café Royal. There was a festive air in the well-known restaurant and, in keeping with the general gaiety that pervaded the place, Westbrook began to tell Plum what he considered to be a particularly amusing story. In the middle of it, Plum fainted. This rather nonplussed Westbrook. He had told Plum funny stories before, and while they had rarely moved the man to convulsions of laughter it was equally true to say that they had never caused him to drop in a dead faint. Conscience-stricken but resourceful, Westbrook removed the recumbent form from the restaurant and bore it away into the night. He remembered that "Plum . . . bore me no ill-will on his recovery. On the contrary, he thanked me for having carried him off in a taxi to the Victoria Hotel." And quite rightly. Westbrook was blameless. It was not his story that had overcome his friend, but a chill contracted aboard ship.

While in England, Plum stayed at sparsely furnished Threepwood; and he was still there when, on the 24th August 1911, *A Gentleman of Leisure* opened on Broadway. He never did manage to see it at its original location, but he finally caught up with it on a later visit to America when the play was on tour and running in Baltimore, Maryland. There he met its leading man, Douglas Fairbanks, Senior, who was just beginning to gain recognition as an actor. (When the show was revived in Chicago in 1913, retitled *A Thief for a Night,* its leading man was John Barrymore, also at the start of an illustrious career.)

With *A Gentleman of Leisure* doing well on tour and his literary affairs in the hands of Seth Moyle, Plum made a speedy return to England in the autumn of 1911 in time to see the performance of a music-hall sketch he had written. It was called *After the Show,* and it had been adapted, in collaboration with Westbrook, from one of his short stories, "Ahead of Schedule."

He was now in the midst of what Ukridge would have called "a vast campaign"—writing numerous short stories, planning a new novel and putting the finishing touches to his latest. Such industry had already become the pattern of his life, but he was especially stimulated by being at Threepwood, where he was always able to work well. That he remained virtually solitary is not surprising. The volume of work that he undertook left him little time for anything else. If he relaxed at all, it was in his attendance at all the Dulwich football matches: but even that eventually led him back to the typewriter when he reported on the games for *The Alleynian.*

The beginning of 1912 saw him with a new literary agent—his first major one in England. It was really a case of Plum's rallying round and showing loyalty to an old friend, Ella King-Hall, who upon marrying Westbrook had set herself up as a literary agent. In the event, his loyalty was not misplaced. She proved so excellent at her job that their association lasted until her death in 1934.

Plum's novel for 1912 was called *The Prince and Betty,* remarkable for being the only one of his books to appear in two completely different versions, but using the same title. The original plot was a combination of love story and crime story, concerning gangsters in New York City and the character Kid Brady invented by Plum for the American market. It was this version that was published in America by W. J. Watt on the 14th February 1912. In England on the 1st May, however, Mills & Boon published *The Prince and Betty* with a plot containing only the love story. But Plum didn't believe in wasting good material. He later rewrote the excised crime story with Psmith as the main character, and the book was published in England in 1915 by Messrs. A. & C. Black under the title *Psmith Journalist.*

In the meantime he remained hard at work on another novel, for which he drew upon his observations at King-Hall's Emsworth House. But this was no reversion to his public school stories. Called *The Little Nugget,* the book was about the precocious son of wealthy parents who was being pursued by kidnappers—and Emsworth House, within such easy reach of Threepwood, provided an eminently suitable background. The importance of this book today is that it introduced Ogden, "the little nugget," who was to reappear some years later in *Piccadilly Jim.*

This was not the first time that Plum had created a character in one book and reintroduced that character at a later date in another book. But what he was really seeking at this time was a continuing character around which a series could be constructed. He had first attempted creating a series with his cricket stories in the *Strand.* Now he wanted to do the same sort of thing with the humorous love stories which he recognised to be his forte, and the need was for a character who would narrate each story and thus provide the link between each book. The first of such characters that he came up with was Reggie Pepper, who could be considered the charter member of the yet-to-be-created Drones Club. Reggie featured in seven short stories before Bertie Wooster made his debut, overran Reggie and finally took him over. But not without complications. For one of Reggie's stories, "Disentangling Old Duggie," written in 1912, truly belongs in the sequence of events to the much later Wooster-Jeeves saga. In the "Duggie" story, Reggie meets Florence Craye for the first time; but in "Jeeves Takes Charge," written in 1916, Reggie has become Bertie Wooster and gets himself engaged to Florence. Furthering this merging of the two characters, two Reggie Pepper stories were later rewritten for Bertie Wooster and Jeeves.

Long before this was to happen, however, in February 1913 Plum was asked to write a long sketch for Lawrence Grossmith, son of the famous singing comedian George Grossmith. Lawrence had just inherited £3,000 and was going to spend some of it on furthering his career. Not averse to being on the receiving end of some of the Grossmith munificence, Plum cast around for ideas and decided that his short story "Rallying Round Old George"—which featured Reggie Pepper and had just appeared in the December 1912 issue of the *Strand*—would adapt well into a long, one-act play. Accordingly, he set to work on it. The original idea for the story had come from Herbert Westbrook and, characteristically, Plum had put Westbrook's name alongside his own in the *Strand.* Now, although he had again done all the writing, Plum saw to it that Westbrook's name appeared with his on the programme for the play: and he also paid half of the fee received to his friend.

The play, called *Brother Alfred,* opened at the Savoy Theatre on the 8th April 1913 and closed two weeks later. It was an inauspicious start to Lawrence's career but not calamitous in its effect. Certainly it in no way lessened his respect for Plum's talents, for he was to win public esteem in later Wodehouse productions.

With the closing of *Brother Alfred,* Plum set off on another of his jaunts to America. On this trip he met Bob Davis, the general editor of Frank Munsey's many publications. Davis had his office on the top floor of the Flatiron Building, then Manhattan's tallest office building, and it was here that Plum sold him *The Little Nugget* as a serial for *Munsey's Magazine.* Plum remembered Davis "as a fellow who would give you a plot and then buy the story you had written for his magazine. You'd call on him and say you wanted a plot. He would take a turn up and down the room and would give you a plot. Then you would write it up for his magazine. I continued to write for the Munsey magazines for the next two years. They didn't pay much, but if you wrote stories in great numbers you could support yourself."

Having written stories in great numbers and thus supported himself for some months, Plum returned to England at the end of October 1913. This time, since he had previously sold Threepwood, he settled himself in a London hotel.

While in London he renewed his acquaintanceship with a former colleague on *The Globe,* Charles H. Bovill. Like Plum, Bovill had written some lyrics for *The Gay Gordons* back in 1907 and, besides writing fiction, was still doing a fair amount of work for the theatre. He had, in fact, just been commissioned to write a revue for the Empire Theatre. Knowing that Plum was not working on anything specific at that moment, it occurred to him that they might collaborate on it. With the suggestion came the invitation for Plum to leave his hotel and move into Bovill's flat at Prince of Wales Mansions, Battersea.

Accepting both offers, Plum made the transfer of accommodation and was soon involved in the writing of the revue. But that was not the only thing to result from this partnership. As their work progressed, Bovill had an inspiration—a series of stories about a young man who comes into a lot of money and is precipitated into various adventures because of it. The idea appealed to Plum—who must have been feeling rather lost at working on only one project at a time—and they began working simultaneously on the revue and the series.

The revue, which was called *Nuts and Wine,* opened at the Empire Theatre on the 4th January 1914; and shortly afterwards the series, entitled "A Man of Means," was sold to the *Strand* in England and the *Delineator* in America. Plum was therefore in sound financial shape, and it could only have added to his general air of well-being to see the publication by Methuen of *The Man Upstairs*—a collection of his short stories, most of which had previously appeared in the *Strand*—on the 23rd January 1914.

It was a promising start to the year, and it meant that he was in a position to take himself off to America again, which he promptly did. Whatever the spell that New York had cast upon him, it had nothing to do with its glamorous night life or high-paced social round. In New York, as in London, he spent much of his time writing. On this visit it was mainly some short stories for *McClure's Magazine;* but he was also commissioned to write light articles for the new American *Vanity Fair* magazine, which pronounced itself to be "Devoted to Society and the Arts." His first contribution was called "The Physical Culture Peril" and it appeared in the May 1914 issue.

By this time he was back in England again on one of his quick hops, allowing himself just about enough time to go with Bovill to see the latter's successor to *Nuts and Wine* at the Empire Theatre before returning to New York to spend a month with Norman Thwaites. These frequent trips across the Atlantic were becoming almost a way of life: and there were more of them in the offing.

"In June," Plum recalled, "a pal of mine, Cameron Mackenzie, editor of *McClure's Magazine,* wanted me to do some stories on John Barrymore. Since I was going back to England and John Barrymore was going to be in England, Mackenzie wanted me to get hold of Barrymore and get all of his reminiscences and so on to make stories out of them. The agreement was that when Barrymore was to come back I was to come back with him and get his stories. Towards the end of July, I got a cable from Cameron Mackenzie saying that John Barrymore was sailing on a German ship on the twenty-seventh of July. War was threatening and the atmosphere was tense, but nothing actually happened to mar the voyage. We landed in New York on the second of August, just two days before war broke out."

But if war was threatening, there was something equally earth-shatter-

ing in store for Plum personally. His solitary way of life was about to undergo a radical change, and the first manifestation of it was to beat the
outbreak of war by one day. For on the 3rd August 1914, the day after his
arrival in New York, at the apartment he was sharing with Norman Thwaites
at 43 East 27th Street, Thwaites introduced him to a lovely young English
widow named Ethel Newton Rowley.

Born on the 23rd May 1885 at King's Lynn in Norfolk, Ethel May
Newton, an only child, had been brought up by her grandmother. At the
age of eighteen, she had married Joseph Arthur Leonard Rowley on the
15th September 1903 and travelled with him to India, where he was an
engineer. A daughter, Leonora, was born to them on the 12th March 1905.
Five years later, Rowley died tragically as a result of drinking infected water
and Mrs. Rowley returned with her child to England. When Leonora was
old enough, she had been safely boarded at Bromley School and Mrs. Rowley
had come to America to visit friends.

From their first meeting, Plum was enchanted with her—no doubt feeling
many of the emotions experienced by the heroes of his novels on that first sight
of the one girl without whom life would not be worth living. And it seemed
that his interest was reciprocated. Certainly Mrs. Rowley was not averse to
going swimming with him every day at Long Beach, Long Island. As Plum
remembered it, "Our visits to Long Beach must have been during the month
of August and the first half of September. We used to go down to the Pennsyl-
vania Railroad Station. We'd ride down to Long Beach to have a swim and
lunch, and then come back on the train. Of course, there were hardly any
motors then. Anyway, I couldn't have afforded that. . . . I remember bathing
once, the ocean being particularly rough that day, and Ethel said, 'Hold on to
me'—and I was then swept away from her by a huge wave. But she always said
I let go of her. . . . We changed and dressed in the bath-houses there. I didn't
remember the place at all when we went down there in the fifties. It was very
primitive in those days."

But the burgeoning of romance, even in primitive places, did not deflect
Plum from his writing; and in that respect there was no disadvantage in sharing
an apartment with Thwaites, who didn't finish his work at the *New York
World* until two o'clock in the morning. Plum's pattern was to spend his days
with Mrs. Rowley and then write after dinner until Thwaites returned from his
office. And at this time, writing for *Vanity Fair* was his only source of income.
The fact is, however, that he wrote almost all of the magazine under a variety

of pen names. He was J. Plum, P. Brook-Haven, Pelham Grenville, C.P. West and J. William Walker. But it was under his own name that he was asked by Frank Crowninshield, *Vanity Fair*'s dynamic editor, to become the magazine's drama critic. Possessing only $50 at the time, Plum readily accepted the offer.

The shortage of funds was, fortunately, only temporary. Money came in from serials sold to *The Captain,* and there was a healthy $2,000 from Bob Davis for *The Coming of Bill*—the plot for which he had himself suggested to Plum.

Plots were now proving a bugbear. With his stories becoming more Americanised, Plum was having difficulty in thinking of suitable backgrounds. He was relieved, therefore, when Bob Davis advised him to stick to writing about the things he knew best. Acting on that advice, he started work on a new serial set in England, with an all-English cast and centring round a peer and his castle. He called it "Something New," and in it he introduced Lord Emsworth and Blandings Castle. It was the beginning of a saga.

While he was thus engaged, in the middle of September 1914, Norman Thwaites, who was British-born, left for England to join the army as a special correspondent. Plum had tried to enlist shortly before this latest trip but "I was rejected for service because of my eyes. They had been bad as a child and I was kept out of the navy because of them. I tried to enlist again over here when America went to war, but I was rejected once more."

If the armies of the allied countries were bent on rejecting Plum, Mrs. Rowley was not. On the 30th September 1914, only two months after their first meeting, they were married in the Little Church Around the Corner, just off Madison Avenue, on 29th Street. To state the fact so simply, however, would be to overlook the fact that the highlights of this romance had had the earmarks of a Wodehouse novel. Plum's proposal to Mrs. Rowley, for instance, had somehow lost some of the solemnity of the occasion by being precipitated by an uncontrollable fit of sneezing, during which Mrs. Rowley had removed herself as far as possible from her stricken suitor. And the marriage ceremony was delayed by the absence of the officiating minister at what should have been the crucial moment. When he did arrive, he was breathless and elated—not at the thought of uniting Plum and Mrs. Rowley in holy wedlock but because he had just made a large sum of money on the stock market.

On the 1st October the newlyweds took up residence in a rented bungalow at Bellport, Long Island—one of Plum's favourite spots. It cost them $25 for the first month and $20 a month thereafter. In addition to this, in November, they also took an apartment at 375 Central Park West in New York City. His recent sales enabled Plum to take on these responsibilities while he finished "Something New" and began work on another serial.

As far as he was concerned, his marriage to Ethel was a turning point. He knew that there were going to be even better times ahead. And in looking back on it all, he said, "It was an awfully curious thing how everything altered just after we got married."

1915–
1918

One of the first things to alter after his marriage was Plum's literary representation in the United States. To see 1915 away to a good start, he signed up with Paul Reynolds, who was soon to become America's foremost literary agent. It was the beginning of a long and fruitful alliance which gave further proof of Plum's reluctance to chop and change when things were running smoothly—the mutually profitable association terminating only with Reynolds's death in 1945.

Reynolds's first act for his new client was to sell "Something New" to George Lorimer, famed editor of the *Saturday Evening Post,* with Plum benefiting to the tune of $3,500. This took care of any worry about immediate finances, for as Plum recalled: "If one could see a few months ahead, one was all right." But in this case it was not only the financial aspect that was important. There was also the enormous prestige of being published in the *Saturday Evening Post*—the ambition of all American writers.

To appreciate the importance of the *Post,* it is necessary to realise that from the turn of the century until World War II magazines reigned supreme as a popular recreation and an influential force in America. The period could properly be called the Age of the American Magazine, and the success of the medium was mainly attributable to publishing magnates S. S. McClure and Frank Munsey. But the rise of the *Saturday Evening Post* above all its rivals to the pinnacle of international prominence was entirely due to George Horace Lorimer, the greatest of the magazine editors. He was a man who knew exactly what he wanted, and he would settle for nothing less. The fiction he chose to publish came from such eminent writers as Mary Roberts Rinehart, Clarence Buddington Kelland, Booth Tarkington, Arthur Train and Rudyard Kipling: but the work had to be of their best. As John Tebbel pointed out in his biography of

Lorimer, no writer was considered to be bigger than the *Post* itself; and Lorimer would not hesitate to turn down a story by the most famous and the most highly paid of them if he felt it to be below standard. Nor was he at all concerned if a well-known writer decided to withdraw his or her services through some real or imagined wrong. There were always plenty of others willing and eager to step in. Not that any of them found it as easy as that to enter. Even the work of regular subscribers had to pass the acid test, for Lorimer was known to read every contribution as though it was the first piece the writer had ever submitted.

It was therefore very much to Plum's credit that in the twenty-two years he wrote for the *Saturday Evening Post* he never received a rejection slip. Remembering this in *Performing Flea*, he wrote:

> *The Boss was an autocrat all right, but my God, what an editor to work for. He kept you on your toes. I had twenty-one serials in the* Post, *but I never felt safe till I got the cable saying each had got over with Lorimer.*

Writing of Lorimer at the time of his death, Edwin Balmer—then editor of *Redbook Magazine*—said that he was "more than a mere editor. He was a veritable tower of strength. He was a man whose fairness and honesty established new and higher standards in the profession. For a writer to be 'accepted by Lorimer' meant to arrive."

It can be understood, then, how honoured Plum felt to receive an invitation from Lorimer to spend a weekend at his home in late May 1915. Plum had just finished writing a serial, "Uneasy Money," and was at loose ends since Ethel had just left for England to bring Leonora back to the States. He therefore accepted the invitation with alacrity and took his completed manuscript with him. On Sunday, Lorimer read "Uneasy Money" with his customary care and concentration, concluded that he liked it better than "Something New" and said that he would buy it for $5,000.

Elated, Plum returned to Bellport to await Ethel's return with Leonora. But the high spirits engendered by the enjoyable and profitable weekend gradually began to dissipate as he contemplated the coming first meeting with his stepdaughter. How would he and the ten-year-old girl get along? Would she like him? Would he like her? And, all things being equal, how did one treat a female child of that age anyway? He knew a great deal about the ways of grubby schoolboys: but a little girl . . . ?

His fears turned out to be groundless. He and Leonora took to each other instantly. Here was an unusual child indeed—a girl whose eagerness for things matched his and who shared his unalloyed fondness for the outdoor life. All of that summer they enjoyed each other's company, taking long walks together and swimming each day in the nearby Atlantic.

Leonora really was an exceptional child. Possessed of wit and tremendous charm, she also had the unique gift of making everyone she met feel that he or she was the finest and most important person in the world. Her effect on Plum was electric, and before she returned to her English school in the autumn, he had formally adopted her.

At the beginning of September, with Leonora gone, Ethel and Plum moved back to their New York apartment, where Plum continued to write articles for *Vanity Fair* and short stories for the *Saturday Evening Post*. One of these short stories, "Extricating Young Gussie," was to have greater significance than its author could have been aware of at the time. It featured a drone—a good-natured but irresponsible young man-about-town—and his manservant. The drone was Bertie Wooster, making his formal bow, not very forcefully assisted by a Jeeves whose potential was yet to be realised.

There had been other comic Wodehouse manservants, of course, starting with Keggs, the butler, in "The Good Angel." But Keggs had been decidedly of the lower classes in speech and manner, with nothing of the smooth and polished performer about him. Closer to the Jeeves concept was the valet Voules in "Rallying Round Old George," whose off-duty manner was rough, but who acted with grace and fluidity in the presence of his master: a curious mixture of Keggs and Jeeves. Then there was Wilson, a manservant of intelligence, who featured prominently in "Ahead of Schedule." But the immediate predecessor to Jeeves was a gentleman's gentleman named Jevons, who appeared in "Creatures of Impulse." He was imperturbable, showed a great deal of tact and, with one exception, performed his duties to perfection. The important point is that Jeeves, like Jevons, was created a gentleman's gentleman, and not merely the butler that so many people imagine him to be. Buttling is but a small part of Jeeves' duties, which encompass all the household functions. For the butler pure and simple, metaphorically speaking, one has to turn to Beach of Blandings Castle, who started out as a Keggs type in "Something New," but who graduated in later stories—as a direct result of the popularity of Jeeves—into a refined, polished and suave butler.

It wasn't until Plum wrote "Leave it to Jeeves" (which became "The Artistic Career of Young Corky" when it appeared in *Carry On, Jeeves*) that he awoke to the fact that he had just the character he needed for a series of books. What he had wanted was someone who could get Bertie and his pals out of their predicaments, not one of them having the mental capacity to manage it himself. And suddenly it was crystal clear: Jeeves was the obvious answer.

Describing his first encounter with Jeeves, Plum wrote in his Introduction to the *Jeeves Omnibus:*

> *I find it curious, now that I have written so much about him, to recall how softly and undramatically Jeeves first entered my little world. On that occasion, he spoke just two lines. The first was: "Mrs. Gregson to see you, sir." The second: "Very good, sir. Which suit will you wear?" That was in a story in a volume entitled* The Man With Two Left Feet. *It was only some time later, when I was going into the strange affair which is related under the title of "The Artistic Career of Young Corky" that the man's qualities dawned upon me. I still blush to think of the off-hand way I treated him at our first encounter.*

But much was to happen before Plum would write these words, by no means the least of events being his entry into the world of the American theatre. Unwittingly instrumental in this was Frank Crowninshield when he appointed Plum drama critic for *Vanity Fair.* For it was in this capacity that Plum attended the opening night of the musical farce *Very Good, Eddie* at the Princess Theatre in New York on 23rd December 1915, thereby meeting an old friend through whose good graces he was to make a new one and start a fresh career.

The Princess, located on the south side of 39th Street, between Sixth Avenue and Broadway, was a small theatre which seated only 299 people. It was owned by Lee Shubert and managed by Elisabeth (Bessie) Marbury and F. Ray Comstock.

Bessie Marbury, a theatrical agent who represented all the European playwrights in the United States, had firm ideas about presenting musical comedy on a miniature scale. As envisaged by her, a show should have no more than two sets, less than the customary minimum of twelve chorus girls, and only eleven musicians in the orchestra pit—the overall cost of the production not exceeding $7,500.

This concept was far removed from what was currently taking place on the stages of Broadway and London. The Broadway musical at this time was a spectacular affair with a budget in the region of fifty thousand dollars. But there was little to commend such a show from the artistic point of view, for the practice was to have a new but not too original book written to encompass the most tuneful arias from an already established light opera. The emphasis would be on scenery, costumes and hordes of beautiful showgirls to back up the glamorous young leading ladies and the all-important comedian, with no great demands being made on anyone's talents. In England, the alternative to using the music from a light opera was to have an original production written and composed on exactly the same lines as an existing work. Again, little was asked of the cast other than they should move gracefully about the stage, leaving the more strenuous efforts to the comedians. The music, though often quite attractive, was of little real merit and was always derivative.

None of this appealed to Bessie Marbury, and she felt it was time for a change, but she found it difficult to acquire original vehicles suited to her intimate theatre. The well-known librettists and composers were not willing to work for the reduced salary that the specifics of her requirements would entail, and she and Comstock were therefore compelled to seek out comparatively unknown people who would be glad of the opportunity of having their work performed. There were many engaged upon altering cumbersome operetta scores for Broadway shows, and there was one in particular of whom she knew. He had frequently been asked to interpolate his own light melodies into the scores he was rewriting, but although he was obviously talented he had not yet gained wide recognition. His name was Jerome D. Kern.

When Bessie asked Kern if he would like to try his hand at her type of small-scale musical, he had just had his first complete musical score, *Ninety in the Shade,* produced and was eager to do something else that would be entirely his own. And when he was further asked if he knew of anyone who could write the book for the proposed show, he was quick to suggest Guy Bolton, who had written the book for *Ninety in the Shade*. Bolton was more than happy to accept the offer.

The result of their endeavours was *Very Good, Eddie*—the second show to be staged at the Princess and thus one of the forerunners of a series of musicals that would revolutionise the American musical comedy theatre. Unlike the offerings on Broadway, the book for this show—written by Guy Bolton and Philip Bartholomae—was strong enough to stand by itself. It was enhanced by, but not dependent on the music—an innovation in itself. But more than this, the show was the first of its kind to rely on situation comedy and humorous characterisation as opposed to the clowning and cross-talk with which the Broadway musicals filled in the gaps between romantic scenes. What the Princess was offering, in fact, was a comedy with music, in which each lady of the chorus was individually dressed to suit her personality, rather than in some kind of uniform costume and which featured the music of one composer throughout. And it was to prove that a small, intimate musical comedy devoid of lavish vulgarity and brash coarseness could become a financial success.

On the opening night of *Very Good, Eddie,* drama critic Plum bumped into composer Kern—his friend from *The Beauty of Bath* days—in the foyer of the Princess Theatre and thereby set in motion another chain of far-reaching events. For after the usual greetings had been exchanged, Jerry Kern invited Plum to his apartment on West 68th Street for the following day. And it was there, on 24th December 1915, that Plum first met Guy Bolton.

Guy Reginald Bolton was born in England of American parents on 23rd November 1884 at Broxbourne in Hertfordshire. His father, Reginald Pelham Bolton, was a well-known engineering expert whose work kept the family travelling frequently between the United States and England. Perhaps somewhat following in his father's footsteps, Guy became an architect. But while helping to design the Soldiers and Sailors Monument on Riverside Drive in New York, he began to write short stories and plays, thereby launching himself on a career that was to be distinguished by such works as *Girl Crazy, Polly With a Past* and *Anastasia.*

On that afternoon in December 1915, however, not one of the three men gathered in Jerome Kern's apartment could have foretold what the future held for all or any of them. They were, in any event, discussing not their own future but that of the musical comedy in general, and they were excited to discover that their ideas coincided. Certainly they were all of the opinion that *Very*

Good, Eddie was along the right lines—that the book of a show had to be independently strong and that the music and lyrics should be integrated to further the plot. It was a concept utterly opposed to the operettas of Victor Herbert and Rudolf Friml, whose works were the mainstay of the American musical theatre as it then was, in which the improbable story would grind to a halt while the stars performed a duet or two.

One thing that came out of the discussion was the dissatisfaction of both Guy and Jerry with the lyrics in *Very Good, Eddie;* and Jerry, who knew Plum to be a superb lyricist, suggested that he and Guy could do a much better job if Plum worked with them. Plum, still enthralled by the theatre and eager to return to it, needed no persuading and it was immediately agreed that the three should join forces.

Word gets around quickly in show business. The partnership had scarcely been formed when two of its members, Guy and Plum, received a summons from Henry W. Savage, one of the top managers of the Klaw & Erlanger combine. If not quite a command from a crowned head, it was the nearest thing to it in the American theatre.

Abraham Lincoln Erlanger, in partnership with Marc Klaw, was the czar of the New York theatres. The only competition to Klaw & Erlanger came from the Shubert brothers—Lee, J. J., and Sam—who were just starting out with the tiny Princess Theatre as one of their first houses. But the Shuberts had a long way to go before they became a serious threat. All the eminent managers—Ziegfeld, Dillingham, Savage, Belasco, Cohan, and Harris—booked their shows into Erlanger's theatres. A call from a Klaw & Erlanger manager was therefore not to be sniffed at.

What Savage wanted was the aid of Guy and Plum in putting into shape a new musical called *Pom Pom* which was due to open at the George M. Cohan Theatre; one of the first things he asked them when they arrived in his office was how much they would require for their services. This was something they had neglected to consider beforehand, and the silence that emanated from Guy indicated that he had no idea. Plum, perhaps with the intention of providing some light relief and a possible chuckle, roguishly suggested one thousand dollars and then wished he hadn't spoken, expecting to be ejected from the office by an irate boot. But Savage was impatient to get to the nub of the matter and instantly agreed to the fee. Guy was greatly impressed with what he took to be Plum's business acumen—and so was Plum. He had never done such a spectacular deal for himself before and would not be likely to do anything to match it in the future.

Although soon busy with *Pom Pom,* Plum and Guy were anxious to get started with Jerry on a musical comedy of their own; and indeed the three spent all the time they could spare on preliminary work for their great venture. On the completion of the doctoring of *Pom Pom,* which opened on 28th February 1916, it seemed that they were all set to go. But again they were forestalled—this time by a call from Erlanger himself. He wanted them to re-write a Viennese operetta he had just acquired. The attractive thing about this offer was that there would be work for all three of them, with Guy writing a new book, Plum writing the lyrics, and Jerry interpolating a few of his own numbers into a score originally composed by Emmerich Kalman. Though not exactly a show of their own, this one—to be called *Miss Springtime*—would be the next best thing.

While all this was going on, another of Plum's serials became a full-length book when *Uneasy Money* was published on 17th March 1916. Although he was now so involved with work for the theatre, Plum was not entirely neglecting his story writing and had a new serial on the boil.

With the summer approaching and another holiday visit from Leonora imminent, Plum and Ethel leased a new bungalow on a creek at Bellport— a delightful place of which Plum would not see nearly enough. He had to work closely with Jerry and Guy on *Miss Springtime,* and was therefore forced to spend much time shuttling back and forth between the bungalow and Jerry's new home in Bronxville, where the three of them were wont to gather. On one of their working nights, Plum remembered, "Jerry wanted to drive down to Bellport to see the new bungalow we had rented. It was eleven o'clock at night, and it's a good two-hour drive from his house and another hour into New York. So we got to Bellport at about three in the morning. We stayed for an hour or so and then we went back to his house. I remember Jerry going fast asleep at the wheel during the ride back. But that's the sort of thing he used to do in those days. He was very much the sort of fellow who would do any-thing on the spur of the moment."

Spending as much time as he could with Leonora, and thus cementing the bond between them, Plum nevertheless finished the serial—called "Picca-dilly Jim"—and sold it to the *Saturday Evening Post* for $7,500 on 1st August 1916. And on that same auspicious day he, Guy and Jerry signed an agreement with Klaw & Erlanger to write an original musical comedy to be produced by Henry W. Savage. It was to be called *Have a Heart,* and they started working on an idea for it while putting the finishing touches to *Miss Springtime.*

It was a busy summer; and when it came to an end, Leonora went back to her school in England and Plum and Ethel returned to New York, where they took a suite of rooms in an apartment-hotel on West 45th Street.

Miss Springtime opened at the New Amsterdam Theatre on 25th September 1916 and was an immediate success. It could hardly have failed, since it had resulted from the combined efforts of some of Broadway's greatest talents. Its director was Herbert Gresham; its choreographer was Julien Mitchell, creator of the Ziegfeld Follies; its sets and lighting were by Joseph Urban, who had revolutionised stage lighting techniques; and its cast was headed by Sari Petrass, George MacFarlane, Jack Hazzard, Georgia O'Ramey and Jed Prouty.

Reviewing the show in *Vanity Fair,* the drama critic—a modest Plum— gave credit where he thought it was due:

> *The man who . . . has revolutionised musical comedy to such an extent that all the other authors will either have to improve their stuff or go back to box-stencilling, is Guy Bolton, author of* Miss Springtime, *at the New Amsterdam. I feel a slight diffidence about growing enthusiastic over* Miss Springtime, *for the fact is that, having contributed a few little lyrical* bijoux *to the above (just a few trifles, you know, dashed off in the intervals of more serious work), I am drawing a royalty from it which already has caused the wolf to move up a few parasangs from the Wodehouse doorstep. Far be it from me to boost—from sordid and commercial motives—a theatrical entertainment whose success means the increase of my meat-meals per week from one to two, but candour compels me to say that* Miss Springtime *is a corker. It is the best musical play in years. . . .*

> *And, good as the Kalman-Kern music
> is, and however excellent Jack Hazzard,
> George MacFarlane, Sari Petrass, Geor-
> gia O'Ramey and the rest of the cast
> may be, the solid rock on which its suc-
> cess is founded is Guy Bolton's book. It
> is sane and sincere, and the humour
> with which it is crammed is distributed
> evenly instead of being laid on in iso-
> lated chunks. This Bolton, as George
> Jean Nathan would say, knows his
> job from the first spoonful of soup to
> the final walnut. His construction is
> perfect, and he has written so many
> good lines that at least half the re-
> viewers, unable to grasp the fact that a
> musical comedy author could be capable
> of real humour, took it for granted that
> J. Hazzard, Esq., the principal co-
> median, had made them up himself as
> he went along—the true fact being
> that, with the exception of three inter-
> polated lines, the script is played ex-
> actly as Bolton handed it in to the
> management. There is no getting away
> from it—the lad swings a wicked pen.*

The critic for the *New York Tribune*, who was not receiving royalties
from the show, backed up Plum's judgment when he wrote:

> *In describing a musical show it is
> customary to remark that the music is
> pretty—very pretty, indeed,—but what
> a book! Therefore it is with no incon-
> siderable relief that one brings up the
> matter of* Miss Springtime, *which is
> endowed with both humour and mel-*

*ody. All of the latter is of an exceed-
ingly high grade, and much of the
former is clever. Still further,* Miss
Springtime *has been staged with the
splendour that one has come to expect
of the K. & E. musical productions, and
the cast contains one or two people who
can sing. So, whatever your tastes, you
are certain to be pleased at the New
Amsterdam.* Miss Springtime *is nothing if not a success. . . . Guy Bolton has
written the book, and* P. G. Wodehouse
*and Herbert Reynolds are responsible
for the lyrics. When a new joke fell upon
the ear early in the evening one felt that
the piece was exceptional, and when it
was followed by others equally new—
to say nothing of a set of workmanlike
and frequently amusing lyrics—the occasion became epochal.*

Miss Springtime ran for 227 performances at the New Amsterdam, had
an even longer run in Chicago, and continued on the road for over four years
with three touring companies. In September 1916, however, it was enough to
know that it had been well received.

Far from resting on their laurels, Plum, Guy and Jerry redoubled their
efforts on *Have a Heart,* and also started work on a new show for the Princess
Theatre. The request for this had come from Ray Comstock, who invited the
trio to his office on 1st October 1916 and stated that he would give them a
contract for a new show without reading it or hearing a note of the score. He
had just seen *Miss Springtime,* and was so impressed that he would take their
work on trust. Their agents, The American Play Company, could, he said, draw
up a contract giving them a seven per cent interest in the show and the right
to choose the director and the cast. . . . The contract was signed on 8th October.

Spurred on to fresh endeavour, the jubilant partners worked so hard on
Have a Heart that by November rehearsals on it had started, with the three of
them taking an active part in preparing the show for the stage. It was exciting

for them to see their ideas taking shape, and everything seemed to be going splendidly when it suddenly became apparent that they were going to have difficulty with their leading comedian. Excellent performer though he was, he was simply too old to be taken for a boy of sixteen, as demanded by the script. Obviously there would have to be a replacement: but who would be able to play the part? Plum knew. He had thought of the one person able to do it to perfection—a vaudeville comedian named Billy B. Van. The matter of casting was, however, the province of Henry W. Savage and the final decision would be his.

When approached, Savage couldn't have agreed more that Billy B. Van would be ideal—but . . . there was the matter of his salary. Savage was sure that they wouldn't be able to get the comedian for less than three hundred dollars a week. This didn't seem much to Guy and Plum, and they said so. "It is to me," replied Savage ("who," according to the two writers in *Bring On the Girls*, "having only twenty-seven million dollars tucked away in blue chip securities, had to be careful"). But he did have a proposition to make. If Guy and Plum would pay half of Billy B. Van's salary for the first three months, it was a deal.

The two looked at each other, both thinking that it was a bit rum for authors to pay out money to the management instead of vice versa. And then they thought of Billy B. Van singing the big song "Napoleon" in the show. . . .

"I'm game," said Guy.

"So am I," said Plum.

And so it was that Billy B. Van was engaged and scored an instant hit with his rendition of "Napoleon" when *Have a Heart* opened at the Liberty Theatre on 11th January 1917. He had the customers rolling in the aisles for the first three months of the run, during which time Plum and Guy dutifully paid half his salary: and then, at the end of the third month, Savage fired him. The fact that with the going of the star the box office takings dropped by several thousand dollars a week didn't seem to bother Savage. He appeared to be more satisfied with the saving of a hundred and fifty dollars a week on the salary of the comedian he chose to replace Billy B. Van. New York runs didn't mean much to him anyway. He was more interested in long tours, and, at any rate, *Have a Heart*—which ran for only five months and two weeks on Broadway—eventually played to crowded houses for six years on the road.

An indication that in this show the three partners had lived up to their ideals was given by the reviewer who wrote:

Have a Heart has the additional asset of a plot—a plot, incidentally, upon which Mr. Kern's music has always a direct bearing.

Shortly after the Broadway opening of *Have a Heart,* Ray Comstock was enquiring about the show for the Princess. *Very Good, Eddie* was now nearing the end of its run (which finally totalled 341 performances) and he was hoping that they would have something ready with which to replace it. They had. Book, music and lyrics had just been completed, and they were calling the piece *Oh, Boy!*—the first of the trio's original musicals for the Princess.

Taking advantage of the terms of their contract, they chose Robert Milton to direct, and Anna Wheaton, Marie Carroll and Edna Mae Oliver to play the leading roles. They were still seeking two young actresses for a couple of small parts, however, when Comstock told them he could get two of the most ravishing of Ziegfeld's Follies girls—Marion Davies and Justine Johnstone—if that was the type they were looking for. Both girls were noted for their beauty and were the type that almost any sane and healthy man would be looking for, and the partners didn't hesitate to accept the offer. But when the show went on the road for its tryout before opening in New York, they had cause to wonder whether they hadn't been too hasty.

At their first stop, Schenectady, the dress rehearsal couldn't have been more disastrous. Apart from everything else that went wrong, when the two Follies beauties appeared on the stage for a brief scene, it was immediately apparent that the blonde and blue-eyed Miss Davies was not at the top of her form. Having suffered an attack of stage fright while awaiting her cue, she had quaffed a glass or two of champagne which, far from calming her nerves, had rendered her utterly incapable of delivering her lines. To overcome this, she and Justine Johnstone had arranged that Miss Johnstone would speak Marion's lines as well as her own. The ensuing scene was therefore as staggering as it was remarkable. For her own lines, Justine used her natural contralto voice; but for Marion's lines she adopted a piping treble. Not wishing to appear uncooperative, Marion mouthed the words whenever the high-pitched voice issued from Justine's lips; but there was an unfortunate lack of synchronisation which lent a bizarre quality to the proceedings and drew shrieks of hysterical laughter from all present.

In the midst of this, there arrived a newspaper reporter and a photographer bent on giving the show some advance publicity. The rehearsal was halted, the stage was cleared, and the stars gathered in small, apparently unconcerned groups, waiting to be called and patently prepared to sacrifice themselves to the camera for the good of the show. But when the stage manager asked the newsmen whom they wanted first, the reply was, "We only want Miss Davies and Miss Johnstone." And they were adamant. Their orders had been to get pictures of the two glamour girls, with an accompanying story, and they had not the slightest interest in the more important members of the cast. The rest of the company had perforce to sit in the orchestra and watch the Follies girls strike pose after pose for the avid photographers, the faces of the female stars becoming grimmer and stonier with each stance taken by the two beauties.

When the rather prolonged session was over, Ray Comstock called for the rehearsal to be continued. But Anna Wheaton and Marie Carroll had already departed, leaving word that if they sat around much longer in the cold they would have no voices for the morrow's opening. The advent of the newsmen and the nature of their assignment had apparently turned the already cold atmosphere absolutely icy.

On the following evening, however, everything went beautifully and the show was a success. Nevertheless, as the tour proceeded to Syracuse, Rochester, Buffalo and Albany, Guy and Plum kept cutting and polishing: and they made two vital changes in the cast, bringing in Tom Powers and Hal Forde to play the leading male roles.

By the time the show was ready for New York, the company had become a unit and everyone was getting along wonderfully with everyone else. The cast had become, in fact, that time-honoured show business cliché—one big, happy family.

Oh, Boy! opened at the Princess Theatre on 20th February 1917 and turned out to be the biggest hit of the season. During its Broadway run there were four road companies on tour, and after the Broadway run had ended, the touring companies continued for another ten years. The show cost $29,262 to produce, including its seven-week tryout, and it made a profit of $181,641.

In a magazine article, Plum wrote:

> *The definition of a smash-hit in the theatre is one that has varied a good deal from age to age. In Shakespeare's time anything that ran two nights was*

*good, and if you did three you went out
and bought a new fur coat. In the nineties authors became offensively con-
ceited if they broke the hundred mark.
Today a musical comedy which runs
less than five years is presumed to have
had some structural weakness in it. It
ought to have been fixed out of town,
people say, even if it meant calling in
a couple of play-doctors.*

But there were no structural weaknesses in *Oh, Boy!* and it had no need
of play-doctors, even if it didn't run for five years. The fact that it achieved 463
performances on Broadway is the measure of its success.

There is no doubt that *Oh, Boy!* and its predecessors established Bolton,
Wodehouse and Kern as the innovators of the American musical comedy in the
form it has taken today. Such was their impact at the time that playwright
George S. Kaufman, then drama critic for the *New York Tribune,* was moved
to write in his "Broadway and Elsewhere" column on 27th May 1917:

The excellence of Miss Springtime *and*
Oh, Boy! *has elevated them* [Guy and
Plum] *in a single season to the envi-
able position of being the most sought
after musical comedy authors in the
land, and advance indications are that
it will be a rare bird among next year's
musical shows which does not have
Wodehouse and Bolton as its authors.*

Their overall success was, of course, also attributable to the music of Jerry
Kern, and Plum worked as closely with him as he did with Guy. Not unnaturally, the Kern-Wodehouse collaboration gave rise to the age-old question
that forever plagues song-writing teams—the one about who writes what first
—and Plum once obligingly explained how he and Kern worked. "Jerry generally did the melody first," he said, "and I put words to it. W. S. Gilbert always

said that a lyricist can't do decent stuff that way, but I don't agree with him—not as far as I'm concerned, anyway. If I write a lyric without having to fit it to a tune, I always make it too much like a set of light verse, much too regular in meter. I think you get the best results by giving the composer his head and having the lyricist follow him. For instance, the refrain of one of the songs in *Oh, Boy!* began 'If every day you bring her diamonds and pearls on a string.' I couldn't have thought of that, if I had done the lyric first, in a million years. Why, dash it, it doesn't scan. But Jerry's melody started off with a lot of twiddly little notes, the first thing being emphasized being the "di" of 'diamonds,' and I just tagged along after him. Another thing . . . is that when you have the melody, you can see which are the musical high-spots in it and can fit the high-spots of the lyric to them. Anyway, that's how I like working, and to hell with anyone who says I oughtn't to."

There was no record of anyone having said he oughtn't to, but there was every indication that his work for the theatre was superseding the writing of novels and short stories. The only reminder of his authorship at this time was the publication in England on 8th March 1917 of *The Man With Two Left Feet* —a collection of short stories which had previously appeared in the *Strand Magazine*—and the fact that he continued to write his regular articles for *Vanity Fair.*

Show business claimed the bulk of his time; and after the completion of *Oh, Boy!,* he and Guy embarked on the writing of several musicals for the coming season. Ray Comstock commissioned them to turn George Ade's successful comedy *The College Widow* into a full-scale musical; Klaw & Erlanger contracted them to rewrite yet another Viennese operetta, obviously hoping to duplicate the success of *Miss Springtime;* and two of the greatest managers in theatrical history, Charles B. Dillingham and Florenz Ziegfeld, invited them to write a revue for their newest and most elaborate showpiece, the Century Theatre.

The adaptation of George Ade's play for Comstock was called *Leave it to Jane,* in which Edith Hallor played the attractive "college widow" of the original title. But it was Georgia O'Ramey, who had been featured in *Miss Springtime,* who provided the comedy highlight of the show when she sang "Cleopatterer," which contained several sets of Plum's funniest lyrics. This number did for *Leave it to Jane* what "Napoleon" had done for *Have a Heart,* and a beautiful Jerome Kern ballad entitled "Wait Till Tomorrow" helped to make the score of this show memorable.

Of Plum's lyrics, critic Gilbert Seldes said:

> *. . . they had the great virtue which*
> *Gilbert's lyrics have and which, I am*
> *told, the comic verses of Molière and*
> *Aristophanes also have: they say things*
> *as simply as you would say them in*
> *common speech, yet they sing prefectly.*
> *There was nothing he [Plum] wanted*
> *to say that he couldn't say to music.*

After attending the first night of *Leave it to Jane* at the Longacre Theatre on 28th August 1917, the drama critic for the *New York Evening World,* Charles Darnton, wrote:

> *Everything at the Longacre Theatre*
> *last night was quite up to date. There*
> *is no reason to take a great deal of*
> *space in saying that the revival of Mr.*
> *Ade's frolicsome affair, in fresh guise,*
> *is quite as enlivening as it was in its*
> *original form. In fact, it gained some-*
> *thing last night by way of Mr. Kern's*
> *sprightly tunes and by verses that added*
> *to the joy of song. You are sure to like*
> Leave it to Jane. *You needn't leave it*
> *to anyone but yourself. A decidedly*
> *clever cast makes this assurance doubly*
> *sure.*

The show ran for 167 performances—not quite another *Oh, Boy!,* but nevertheless a good run. (Its durability was proven forty-two years later when, in a 1959 revival, it chalked up a spectacular 928 performances.)

With *Leave it to Jane* under way, Plum gave a helping hand to Guy in an adaptation of David Belasco's *Sweet Kitty Bellairs,* writing the lyrics to Rudolf Friml's music. The resultant show was called *Kitty Darlin'* and it opened on 10th September 1917 at the Teck Theatre in Buffalo, New York. It was immediately apparent that a good deal more work would be needed on it to turn it into a success, but Plum and Guy had other commitments and so Otto Harbach was called in to take over from them.

Their main reason for abandoning *Kitty Darlin'* was that they had to put the finishing touches to Klaw & Erlanger's reworked Viennese operetta, now called *The Riviera Girl,* which was due to open on 24th September. Like *Miss Springtime,* it was going into the New Amsterdam Theatre, and indeed, everyone who had worked on *Miss Springtime,* apart from the cast, was working on *The Riviera Girl.* Herbert Gresham was directing; Julien Mitchell was the choreographer; Joseph Urban was in charge of the sets and lighting; and the score was by the gifted Hungarian Emmerich Kalman, with a few interpolated numbers by Jerome Kern. But when the show opened on its due date, the efforts of the most talented group of theatre people in New York failed to ensure a repeat of their previous success. *The Riviera Girl* was a flop.

To complete their theatrical year, Guy, Plum and Jerry wrote the promised revue for Charles B. Dillingham and Florenz Ziegfeld, *Miss 1917.* Dillingham and Ziegfeld had gone into partnership the previous year to produce a spectacular show at their Century Theatre and now planned to make this an annual event, with each show more stunning than the one before. They therefore expected something special from the trio. Certainly they did not stint themselves in assembling a glittering array of stars which included Lew Fields as principal comedian, Irene Castle, Bessie McCoy, the famous Spanish dancer Valencia, Ann Pennington, Vivienne Segal, Harry Kelly and his dog, Van and Schenck, Marion Davies and George White. And Joseph Urban excelled himself in devising costumes that blended with landscape scenery, thus providing a special task for the lyricist. Each of the twelve chorus girls had an individual costume for this scene, and Plum was called upon to write a lyric comprising a verse and twelve choruses—a chorus for each girl in which she would describe what she was wearing.

The rehearsal pianist earned his thirty-five dollars a week by coaching the chorus, working on the ensemble numbers and rehearsing the principals. When not so engaged he would idle away the moments, to the delight of the cast and the stagehands, by playing his own compositions. Accompanying the rehearsal for *Miss 1917* was his first professional job in the theatre. His name was George Gershwin.

Miss 1917 opened on 5th November 1917 to the acclaim of the critics, but not that of the public. To quote whoever said it first, the public stayed away in droves; and the show closed after only forty-eight performances. It was probably just as well. A postmortem revealed that, because of the tremendous expenses involved, the revue would have run at a loss of between three and four thousand dollars a week even if it had played to capacity houses. Another flop—but a lavish one.

Although clearly uneasy about the failure of *Miss 1917,* Guy, Plum and Jerry had another idea for a musical and had started to work on it when they had a call from Ray Comstock. He wanted them to do another *Oh, Boy!* for the Princess Theatre, and his timing couldn't have been better. His offer was a much-needed morale booster to the men with two successive flops behind them. They hadn't been admitting it to each other, but both Plum and Guy had begun to fear that they were through in the theatre. What Comstock proposed soon reassured them. He was raising their cut to seven-and-one-half per cent and would pay them an advance of one thousand dollars. The title of the show was to be *Oh, Lady! Lady!!*—the currently popular catch-phrase of vaudeville star Bert Williams.

At this time, Ethel had just rented a studio apartment at the Beaux Arts in Greenwich Village. It was close to the Princess Theatre and a convenient place at which the team could get together to write the show. Things were not going too smoothly from the plot point of view, and the authors had not even decided where the action of the piece should take place. But their biggest problem was how to introduce a romantic theme that was to run secondary to the main love story. Ethel was accustomed to the ways of writers by now, and she knew instinctively when to make herself scarce. She therefore took herself off one morning, leaving Plum and Guy to grapple with their problem undisturbed. Before going, however, she reminded Plum that a young lady would be calling to inspect and take away a settee that needed renovating.

Not long after Ethel's departure, the two men discovered that they had run out of tobacco—without which all inspiration would wither—and Guy was elected to go and buy some. He left the studio apartment, which had recently been occupied by well-known artist Leon Gordon, and was making his way from the building when he ran into Audrey Munson, New York's leading artist's model, with whom he was already acquainted. Having passed the time of day with her, he asked her what she was doing and she told him that she was making the rounds of the artists' studios. "In my line," she confided, "you've got to make the most of what you've got while you've still got it."

Guy went on his way and Audrey went on hers, making one or two unproductive calls and eventually arriving at what she had been told was the door of Leon Gordon's studio. In response to her ring, Plum opened the door and ushered her in. There then followed the sort of conversation that is sup-

Plum's mother at Cheltenham.

Eleanor and Ernest Wodehouse's
wedding picture,
taken on February 3, 1877
in Hong Kong.

Plum Wodehouse
at twenty-one,
at the beginning
of his writing career.

breeze. But when it did, he leaped from his chair in much the same way that Archimedes must have leaped from his bath: and only the fact that he was an originator rather than a copyist prevented him from shouting "Eureka!" He had realised, of course, that what had just taken place would provide the scene and the setting that had been holding up their work. To introduce the secondary love interest, they could have their artist-hero leave his friend in his studio to deal with a lady decorator and have said friend fall in love with a model who calls and is mistaken for the decorator—and it could all take place in Greenwich Village. It was a matter of turning fact into fiction.

On 22nd December 1917, *Oh, Lady! Lady!!* opened at the Dupont Theatre, Wilmington, Delaware, for its first tryout, and its authors were highly pleased with it. They felt that the integration of book and music was better than it had been for *Oh, Boy!*, and they were convinced that the story was exceptionally strong for a musical comedy. Plum was so well satisfied with the story, in fact, that he used it later for his novel *The Small Bachelor.*

Both Plum and Guy remembered this show with great fondness, recalling how fortunate they had been in the matter of the cast. The heroine, Molly, was played by Vivienne Segal, an extremely pretty girl who could sing, dance and play comedy roles with a natural flair; her leading man was Carl Randall, a specialty dancer successfully performing his first acting part. They were supported by Harry Brown, Carroll McComas, Edward Abeles, Florence Shirley, Reginald Mason, Margaret Dale, and Harry Fisher. The tiny part of a maid in the first act was played by Constance Binney, who later became a Hollywood star.

"It was probably the first—one might almost say only—occasion," said Plum, "on which a musical play had in the matter of cast an absolutely full hand."

The Wednesday performance of the tryout at the Dupont Theatre coincided with Christmas Eve and the auditorium was consequently almost empty: so empty that at one point Guy, forgetting that there *was* an audience, rose and interrupted a scene to correct a mistake. His voice trailed off as he realised what he had done, but Plum surprisingly came to the rescue by addressing the thirty-six members of the public who had ventured into the theatre and explaining that the show had to be put into shape for New York. Emboldened by the audience's sympathetic response to this, Guy said, "There are so few of you and you were keeping so quiet that I had quite forgotten you were there." This raised a bigger laugh than any of the lines in the show had managed to posed to take place only in the wildest of farces. Plum, mistaking Miss Munson for the settee lady, rambled on about arms, legs and seats; and Audrey, not unused to the eccentricities of artists, but nevertheless slightly taken aback by what she considered a most unusual approach, came to the conclusion that Plum wanted her to pose for him there and then. Consequently, at a convenient break in their improbable conversation—and since he had expressed an urgent desire to get on with his work—she excused herself and disappeared into the bedroom . . . where, Plum imagined, she must be inspecting some furniture Ethel had forgotten to mention. He was therefore a little nonplussed when, he having sat himself down and proceeded with his writing, the bedroom door opened and Audrey Munson was revealed in a state of near-nudity. It struck him as rather odd behaviour, even for a female renovator, and he might have made some passing reference to it along those lines if the door bell hadn't chosen that moment to ring again.

This time he was confronted by a fully dressed young lady accompanied by a very large man in overalls, and his reeling mind managed to grasp the fact that this must be an authentic lady renovator with assistant—although he could not yet find a logical explanation for the almost naked creature still poised in the bedroom doorway.

Rarely at a loss for words, he said, "Oh, good morning . . ."; but the newcomer, muttering frigidly that she had better look in again at a more convenient time, whirled away with her assistant in tow.

Towards the end of this interlude, Audrey Munson—beginning to suspect that her professional services would not be required after all—retired once more to the bedroom. And at this juncture, to Plum's vast relief, Guy returned with the tobacco. Guy, Plum knew, was a man of the world and would know exactly how to cope with the strange young person in the bedroom who seemed disposed to remove her clothes for no particular reason and without any warning: and there was now a certain urgency in coming to grips with the problem since Ethel might be back at any moment. But Guy's agile mind was only just starting to assimilate the incoherent details of Plum's adventure when the bedroom door opened and Audrey Munson, with her clothes on, presented herself.

It took but moments for everything to be made clear after Guy had performed the introductions, and when Audrey left she was still chuckling over the mutual misunderstanding. The full import of the incident didn't strike Guy, however, until Miss Munson and her chuckle were a mere echo on the

Plum's father at retirement.

Above: Armine, Plum on Eleanor's lap, and Peveril, April 9, 1884.
Below: Armine, Peveril, and five-year-old Plum, in January 1887.

Above: Plum aged seven.
Below: Plum seated on tree, Armine and Peveril during school holidays in April 1895.

Plum on Dulwich grounds in 1898.

The first cricket team at Dulwich, with Plum standing second from right, 1899.

THE SATURDAY EVENING POST

An Illu_____ Weekly
Founded A_____ i. Franklin

JUNE 26, 1915   5c. THE COPY

Beginning

Something New—By Pelham Grenville Wodehouse

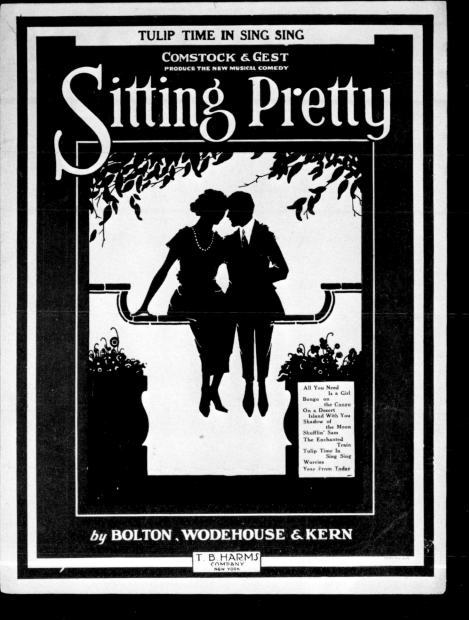

Plum's famous comedy lyric in the last of the Bolton-Wodehouse-Kern shows.

Above: Plum's first appearance in an important magazine.
Below: His first appearance in Punch, which relationship would continue for sixty-five years

Above: Plum's entry into the adult literary world.
Below: Title page of Plum's first published book.

Period jackets from his famous books.

From the first to the latest of the Jeeves novels.

Family portrait taken in the early twenties.

achieve so far, and Guy was encouraged to continue by saying, "I thought we were having a rehearsal. If you don't mind, we'll have one now."

There could never have been a rehearsal quite like it in the history of show business. The audience sat enthralled, paying rapt attention to every alteration the authors made and occasionally contributing suggestions of their own. At the end of it all, the cast went down to the footlights to autograph programmes for the select group, and Vivienne Segal said wistfully, "If only we could have you people with us for our first night in New York."

But she needn't have worried. When *Oh, Lady! Lady!!* opened at the Princess Theatre on 1st February 1918, the critics were unanimous in their praise and it was obvious that Ray Comstock had indeed acquired another *Oh, Boy!* It inspired an unnamed but lyrical critic for *The New York Times* to write:

> *This is the trio of musical fame*
> > *Bolton and Wodehouse and Kern;*
> *Better than anyone else you can name,*
> > *Bolton and Wodehouse and Kern.*
> *Nobody knows what on earth they've*
> > *been bitten by:*
> *All I can say is I mean to get lit an' buy*
> *Orchestra seats for the next one that's*
> > *written by*
> > *Bolton and Wodehouse and Kern.*

And Dorothy Parker, who replaced Plum as drama critic for *Vanity Fair* and into whose soul the acid had not yet entered, wrote:

> *Well, Bolton and Wodehouse and Kern*
> *have done it again. Every time these*
> *three gather together, the Princess Thea-*
> *tre is sold out for months in advance.*
> *You can get a seat for* Oh, Lady! Lady!!
> *somewhere around the middle of Au-*
> *gust for just about the price of one on*
> *the Stock Exchange. . . . If you ask me,*
> *I will look you fearlessly in the eye and*
> *tell you in low, throbbing tones that it*

has it over any other musical comedy in town. . . . But then Bolton and Wodehouse and Kern are my favourite indoor sport, anyway. I like the way they go about a musical comedy. I like the way the action slides casually into the songs. I like the deft rhyming of the song that is always sung in the last act by two comedians and a comedienne. And oh, how I do like Jerome Kern's music. And all these things are even more so in Oh, Lady! Lady!! *than they were in* Oh, Boy!

There has always been praise in plenty for Plum's lyrics. In *The World of Jerome Kern,* David Ewen described them as being years ahead of their time in almost every way, adding that later songwriters often expressed their indebtedness to and appreciation of Wodehouse. Richard Rodgers wrote, "Before Larry Hart, only P. G. Wodehouse had made any real assault on the intelligence of the song-listening public." And Howard Dietz, lyricist for many outstanding Broadway musicals, wrote to Plum: "Perhaps you did not know it, but over the years I have held you as the model of light verse in the song form. I believe I know more of your phrases than you would remember yourself."

Oh, Lady! Lady!! ran for 219 performances at the Princess while a second company was performing it simultaneously at the Casino Theatre in New York. And on one occasion it was put on at Sing Sing Prison with an all-convict cast.

It is interesting to recall that "Bill," the song distinguished by Plum's most famous lyric, was written for *Oh, Lady! Lady!!* but was dropped during the tryout period when it proved to be unsuited to Vivienne Segal's voice. (Nine years were to pass before the song found its singer in Helen Morgan, who immortalised it in *Showboat.*)

At the beginning of March 1918, Ethel and Plum moved to Great Neck, Long Island, to be near Guy. Plum remembered that "We had a house which was nicely situated. It was in the middle of a lot of property owned by the Grace (shipping magnate) family and it wasn't built over at all. In fact, Great Neck was an absolute village when we were there. You know, there was a general store where you bought everything, and they had a wooden railroad station. We were more towards King's Point, at a place called Arrandale Avenue. It was rather a bit outside Great Neck proper. Scott Fitzgerald and his crowd lived about three miles from us. I loved Great Neck in those days. There were an awful lot of actors there. Ed Wynn was there and so were Roy Barnes, Donald Brain and Ernest Truex. I used to play golf with them at the Sound View Golf Club. That's the place where I wrote about the Oldest Member and all my golfing stories. The golf course was awfully nice. However, I wasn't any good at golf. I suppose I ought to have taken lessons instead of playing. I didn't mind losing, because it was such good exercise walking round the holes. If only I'd taken up golf immediately after I left school instead of playing cricket . . . but then I hadn't really much time for doing anything because I was writing all the time."

And he was still writing all the time. For even as they were getting settled in Arrandale Avenue, a producer named Al Woods asked Guy and Plum to adapt a farce called *The Girl from Rector's* into a musical. The resultant show was called *See You Later,* and it had music by Joseph Szulc and Jean Schwartz. Starring Roy Barnes, Charlie Ruggles and Victor Moore, it had its out-of-town opening at the Academy of Music in Baltimore on 15th April 1918. But the long trek to Broadway was never completed. The show died en route.

Not long after this, Ethel and Plum went to England and rented a house, number 16 Walton Street, in southwest London to be near Leonora while she was finishing her current term at Bromley. Frances Donaldson, who was a schoolfriend of Leonora's, told in her book *Freddy* of her first sight of Plum on one of his visits to the school. She was in a classroom at the front of the house with Leonora and some other girls when one of them called the others to the window to see "the most extraordinary man coming down the drive." What Frances Donaldson saw was a broad-shouldered, red-faced man riding down the school drive on a bicycle, a white handkerchief over his head tied in a knot at each corner. "That," Leonora told her friends, "is Plum." As they continued to watch, they were astonished to see Plum dismount some distance from the house and wheel his bicycle into the shrubbery that lined the drive, where he crouched beside it as though in hiding. This didn't surprise Leonora at all. On the contrary, she explained to her bewildered classmates that Plum was frightened of Miss Starbuck, the headmistress, and had therefore arranged to hide in the bushes until Leonora could get out to meet him.

Such fraught meetings were soon forgotten when the term ended and Leonora returned with Plum and Ethel to America to spend the summer at Great Neck. Not that it was to be a summer of complete repose for Plum. Guy greeted him with the news that A. L. Erlanger wanted them to write a musical for the New Amsterdam Theatre in collaboration with composer Ivan Caryll.

Caryll had already written many musicals, including the extremely successful *The Pink Lady* from which had come the evergreen "Beautiful Lady" waltz, and he had a basic idea for this one. It would be about a star of the Paris stage who becomes "godmother" to an unknown soldier, writing to him and sending him food parcels and cigarettes; but the soldier is really a struggling playwright who wants to get acquainted with her in order to persuade her to act in one of his plays. It seemed viable to Plum and Guy, and they set to work on it. By July the show was in rehearsal, and it eventually opened at the New Amsterdam on 16th September 1918. Called *The Girl Behind the Gun,* it ran for 160 performances.

In October, a young English actor-manager, George Grossmith, arrived in New York to bid for the rights of *Oh, Boy!,* which he wanted to put on in London. Although considered generally as something of a snob, Grossmith's attitude to Plum could not have been too off-putting, for Plum found him thoroughly likeable—which was just as well since their paths were to cross again in the future. A deal was concluded and *Oh, Boy!* crossed the Atlantic to appear as *Oh, Joy!* on the London stage, with Beatrice Lillie and Tom Powers as its stars.

While working on *The Girl Behind the Gun,* Guy and Plum had started on what was to be their last show for the Princess Theatre. This they now brought to fruition in collaboration with Louis Hirsch, composer of "The Love Nest," because Jerry Kern was unavailable due to prior commitments. The show was called *Oh, My Dear.* It was the only one of their pieces for the Princess that did not have music by Jerome Kern, and it was noticeable.

The show opened on 27th November 1918 and had a successful run of 189 performances. But that the music was the least of its ingredients was noted by Dorothy Parker in her *Vanity Fair* review:

> *His [Hirsch's] music is so reminiscent that the score rather resembles a medley of last season's popular songs, but it really doesn't make any difference—*

Mr. Wodehouse's lyrics would make
anything go.

With *Oh, My Dear* well and truly launched, Plum, Ethel and Guy went to Palm Beach, Florida, for a rare vacation, but they were not given much opportunity of forgetting about work. They had been there only a few days when they ran into Florenz Ziegfeld, who not only told Plum and Guy that he wanted them to write a show for Marilyn Miller but also sent a wire to Jerome Kern asking him to join them right away for a joint discussion.

On Jerry's arrival, they were all whisked away on a yachting trip by Ziegfeld, whose other guests included millionaires Messmore Kendall, Paul Block and Walter Chrysler, novelist Arthur Somes Roche and his wife Ethel Pettit, who had replaced Sari Petrass as the heroine of *Miss Springtime* during its New York run. The full story of that trip is told by Guy and Plum in *Bring On the Girls,* but the upshot of it was that when Jerry Kern sat at the piano and played "Bill" everyone was impressed with the melody. Ethel Pettit asked if there was a lyric, and when Plum had obligingly scribbled it down for her she sang:

I used to dream that I would discover
   The perfect lover
     Some day:
I knew I'd recognize him if ever
He came round my way:
He'd have hair of gold
   And a noble head
Like the heroes bold
   In the books I'd read.
Then along came Bill,
   Who's not like that at all,
You'd pass him on the street and never notice him.
   His form and face,
   His manly grace,
   Are not the sort that you
   Would find in a statue:
I can't explain...
It's surely not his brain
   That makes me thrill:
I love him because...oh, I don't know,
   Because he's just my Bill.

Ziegfeld immediately wanted to buy the song, but Jerry told him that it was not for sale. It was then explained how it had been written for but dropped from *Oh, Lady! Lady!!;* that it was a situation song; that it had to be featured in a book show, where it would be pertinent to the plot. No one disputed this. Indeed, the assorted millionaires each asserted that he would be willing to back a show with that song in it and a star to sing it such as Ruth Etting . . . Nora Bayes . . . Fanny Brice. . . . But this trio remained cautious, merely reflecting on how easy it was to get backing for a show if one had a song, a lovely and talented woman to sing it, and a handful of wealthy men to listen to it in a conducive atmosphere. They were not too concerned about "Bill." They knew they would be able to use it in a show some day.

7 1919– 1929

The experience gained from his work in the musical comedy theatre was to have a marked effect on Plum's writing. Collaborating with Guy Bolton and Jerome Kern in the creation of a show—which meant integrating story, music and lyrics into an uninterrupted whole—had given him the insight to a technique which could be adapted to suit the construction of his novels. As he wrote to William Townend:

> *The more I write the more I am convinced that the only way to write a popular story is to split it up into scenes, and have as little stuff between the scenes as possible. The principle I always go on in writing a long story is to think of the characters as if they were living salaried actors. The one thing actors—important actors, I mean —won't stand is being brought on to play a scene which is of no value to them in order that they may feed some less important character, and I believe this isn't vanity but is based on an instinctive knowledge of stagecraft. They*

kick because they know the balance
isn't right.

Plum's object was to give his novel characters the balance they would have expected had they been actors on a stage; and he has himself described his books as musical comedies without the music. All of his full-length plots can be broken down into their component parts of acts, chorus numbers, duets and solos, with dialogue that is always crisp and concise, and entrances and exits that are carefully planned and vividly accomplished. There is no waste. And indeed almost any Wodehouse plot has the aura of the musical comedy theatre, with its youthful lovers befogged by mistaken identity or other innocent —but never deliberately evil—misunderstanding which is always happily resolved in time for a happy ending, or final curtain.

Another inheritance from the theatre was the jargon of stageland, which slid easily into Plum's already wide and varied vocabulary and automatically found its way into his writings along with quotations from Greek mythology and classical poets, the new words of his own invention, and the slang and clichéd figures of speech which he used so ingeniously.

It could be said that, from this time on, Plum's literary work had a rag-time air about it. Ragtime music had taken root in America at about the time that Plum started writing there, and it is not illogical to compare his style with the style of the music when one considers the makeup of each. Although apparently wild and uncontrolled, with its syncopation and intricate secondary notes, ragtime was precisely written and needed to be precisely executed. In the same way, Plum's writings seemed to flow unchecked—and yet his plots, syncopated with subplots, required the most disciplined kind of thinking and execution. To take the analogy further, Plum's dialogue is akin to the cross-current in syncopation. His distortion of famous quotations intermingled with clichés is a direct parallel to the secondary improvisation which is basic to ragtime. And in the final analysis, Plum's novels and ragtime were products of a particular age—a reflection of their environment—which had the timelessness to endure when all that they had represented was long gone.

During the latter part of 1918 Plum had again been writing for publication, but it was the call of the theatre that brought him and Ethel to England in January 1919. They came for the rehearsals of *Kissing Time*—which had been *The Girl Behind the Gun* in the States—and again they rented the house in Walton Street. Considerable changes had to be made for the London presentation of the show, and Clifford Grey was called in to write lyrics to new music by Ivan Caryll while Plum anglicised the book. It was hard work but worth while, for when *Kissing Time* opened at the Winter Garden Theatre on 20th May 1919 it was an overwhelming success, eventually achieving 430 performances.

While Plum was in England, in May 1919, came the publication of *My Man Jeeves*—a volume containing eight short stories of which four were about Bertie Wooster and Jeeves and the other four about Reggie Pepper. It was the first time a collection of Wooster-Jeeves stories had appeared in Britain, but the book didn't do them or their author much credit. Printed on cheap paper, it was a small volume with cardboard covers and it sold at a shilling a copy. Consequently, it did not attract much attention.

Also published in 1919, in America, was *Their Mutual Child,* which had originally appeared as a serial in *Munsey Magazine* in 1914. There was no knowing why it had taken five years to progress to volume form; but yet another year was to pass before it was published in England as *The Coming of Bill.*

Before then, however, Plum and Ethel had returned to America, taking Leonora with them, to spend the summer at Great Neck. For once, it was a time of greater relaxation for Plum; he made the most of it—playing golf and swimming as often as he could. But as the summer drew to a close, work beckoned again and he and Guy started to write a musical based on Samuel Shipman's play *East is West.* They called it *The Rose of China* and turned to the well-known conductor of the Ritz Hotel orchestra, Armand Vecsey, for the music.

This work for the theatre was punctuated by the publication, on 4th October 1919, of *A Damsel in Distress.* Over the years, Plum's writing had been progressing towards a unique style that was fully achieved in this novel. Remembering the edict on writing only about the things of which he had personal knowledge, he had characteristically chosen the musical comedy theatre for his background and had made his hero an American playwright in England who courts an English titled lady. The secondary love interest concerned an American chorus girl who finally lands herself an English peer. This involvement of Americans in England and Englishmen in America was no new ploy. Plum had used it before in *A Gentleman of Leisure,* the Jeeves stories, *Psmith Journalist, Uneasy Money* and *Piccadilly Jim:* and it was a clear indication that he was making a conscious effort to appeal to readers on both sides of the Atlantic.

Meanwhile, back at the theatre, *The Rose of China,* starring Oscar Shaw, Jane Richardson and Frank McIntyre, opened at the Lyric in New York on 25th November 1919 and proved a sad disappointment to all concerned. It was generally considered to be not musical enough, and it closed after only forty-seven performances.

For the next few months the Wodehouses remained in America, but on 25th April 1920 they embarked on the S.S. *Adriatic* for another visit to England, where they once again rented the house at Walton Street in London. And almost as soon as they had arrived, Plum was busy on a novel which he was calling *The Little Warrior.* Like *A Damsel in Distress,* it had the world of musical comedy as its background; and work on it progressed rapidly, obviously due to a change in his writing methods as outlined in a letter to William Townend:

> *I now write stories at a terrific speed. I've started a habit of rushing them through and then working over them very carefully, instead of trying to get the first draft exactly right, and have just finished the rough draft of an eight-thousand-word story in two days. It nearly slew me. As a rule, I find a week long enough for a short story if I have the plot well thought out. On a novel I generally do eight pages a day, i.e. about 2,500 words. As a rule I like to start work in the mornings, knock off for a breather, and then do a bit more before dinner. I never work after dinner. Yet in the old days that was my best time. Odd. Plots: they've been coming along fine of late.*
>
> *Funny you should have had that trouble about a story getting longer and longer in spite of yourself. I'm suffering that way now. This new novel of mine is already 15,000 words longer than*

anything I have done, and the worst is
yet to come.

Leonora remained at school that summer while Ethel and Plum stayed at Quinton Farm, Felixstowe. But the bond between Plum and Leonora, or "Snorkles," was as firm as ever and he was inclined to make her his confidante. The extent to which he discussed his work with her can be judged from a letter dated 7th August 1920:

> *Darling Snorkles,*
> *At last I'm able to write to you!*
> *I finished the novel yesterday,* Girl on
> a Boat, *and I wish you were here to*
> *read it, as I think it's the best comic*
> *one I've done. It's not meant to be in*
> *the same class as* The Little Warrior,
> *but as a farce I think it's pretty well to*
> *the mustard. I've done it in such a*
> *hurry, though, that there may be things*
> *wrong with it. Still, I'm going to keep*
> *it by me for at least two weeks before*
> *sending it off to America, so perhaps*
> *you'll be able to see it after all before it*
> *goes. If not, you can read the original*
> Mss.
> *I have now got three more Archie*
> *stories to do and then I shall have*
> *worked off all my present contracts. I*
> *haven't a plot yet for the tenth Archie*
> *story, but they are using a golf story of*
> *mine in the Christmas* Strand, *which*
> *will give me a fair amount of time to*
> *think of one.*
> *Mummie has taken up golf and is*
> *very keen on it and is really getting*
> *quite good. You must start as soon as*
> *you can.*

*Don't you think this is a good line
in the book? Chap who's always thinking himself ill says to a chap who is
having a row with him "My face hurts!"
Other chap says "You can't expect a
face like that not to hurt!" I thought
it was not only droll, but whimsical
and bizarre, but Mummie said it was
obvious! No human power, however,
will induce me to cut it out.*

*I really am becoming rather a
blood these days. In a review of Wedding Bells at the Playhouse the critic
says "So-and-so is good as a sort of
P. G. Wodehouse character." And in a
review of a book in the Times, they
say "The author at times reverts to the
P. G. Wodehouse manner." This, I need
scarcely point out to you, is jolly old
Fame. Once they begin to refer to you
in that casual way as if everybody must
know who you are all is well. It does
my old heart good.*

*Well, cheerio, old fright. Write
again soon.*

Your loving
Plummie

At the end of the summer, Plum and Ethel returned to 16 Walton Street, and Plum resumed work on a number of short stories which had been commissioned by *Cosmopolitan* and the *Strand*. Although writing at a furious rate, he nevertheless found time to read many books—one of which particularly impressed him. It was called *What Next?*, and it was a first book by a young man named Denis Mackail. Its plot concerned an ingenious butler coming to the aid of his former master, and though it was an unusual and clever permutation of Plum's Jeeves formula it was certainly not imitative. Plum loved it.

The outcome of Plum's appreciation of *What Next?* is told by Denis

Mackail in his highly amusing and interesting book *Life With Topsy:*

> *It* (What Next?) *had been published some months when a letter reached me which I found it hardly possible to believe. For it was signed P. G. Wodehouse . . . he had read that novel and he had actually written to praise it. . . . And a little later, as if this weren't enough, he wrote again and asked me to dinner at one of his clubs. As I need hardly tell anyone of his acquaintance, by the time I reached the club in question he had already become disgusted with it, and rushed me off to the Savoy Grill-Room instead. There he provided a considerable banquet and immediately started talking about writing, without a moment's delay. For this—apart from Pekes, and cricket and football matches at his old school, with which he also seemed obsessed—was his own great, unending topic; and at all the evenings that we have spent together I can't remember him ever lingering, for more than a few seconds, on anything else.*

That first meeting with Denis Mackail was to mark the beginning of another of Plum's rare, but lifelong friendships. Acceptance was complete and Mackail was admitted to the family circle, thereby witnessing the affectionate camaraderie that existed between Plum and his adopted daughter. "They got on gloriously," he recalled in more recent times. "Plum created Leonora. Her mind was delicious."

In November 1920 Plum's American publisher, George Doran, complained about the poor market for short stories in volume form and suggested that the Archie Moffam stories should somehow be amalgamated into a full-length novel. Co-operatively, Plum settled down to study the problem and then wrote to tell Leonora how he was setting about it:

> *I am at present moulding the Archie stories into a book. The publisher very wisely says that short stories don't sell, so I am hacking the things about putting the first half of one story at the beginning of the book and putting the finish of it about a hundred pages later, and the result looks very good. For instance, I blend the Sausage Chappie story and Paving the Way for Mabel rather cunningly. You remember that the blow-out of the latter takes place in the grill-room. Well, directly it has happened there is a row at the other end of the grill-room, which is the Sausage Chappie having the finish of his story. Rather ingenious, what!*

At this time, back in the States, Guy Bolton and Jerome Kern were writing a musical called *Sally* at the behest of Florenz Ziegfeld. Plum had been given to understand that he was to write the lyrics—had, in fact, written them and sent them over—only to discover that, in his absence, Ziegfeld had contracted lyricist Clifford Grey to do the work. And again it was to Leonora, in a letter dated 28th November 1920, that Plum wrote of the tempest in a teapot that followed:

> *I forgot to tell you in my last letter the tale of the laughable imbroglio—or mix-up—which has occurred with Jerry Kern. You remember I sent my lyrics over, and then read in* Variety *that some other cove was doing the lyrics and wrote to everybody in New York to retrieve my lyrics. Then that cable came asking me if I would let them*

*have "Joan of Arc" and "Church Round
the Corner," which, after a family coun-
cil, I answered in the affir. Well, just
after I had cabled saying all right, I got
a furious cable from Jerry—the sort of
cable the Kaiser might have sent to an
underling—saying my letter withdraw-
ing the lyrics was "extremely offensive"
and ending "You have offended me for
the last time!" Upon which, the manly
spirit of the Wodehouses (descended
from the sister of Anne Boleyn) boiled
in my veins—when you get back I'll
show you the very veins it boiled in—
and I cabled over "Cancel permission
to use lyrics." I now hear that Jerry is
bringing an action against me for royalties on* Miss Springtime *and* Riviera
Girl, *to which he contributed tunes.
The loony seems to think that a lyricist
is responsible for the composer's royalties. Of course, he hasn't an earthly, and
I don't suppose the action will ever
come to anything, but doesn't it show
how blighted some blighters can be
when they decide to be blighters?*

The rift was not serious, however, and there was naturally no court case. In the event, when *Sally*—starring Marilyn Miller and Leon Errol—opened in New York on 21st December 1920, Plum's lyrics to "Joan of Arc" and "Church Round the Corner" were present in all their glory.

It wasn't until 23rd March 1921 that Ethel and Plum set sail again for America, this time for the purpose of selling their house at Great Neck. Since it was hoped that their stay would be of short duration they booked in at the Hotel Biltmore, about which Plum was quick to write to Leonora:

Mummie hunted all round New

York for a hotel. We finally settled on this at fourteen seeds a day, which won't do a thing to the old bank-balance. We've got a nice room, looking down on to the roof garden and three pigeons (which are thrown in free).

We had an awfully nice trip. Fred Thompson was a wonderful chap to have with us. Full of funny stories and a most awfully good sort. We are all tremendous pals. The journey didn't seem a bit long, though it took nine days. I sweated like blazes at the novel and wrote and revised another 12,000 words, so that I now have about 70,000 words of good stuff, and am going to shoot it in without waiting to finish the thing. I shall finish it bit by bit while I am here. I'll keep a copy for you. The scene at the boxer's training camp came out splendidly, though it was very hard to write. I had a wobbly table, which I had to prop up with trunks, and writing wasn't easy. I generally worked every afternoon from three to half-past six. I did a good scene for Sally and Ginger. There are some fairly difficult bits still to do, but I hope I shall polish them off all right. It ought to be easier doing them in New York.

Referring to things in New York with Prohibition very much in force, he continued:

Our first act was to summon a bell-boy and give him the Sinister Whisper, to which he replied with a conspiratorial nod and buzzed off, returning later with a bottle of whisky—at the nominal price of seventeen dollars!!! I suppose if you tried to get champagne here you would have to throw in your Sunday trousers as well. Apparently you can still get the stuff, but you have to be darned rich.

Well, cheerio, old scream. We're thinking of you all the time.

Your loving
Plummie.

With the Great Neck house sold, Plum and Ethel returned to England to stay at Baldwin King-Hall's house at Emsworth. From there, Plum again wrote to Leonora:

I crammed a frightful lot of business into my twenty days in N.Y. Everybody I met wanted me to do a play. I am going to do one with Guy and Jerry, this one for Savage, and maybe another. What I would like to do would be to stick to lyrics, which I can do on my ear. Dialogue is too much like work.

I worked like the dickens going over and wrote twelve thousand words of the Sally novel. Also another chunk in N.Y., so that now I only have about five thousand to do, and shall polish that off directly I get free of these plays. I have to stick to the Adelphi show for a while, as I promised Fred Thompson I would work at it on the boat and I didn't touch it. Another three days ought to see me nearly through. I've done about half of it, but it has been an

awful fag. I've now got to the point
where Grossmith and Jerry come on
and I have to be frightfully funny. Un-
fortunately, I feel very mirthless and
my comedy will probably be blue round
the edges.

The show for the Adelphi Theatre referred to in the letter was *The Golden Moth,* with a book by Fred Thompson (assisted by Plum), music by Ivor Novello and lyrics by Plum. It opened in London on 5th October 1921 and ran successfully into 1922 with 281 performances.

Not long after the opening, Ethel bought herself a racehorse—which soon gave Plum cause to write elatedly to Leonora:

Darling Angel Snork,
   The Wodehouse home is en fete
and considerably above itself this p.m.
Deep-throated cheers ring out in Flat
43, and every now and then I have to
go out on the balcony to address the
seething crowds in St. James Street.
And why? I'll tell you. This afternoon
at Hurst Park dear jolly old Front Line
romped home in the Hurdle Handicap
in spite of having to carry about three
tons weight. The handicappers crammed
an extra ten pounds on him after his
last win, so he had to carry thirteen
stone three pounds, and it seemed im-
possible that he could win that record
—the Evening Standard *says there has*
never been a case before of a horse win-
ning a good race under such a weight.
We get four hundred quid in stakes—
minus fifty quid which we have to
cough up to the second horse and
twenty-five to the third. Still, with what

*Mummie (the well-known gambler)
got on at six to one, we clear five hundred quid on the afternoon.*

*My first remark on hearing the
news was "Snork will expect something
out of this!" It seemed to me that the
thing must infallibly bring on a severe
attack of the gimmies in the little darling one. Mummie says that when you
come back you shall collect in the shape
of a rich present. (A box of candy or a
fountain-pen or something lavish like
that. Or maybe a string of pearls.
Maybe, on the other hand, not.) Well,
that's that. So Mummie has started her
career as the Curse of the Turf in great
style.*

This unexpected affluence by way of the racecourse didn't mean that Plum
was ready to trade in his typewriter for a pair of binoculars and a top-hat. The
triumph was Ethel's. He had work to do and, as ever, his only race was to be
against time—for another stage proposition was about to be made to him.
Starring in *The Golden Moth* was George Grossmith, with whom Plum had
become well acquainted since their initial meeting in America. Although appearing at the Adelphi, Grossmith was also managing the Winter Garden
Theatre at which *Sally* was enjoying a fantastically successful run. It was to
eventually achieve 383 performances, but at this time Grossmith knew that the
end was in sight and was anxious to have another musical ready to take its
place. He therefore asked Plum to collaborate with him on a book and also
help with the lyrics. Additionally, he wrote to Jerome Kern and invited him
to compose the music.

As soon as *The Golden Moth* had ended its run, Grossmith and Plum set
sail for America on the *Aquitania* to work with Jerry. They had planned most
precisely how they would spend their days at sea: discussing the story during
morning walks around the deck; writing scenes in the afternoons; relaxing in
the evenings, with a final conference before retiring. And it all went accordingly—until the evening of the inevitable ship's concert, when all the celebrities

aboard were expected to contribute their services. Nothing had been permitted to disturb Plum's concentration until now; but he found it impossible to deny himself to a persistent public when all around him were ready, willing and extremely able. He felt neither ready nor willing, and had grave doubts about being able. What, after all, could he do to entertain? To the first suggestion that he should simply "say a few words" he gave a flat refusal; but he grudgingly agreed that he might give a reading of one of his stories, although he had never done such a thing before.

George Grossmith, experienced in these matters, advised Plum to choose something short and fitting. Pointing out that Plum would be the last performer on the bill, he mentioned kindly that the audience would be a bit restive by then and rather keen to get back to the dancing or whatever. The thing to do, he opined—ignoring what he had imagined to be a hurt look on Plum's face—was to get it over quickly; make it, in other words, snappy.

Grossmith was therefore faintly disturbed when in the due course of events Lillian Russell, who was in the chair for the concert, announced the last turn and Plum mounted the rostrum carrying a copy of his latest 90,000-word novel. It wasn't quite what Grossmith had had in mind. He was further discomfited, however, when Plum solemnly opened the book at the first page of Chapter One and, without preamble, began to read in an intimate mumble that barely reached the second-row seat in which Grossmith was huddled. After about twenty minutes of this, large numbers of the audience began to creep quietly away and Grossmith was able to move into the front row. He still couldn't hear too well, but it was obvious to him that Plum was thoroughly enjoying himself. Whatever his original motive may have been in the way of entertainment, Plum was no longer aware of the audience—or its rapidly decreasing size—and was reading now entirely for his own pleasure, interpolating such remarks as "By Jove, that's good. I'd no idea . . ." and "Devilish funny; I'd forgotten that bit . . ."

Exactly how the evening ended evaded Grossmith's memory—he having become engrossed in a game of bridge as Plum read on—but he knew that there must have come a point at which Plum stopped, because he clearly recalled arriving in New York and proceeding to Jerry Kern's house in Bronxville, where he and Plum stayed while working on the show.

As cabarets were just becoming popular in England at the time, Grossmith decided to give his show an ultra-modern touch by calling it *The Cabaret Girl.* He and Plum had managed to achieve a great deal of writing on the outward journey, and he was delighted with the way in which Kern collaborated. For Jerry did the main part of his task in little over a week, enabling the two authors to return to England with enough music to get rehearsals started, promising to bring the completed score to London within a few more weeks.

The Cabaret Girl went into rehearsal as soon as Plum and Grossmith arrived back in London at the beginning of August, and it opened at the Winter Garden Theatre on 19th September 1922 with Grossmith starring. On the next day, 20th September, Plum was already writing to Leonora about it:

> *Honestly, old egg, you never saw such a first night. The audience were enthusiastic all through the first and second acts, and they never stopped applauding during the cabaret scene in act three—you know, the scene with no dialogue but all music and spectacle. I knew that scene would go big, because the same thing happened at the dress rehearsal. Grossmith was immense, so was Heather Thatcher. As for Dorothy Dickson, she came right out and knocked them cold.*
>
> *This morning Mummie and I are not our usual bright selves, as we didn't get to bed till six and woke up at nine! William Boosey gave a party at the Metropole and we didn't leave till 5.30. There isn't any doubt that we've got an enormous hit. Jerry's music was magnificent. Every number went wonderfully, especially "Dancing Time."*

Flushed with success, Plum returned to America almost at once to work with Guy Bolton on a show commissioned by Florenz Ziegfeld. At Guy's home at Great Neck the two of them concentrated on finishing the book in record time, and then they went to Palm Beach to read it to Ziegfeld. A disgruntled Plum told William Townend of the outcome in a letter written in December 1922:

Life has been one damned bit of work after another ever since I landed here. First, Guy Bolton and I settled down and wrote a musical comedy—tentatively called Pat, *a rotten title—in two weeks for Flo Ziegfeld. It has been lying in a drawer ever since, Ziegfeld having been busy over another play, and doesn't look like getting put on this year.*

This, I should mention, is the play Ziegfeld was cabling about with such boyish excitement—the one I came over to do. You never heard anything like the fuss he made when I announced I couldn't make the Wednesday boat but would sail on the Saturday. He gave me to understand that my loitering would ruin everything.

I then sat down to finish Leave it to Psmith, *for the* Saturday Evening Post. *I wrote 40,000 words in three weeks.*

Since then I have been working with Guy on a musical comedy, Sitting Pretty, *for the Duncan Sisters, music by Irving Berlin. This is complicated by the fact that Guy's new comedy has just started rehearsals, and he is up to his neck in it. So the work is proceeding by jerks.*

The Saturday Evening Post *has done me proud. Although they never commission anything, they liked the first 60,000 words of* Leave it to Psmith *so much that they announced it in the papers before I sent in the* *remainder. I mailed them the last part on a Wednesday and got a cheque for $20,000 on the following Tuesday.*

When it was realised that Plum would not be able to return to London right away, Ethel joined him in New York. He was now working on another series of short stories, this time featuring Stanley Featherstonehaugh Ukridge of *Love Among the Chickens* fame, for which the going had not been easy. But only a fellow-author could fully appreciate the difficulties of writing a series of stories about one character and maintaining a high level of interest and humour throughout, and it was therefore understandable that Plum should use William Townend as a sounding board. In a letter to Townend at this time, he wrote:

I was awfully glad to get your letter containing the welcome statement that you thought on reading it again that "Ukridge's Dog College" was all right. I had to rush that story in the most horrible way. I think I told you that the Cosmopolitan *wanted it for the April number, and I had about five days to deliver it and got it all wrong and had to write about 20,000 words before I got it set. And then, when I reached Palm Beach I found that the artist had illustrated a scene which was not in the final version, and I had to add a new one by telephone!*

I have done two more stories in the last three weeks, and am now well ahead again, having completed eight. I'm so glad you like the series. Now that I've got well into it, I think it better than any of the others. It was difficult at first having the "I" chap a straight character instead of a sort of

Bertie Wooster, but now I find it rather
a relief, as it seems to make the thing
more real.

In May 1923 Herbert Jenkins Limited—which had previously published *Piccadilly Jim, The Coming of Bill, A Damsel in Distress, Jill the Reckless* (the British title for *The Little Warrior*) and *The Indiscretions of Archie*—brought out *The Inimitable Jeeves,* which had been blended into a novel from a number of short stories in the same way as *The Indiscretions of Archie.* It was the first all-Jeeves book, and it has remained a perennial best-seller—particularly in America—with more than three million copies sold in hard-cover and paperback editions.

Perhaps the publication of the book reminded George Grossmith of Plum, or it may just have been that *The Cabaret Girl* was nearing the end of its run, but certainly at this time Grossmith cabled Plum and Jerry to ask if they would collaborate with him on another show. And with their acceptance, he set sail for America on what was to be a working holiday.

Ethel and Plum had taken a house at Easthampton, Long Island, for the summer, and this year Leonora was with them. Apart from swimming, playing golf and being a companion in general to Plum, she was also a great help in entertaining her parents' guests. For in addition to Grossmith, they were also playing host to Robert Denby and Lord and Lady Ilchester. Of the titled couple, who were friends of Grossmith, Lady Ilchester was a very genial red-faced woman who gave, in Plum's words, "just a hint as to how to draw the character of Aunt Dahlia. I always thought of her when I was doing Aunt Dahlia."

But Aunt Dahlia was not very much on his mind just then. The business in hand was Grossmith's show, which he was calling *The Beauty Prize* and in which—to be topical—the new craze mah-jong would be featured. Its conception really was a holiday task. Wherever they happened to be— on beaches, porches or shady lawns; in the back of a car or the front of a launch—they were working on the script. And the work went well. By the end of July, Plum, Grossmith and Jerry were on their way to England to start rehearsals.

The Beauty Prize opened at the Winter Garden Theatre on 5th September 1923: and Plum marked the occasion by choosing to start the return trip to America on that day, taking Ethel with him. Staying with Guy Bolton at Great Neck, he went all out to complete the necessary revision of the ending of *Leave it to Psmith* for book publication. When it was done, he touched on the agony of it in a letter to Townend:

> *If one has finished a long story, one goes cold on it and alterations are a torture. I had this experience with* Leave it to Psmith. *You and a number of other people told me the end was wrong, as I had already suspected myself, but I couldn't muster up energy and ideas enough to alter it. I finally did it, and it has held up the publication of the book and caused much agony of spirit at the Herbert Jenkins office. Still, it is all right now, I think.*

For the American publication of the book, he was asked to write a publicity blurb on how it came to be written. His explanation was:

> *I am not one of those authors to whom mere material gain is everything: and it was not entirely the thought of the box of cigars which the proprietor of the* Saturday Evening Post *had promised me for the serial rights nor the reflection that, if he brought it out as a book, George H. Doran would be practically bound to send me a card next Christmas that induced me to write* Leave it to Psmith. *I was urged to the task principally by the importunity of my daughter Leonora, who, if I may coin a phrase, is my best pal and severest critic. It was the fact that she kept after me like a*

bloodhound to write another Psmith story that at length induced me to set typewriter to paper.

Psmith—the p is silent as in pshrimp—was the hero of a book for boys which I wrote in the year 1909 when I was young and slim and had quite a crop of hair. I had always intended some day to write of his after-school life, but never quite got down to it till my golden-haired child, who is the world's worst pest, harried me day by day in every way to such an extent that I saw the thing had to be done. So I did it.

And it was as well that he did, for it turned out to be one of the most amusing of the Blandings Castle novels and his most successful book in England.

During the latter part of November 1923, while plotting *Bill the Conqueror,* Plum again unburdened himself to Townend:

I am half way through mapping out a new novel which looks like being a pippin. I am going on a new system this time, making the scenario very full, putting in atmosphere and dialogue, etc., so that when I come actually to write it the work will be easy. So far I have scenarioed it out to about the 40,000-word mark; and it has taken me 13,000 words to do it! I have now reached a point where deep thought is required. I am not sure I haven't got too much plot, and may have to jettison the best idea in the story. I suppose the secret of writing is to go through your stuff till you come on something you think is particularly good, and then cut it out.

Plum and Ethel continued to stay with Guy Bolton as the old team of Plum, Guy and Jerry worked on a musical, *Sitting Pretty,* which had been commenced late in 1922 under quite different circumstances. The show's history to date had been one of turmoil and, although it had brought the trio back into harness for their first musical together since the Princess days—and for their producer from those days, Ray Comstock—Plum viewed its prospects with a certain amount of gloom. In a letter to Townend, he explained why:

Do you remember me telling you that Guy and I were doing a show for the Duncan Sisters with Irving Berlin? This is it. What happened was that we didn't plan to produce till October or later and the Duncans asked Sam Harris, our manager, if they could fill in during the summer with a little thing called Topsy and Eva—*a sort of comic* Uncle Tom's Cabin *which they had written themselves. They just wanted to do it out on the coast, they said. Sam said that would be all right, so they went ahead, expecting to play a couple of months or so, and darned if* Topsy and Eva *didn't turn out one of those colossal hits which run forever. It's now in about its fifteenth week in Chicago with New York still to come, so we lost the Duncans and owing to losing them lost Irving Berlin, who liked* Sitting Pretty *but thought it wouldn't go without them. So we got hold of Jerry and carried on with him.*

He has done a fine score, but it still remains to be seen whether or not the show—written as a vehicle for a sister act—will succeed with its present cast. We have Gertrude Bryan and Queenie Smith for the two Duncan parts, and they are both very good, but they aren't a team and this may dish us. A pity if it happens, as it's really a good show.

Unfortunately, Plum's fears were realised. *Sitting Pretty* opened at the Fulton Theatre, New York, on 8th April 1924 and ran for only 95 performances.

Once the show was on, the Wodehouses returned to London and bought a very fashionable house at 23 Gilbert Street, Grosvenor Square, where Leonora joined them. It was the right sort of address for a successful author, and Plum settled in to start on a new novel, *Sam the Sudden,* using his system of first writing a 30,000-word scenario. But it was slow going, and he soon realised that living in Mayfair was not conducive to concentration. He wrote to Townend:

How is the cottage working out? One thing about living in the country is that, even if the windows leak, you can get some work done. I find it's the hardest job to get at the stuff here. We have damned dinners and lunches which just eat up the time. I find that having a lunch hanging over me kills my morning's work, and dinner isn't much better. I'm at the stage now, if I drop my characters, they go cold.

From the end of 1924 to the end of 1925, Plum was busy with the writing of *Sam the Sudden* and the filling out of a collection of Wooster-Jeeves stories for a volume to be called *Carry On, Jeeves.* To this end, in addition to including the four original Jeeves stories that had appeared in

My Man Jeeves, he rewrote "Helping Freddie"—which had been a Reggie Pepper story in that volume—and turned it into a Wooster-Jeeves adventure called "Fixing it for Freddie."

Although so fully occupied, and in any event still not one for gadding about socially, Plum was not entirely a recluse. He did see people sometimes, and he particularly enjoyed meeting those with whom he could discuss writing. Such a one was his boyhood literary hero, Sir Arthur Conan Doyle, about whom he wrote to Townend:

> *Don't you find as you age in the wood, as we are both doing, that the tragedy of life is that your early heroes lose their glamour? As a lad in the twenties you worship old whoever-it-is, the successful author, and by the time you're forty you find yourself blushing hotly at the thought that you could ever have admired the bilge he writes.*
>
> *Now, with Doyle I don't have this feeling. I still revere his work as much as ever. I used to think it swell, and I still think it swell. . . .*
>
> *And apart from his work, I admire Doyle so much as a man. I should call him definitely a great man, and I don't imagine I'm the only one who thinks so. I love that solid, precise way he has of talking, like Sherlock Holmes. He was telling me once that when he was in America, he saw an advertisement in a paper: "Conan Doyle's School of Writing. Let the Conan Doyle School of Writing teach you how to sell" or something to that effect. In other words, some blighter was using his name to swindle the public. Well, what most people in his place*

*would have said would have been
"Hullo! This looks fishy." The way he
put it when telling me the story was:
"I said to myself, 'Ha! There is vil-
lainy afoot.' "*

On 15th April 1926 Herbert Jenkins published *The Heart of a Goof,*
which was the second collection of golf stories narrated by the Oldest Member. It was the only new Wodehouse book to appear in this year. But the
world of the theatre was still crying out for the Wodehouse touch, and
early in the month of the book's publication Plum was commissioned to
adapt a Russian light opera for the musical comedy stage. He found that
he was expected to write not only an entirely new book but also sets of lyrics
to the music of Bruno Granichstaedten. It proved too much, even for the
prolific Plum, in the limited time allotted to him, and he had to ask Graham
John to provide the lyrics. The show, called *Hearts and Diamonds,* marked
the debut in Britain of the famous Russian director Kommisarjefski—but,
unfortunately, not to any great degree. It opened on 1st June 1926 at the
Strand Theatre, London, and closed after only forty-six performances.

Immediately after the opening of *Hearts and Diamonds,* Plum and Ethel
availed themselves of an invitation to spend the summer at Hunstanton Hall
in Norfolk. Charles Le Strange, owner of the Hall, was a friend of Ethel's,
and his invitation couldn't have come at a more opportune time. For Plum,
naturally, had work to do—and as soon as he saw the Hall and its grounds,
he knew that this would be the ideal place in which to do it. Producer
Gilbert Miller had asked him to do an adaptation of Ferenc Molnar's *Spiel
im Schloss,* and Plum just happened to have a translation of the play with him.

Everything about Hunstanton Hall appealed to him. It was a real-life
Blandings Castle, the estate encompassing more than a thousand acres, which
included a lake, a park, many gardens and a moat. Part of the original
mansion, built in 1623, had been destroyed by fire in the early nineteenth
century and rebuilt in Victorian style. The house was so large that at least
two-thirds of it hadn't been lived in for almost a century.

Plum spent much of his time on the moat, sitting in a punt with his
typewriter on a small bedside table and wishing that he could settle down
permanently in a place like this—the Hall, of course, not the moat. And
he watched in wonderment the way that life was lived there, regretting only

that he couldn't use any of it in a story because no one would believe it. By this he meant such things as the late arrival of an unexpected guest because of car trouble—said guest arriving eventually at three o'clock in the morning to find that his host had roused the entire household and had a five-course dinner waiting for him.

It was a delightful interlude while it lasted—but life was real, life was earnest, and there was always work to be done.

Towards the end of July 1926, Plum received a cable from Guy Bolton urging him to make his way to the States and help with the writing of a musical comedy called *Oh, Kay!* It was to star the effervescent Gertrude Lawrence, who was currently taking New York by storm in an imported London revue. To date, Miss Lawrence had never appeared in a musical comedy, having made her name in London in revues with titles such as *Rats!* and *Buzz-Buzz.* She had first been seen in New York in the *Charlot Revue of 1924* at the Times Square Theatre, in company with Jack Buchanan and Beatrice Lillie, and had even then made it plain that there was nothing on the stage she would not be capable of doing. Now, in 1926, she had placed her affairs in the hands of Guy Bolton and he had taken her to the management of Alex Aarons and Vinton Freedley—much to the chagrin of Florenz Ziegfeld, who had been hoping to star her in one of his shows. The next step was a musical comedy.

"The thing I remember most vividly about *Oh, Kay!,*" Plum was to recall, "is the period of what is known as gestation—that is to say, the summer months during which Guy and I were writing it at his home in Great Neck. The summer of 1926 was considerably hotter than blazes, and it is not too much to say that I played like one of those fountains at Versailles, taking off some fourteen pounds in weight. It seemed for a time as though those lovely billowy curves of mine would be lost to the world forever, but fortunately they came back during rehearsals." Reminiscing further, it was his opinion that "Gertie was angelic to work with, and I cannot remember even one of those devastating rows which usually occur in the rehearsal period. And when we opened in Philadelphia in November, we were fortunate enough to have the customers rolling in the aisles. Gertie and Oscar were, as always, superb."

The Oscar referred to was Oscar Shaw, who had been in four of the Bolton-Wodehouse-Kern musicals and who was the best all-round light-comedy juvenile lead of the period. He had been the unanimous choice to play opposite Gertrude Lawrence.

Contemporary in plot, *Oh, Kay!* was principally concerned with prohibition and bootlegging; and for the part of a bootlegger-turned-butler both Plum and Guy had opted for Victor Moore, who had been so good in *See You Later.* At rehearsals, however, Moore's mild and deprecating manner led Aarons and Freedley to believe that he couldn't possibly be very amusing. So sure were they that they were prepared to pay him off and replace him with someone more impressive before the show opened its two-week pre-Broadway run in Philadelphia. But Plum and Guy stood firm. They knew Moore's work, and they were not at all perturbed because he didn't seem to come across at rehearsals. It was therefore the management and not they who were amazed when on the opening night of the tryout Victor Moore brought the house down with his performance. All he had needed was the 'feel' of an audience to get him going.

Not the least memorable thing about *Oh, Kay!* was its music. With melodies by George Gershwin and lyrics by his brother Ira, the show contained six songs that have become evergreens: "Someone to Watch Over Me," "Fidgety Feet," "Maybe," "Clap Yo' Hands," "Do, Do, Do" and the title song, "Oh, Kay!."

When it had its Broadway opening at the Imperial Theatre on 8th November 1926, the show scored an instant hit. The reviewers were full of praise. J. Brooks Atkinson of *The New York Times* wrote:

> *Musical comedy seldom proves more intensely delightful than* Oh, Kay! . . . .
> *Usually it is sufficient to credit as sponsors only the authors and the composer. But the distinction of* Oh, Kay! *is its excellent blending of all the creative arts of musical entertainment.*

And the noted drama critic of the *New York Daily News,* Burns Mantle, said:

> *Farseeing are Aarons and Freedley, too, in the employment of the best talent they can buy. The book of* Oh, Kay! *was written by Guy Bolton and P. G.*

Wodehouse, than whom there are no
better librettists writing for our stage.

Only five days earlier, on 3rd November, Plum's adaptation of *Spiel im Schloss,* called *The Play's the Thing,* had opened at the Henry Miller's Theatre in New York—having had its first-ever performance at the Great Neck Theatre, Long Island, on 21st October—and had also been well received. So Plum was in the happy position of having two hits playing concurrently in New York. And both were to enjoy long runs—*Oh, Kay!* totalling 256 performances and *The Play's the Thing* achieving a not inconsiderable 326.

No sooner were Plum and Guy giving every appearance of sitting back and basking in their success than the Shuberts were commissioning them to write a musical romance based on the life of Jenny Lind, the music to be composed by Armand Vecsey. The show, called *The Nightingale* and starring Eleanor Painter and Stanley Lupino, opened at the Jolson Theatre, New York, on 2nd January 1927 and ran for ninety-six performances.

Again there was no breathing space. With the opening of *The Nightingale,* Plum received an urgent call from Gilbert Miller and Al Woods who, with *The Play's the Thing* away to such a magnificent start, were now in the throes of producing a play called *The Cardboard Lover.* This adaptation by Valerie Wyngate of an original French work by Jacques Deval was already on the road—starring Laurette Taylor, and with Leslie Howard making his debut in America as her leading man—but it had become obvious that it would have to be completely rewritten before it could be put on in New York. It meant exhaustive work at a non-stop pace which might have daunted anyone but Plum. But he accepted the challenge and did what was necessary with all the skill that had been expected of him.

By the time his version of the play opened in New York at the Empire Theatre on 21st March 1927, Jeanne Eagles had replaced Laurette Taylor and the title of the piece had become *Her Cardboard Lover.* An unnamed critic included in his review the comment:

> *Mr. Wodehouse's fine hand is notice-*
> *able in some dialogue, the main in-*
> *gredients of which are bestowed on*
> *Mr. Howard. Howard utters these lines*
> *as though he wrote them. And how*

sweet they are to the ear.

The play ran for 152 performances and rocketed Leslie Howard to star status.

With *Her Cardboard Lover* safely staged on Broadway, Plum and Ethel returned to England. This time Ethel rented a magnificent sixteen-room house at 17 Norfolk Street, just off Park Lane, in the heart of Mayfair. The rental was £450 a month, and the running of the establishment called for a retinue of servants such as the Wodehouses had never before required. There was a morning secretary to keep the household-expenses books, an afternoon secretary to deal with Ethel's many business interests, a cook, a butler, a kitchen maid, a footman, two housemaids, one lady's maid, one odd-job man, and a chauffeur for the new Rolls-Royce. Out of this motley crew, the servants of prime importance were, of course, the butler and the cook.

Amid all this luxury, Ethel took it upon herself to supervise the decorating and furnishing of a super-ideal study-cum-library in which Plum would be able to work undisturbed. Rare and costly books lined its shelves, and beautiful prints and paintings relieved the panelled walls. Its draperies were rich but subdued, and expensive but comfortable furniture completed a workroom to pique the envy of any garret-ridden writer.

When everything was in its place and the room was ready for occupation, Ethel happily escorted Plum across its threshold and waited for his reaction. Plum took one look, complimented Ethel warmly on her excellent taste, and then asked if he might be allowed to go down to the kitchen. There he decided to borrow a small deal table and a chair which he personally transferred one at a time to his bedroom, installing his beloved Monarch typewriter on the one and himself on the other. He then settled down to do some work, beginning as and where he meant to carry on. It was clearly far too late to teach this old dog new tricks.

Ethel had always loved to entertain, and now she gave frequent cocktail parties for as many as twenty or thirty guests at a time. She also took to giving a dinner party once a fortnight to which eight couples would be invited. Plum truly hated these dinners and would absent himself from the company as soon as he decently could, taking his pet Peke under his arm and going out for a stroll across Hyde Park. Beverly Nichols once wrote that he saw Plum's well-known disappearances from parties as the key to his character, "which is dominated by a loathing for display."

It wasn't always to the park that Plum went when he'd managed to sneak away from a gathering. Sometimes he was able to slip unobserved into his bedroom, there to get on with some writing. There was always plenty of that to be done. Even while engrossed with *Oh, Kay!*, *The Play's the Thing*, *The Nightingale*, and *Her Cardboard Lover* he had been stolidly working away at the novel he was weaving from Guy Bolton's plot for *Oh, Lady! Lady!!* and which he was calling *The Small Bachelor*. The shows were mere interludes during his work on the book. As Leonora once wrote, Plum's idea of a vacation was to write a play or short story in between his novels. The 'vacations' certainly didn't prevent him from completing *The Small Bachelor*, which was published first in England on 28th April 1927.

For the summer of 1927 the Wodehouses rented Hunstanton Hall from Le Strange and moved in with the latest addition to the family—a three-month-old Pekingese named Susan. Both Ethel and Plum were inveterate animal lovers, with a special addiction to Pekingese dogs; and Susan was their particular favourite. Plum took her everywhere with him, as a result of which she became a very well known Peke indeed. The bond between master and dog was so great that Leonora was prompted to write:

> *Susan is our Pekingese, and Plum adores her. Just as we have planned glorious voyages round the world, we remember that Susan would have to be left behind, so we stay in England to keep her amused, or see the world in relays. She is very pretty, small with a chestnut coat and that dancing way of walking that Pekingese have. Plum will leave anyone in the middle of a conversation to ingratiate himself with Susan if she gives him the slightest smile; and a man may be without morals, money, or attractions, but if the word goes round that he's "sound on Pekes" Plum will probably somehow find excuses for his lack of morals, lend him money, and invent attractions for him.*

In July 1927 Plum was working on another novel, about which he wrote to Townend:

> *I am sweating blood over* Money for Nothing *and have just finished 53,000 words of it. Meanwhile, I have to anglicise* Oh, Kay! *by August 9th, attend rehearsals, adapt a French play, write a new musical comedy and do the rest of* Money for Nothing, *as far as I can see, by about September 1st. It'll all help to pass the time.*

Just another typical Wodehouse working period, in fact.

On the 21st September 1927 the London presentation of *Oh, Kay!* opened successfully at His Majesty's Theatre, to eventually enjoy a run of 213 performances, and on 27th September Herbert Jenkins published *Meet Mr. Mulliner*—a collection of short stories which had previously appeared in the *Strand* and in each of which Mr. Mulliner told one of his tall stories to the regulars in the bar-parlour of The Angler's Rest.

Soon after this, Plum was on his way back to America at the behest of Florenz Ziegfeld; and in a letter from New York dated 28th November 1927 he told Townend all about it:

> *I would have written before this, but ever since I landed I have been in a terrible rush. I came here with George Grossmith to do* The Three Musketeers *for Flo Ziegfeld, and we finished a rough version on the boat. But like all work that is done quickly, it needed a terrible lot of fixing, which was left to me as George went home. I was working gaily on it when a fuse blew out in Ziegfeld's Marilyn Miller show—book by Guy Bolton and Bill McGuire—owing to the lyricist and*

composer turning up on the day of the start of rehearsals and announcing that they had finished one number and hoped to have another done shortly, though they couldn't guarantee this. Ziegfeld fired them and called in two new composers, Sigmund Romberg and George Gershwin, and asked me to do the lyrics with Ira. I wrote nine in a week and ever since then have been sweating away at the rest. Meanwhile Gilbert Miller wanted a show in a hurry for Irene Bordoni, so I started on that, too—fixing the Musketeers *with my left hand the while. By writing the entire second act in one day I have managed to deliver the Bordoni show in time, and I have now finished the lyrics of the Flo show and the revised version of the* Musketeers, *and all is well—or will be until Flo wants all the lyrics rewritten, as he is sure to do. We open the Bolton-McGuire-Ira Gershwin-Wodehouse-George Gershwin-Romberg show in Boston next week. It's called* Rosalie, *and I don't like it much, though it's bound to be a success with Marilyn and Jack Donahue in it.*

Just at present I feel as if I would never get another idea for a story. I suppose I shall eventually, but this theatrical work certainly saps one's energies. As I write this, it is six o'clock, so the play I wrote for Ernest Truex, Good Morning, Bill, *must just be finishing in London. I hope it has got*

over, as I know Gilbert Miller is wait-
ing to see how it is received in London
before putting it on here.

New York is noisier than ever. I
found my only way of getting any
work done on the Flo lyrics was to
take a room at the Great Neck Golf
Club and work there. So I am the only
man on record who commutes the
wrong way. I catch the twelve o'clock
train from New York every day and
return after dinner. Flo thinks I play
golf all day out there and is rather
plaintive about it, but I soothe him by
producing a series of lyrics.

Good Morning, Bill, which had its first night at the Duke of York Theatre on 28th November while Plum was writing to Townend, was joyously
received. One critic wrote:

How refreshing it is to laugh in a
theatre with one whose humour is
neither blatant nor coarse nor cruel;
whose silliness, when he is silly, has
the good sting of character to save it,
and whose sense of nonsense has an
easy, graceful good-humour which
makes unnecessary the noisy violence
that is too often the only support of
fame. The matter is thus—Mr. Wode-
house is a stylist.

In the cast headed by Ernest Truex was Lawrence Grossmith—brother
of George, and the first man ever to have commissioned Plum to write a
play. But players and play, though successful, were doomed to a limited run
of 146 performances because the theatre had been previously booked for
another presentation.

As a sort of bonus to round off Plum's year, the end of 1927 saw the production in New York of *Show Boat,* with which he had had no direct connection but in the score for which Jerome Kern had included "Bill," with Plum's lyric. The show, the song and its singer, Helen Morgan, were all smash hits.

It was on 10th January 1928 that *Rosalie* opened at the New Amsterdam Theatre, with Marilyn Miller and Jack Donahue scoring the success that Plum had predicted for them. Indeed—despite Plum's distaste for its plot—the show ran for 335 performances, and the film rights in it were snapped up by Metro-Goldwyn-Mayer.

The Three Musketeers, after the frenetic activity that had attended its creation, opened at the Lyric Theatre in New York on 13th March 1928 and proved that all the effort had been worth while. With Dennis King as its star, it romped away to 318 performances.

So many shows in so short a time meant extremely hard work, but it paid off. Plum's market value had zoomed, and his agents were able to demand and get for him the highest fees ever paid to a writer. But even so, he was now anxious to resume his other writing career. An idea for a new Blandings Castle story had been simmering within him for the past sixteen months and he felt it was about ready to be brought to the boil. With the shows behind him, he wanted to devote all his time to straightening out the plot in his mind before committing anything to paper. He had already decided on its title—*Summer Lightning.*

Plum returned to England to write this book, and while engaged on it he began to make notes for another novel to be called *Big Money.* Since there was no intention of actually writing it until he had finished *Summer Lightning,* he contented himself with a very short scenario that would cover the gist of the plot.

Being in London meant seeing old friends, and Denis Mackail was one with whom Plum spent much time. The pattern of their meetings was described thus by Mackail:

> "*I say, touching this matter of Pekes . . .*"
> "*I say, when you get absolutely stuck in a story . . .*"
> "*I say, what do you* really *make*

of old Somerset M.?"

These were all Plum's openings, as we smoked and sipped, and hammered each subject with our mighty brains. Most enjoyable, I can tell you. At about half-past ten—for we always dined early—we suddenly started rushing through the streets, at Plum's prodigious pace, until a point where, just as suddenly, he had vanished and gone. No lingering farewells from that quarter. I might hear him saying Goodnight, from the middle of the traffic; I might catch a glimpse of his raincoat swinging across the road. But the general effect was that he had just switched himself off. It was the custom. And in those days, of course—unless he were also dashing off to America—there would always be another of these evenings quite soon.

Apparently never content unless he had more than one project going at a time, Plum found that the writing of *Summer Lightning* did not prevent him from brewing up another Lord Emsworth plot in short-story form. But it seemed to give him much more trouble than the full-length work which was his main task, and he mentioned it to William Townend in a letter dated 30th April 1928:

So sorry not to have written before, but I have been much tied up with a very difficult story. "Company for Gertrude," I'm calling it. . . . It's one of those maddening yarns where you get the beginning and the end all right, and only want a bit in the middle.

That summer, Plum and Ethel rented Rogate Lodge in Sussex. It was a large furnished country house with its own beautiful park—and it was well equipped for entertaining. Denis Mackail, Michael Arlen, and John Galsworthy, who lived nearby, were frequent luncheon guests. But their host, even with a country estate and a butler, remained the Plum they had always known. Unimpressed by the grandeur of his surroundings, he was as sloppily dressed as ever; still determined to talk of nothing but writing, and still adept at vanishing into thin air whenever he felt like being alone.

A house guest at Rogate Lodge was novelist-playwright Ian Hay, whose real name was John Hay Beith. He was there to work on a dramatization of *A Damsel in Distress* and would spend the mornings discussing the characters and planning the show with Plum. In the afternoons, Hay would work on the dialogue by himself. It was a collaboration in which, as Plum was later to explain, Hay "hogged all the writing": quite different from Plum's earlier collaboration with Herbert Westbrook. Writing to Townend about the play on 26th July 1928, Plum said:

> *Ian Hay has been here, too, dramatising* A Damsel in Distress. *Tom Miller and Basil Foster are putting it on. It opens in London on August 14th. We have formed a syndicate—the management, Ian, and I each putting up five hundred quid. We needed another five hundred to make up the necessary two thousand, and A. A. Milne gallantly stepped forward and said he would like to come in. I don't think we shall lose our money, as Ian has done an awfully good job.*

If Plum had delayed his letter by another day he would have had another piece of news for Townend; for on 27th July 1928 Herbert Jenkins published *Money for Nothing*—the novel in which Plum had fictionalised Hunstanton Hall.

In that letter to Townend, Plum miscalculated the opening of *A Damsel in Distress* by a day. It opened, in fact, on 13th August at the New Theatre in London and made an instant impact, eventually chalking up 242 performances.

With the play successfully staged, Plum and Ian Hay took a short holiday together, about which Plum wrote to Townend:

> *He and I went off to Scotland on a golfing tour, which I loved. Hay had this little car . . . of his, and we went up to Edinburgh and then to a different golf course every day. We went to Glen Eagles and St. Andrews too. It was awfully nice. Ian had a lot of interests in common. We were both keen on golf and public schools. I read all his stuff and liked it enormously. I liked collaborating with Ian because it's like collaborating with Guy. He liked doing all the stuff himself. I was just to contribute the book. We talked it all over and got our scenario and the characters and everything and then he wrote it.*

On 21st August 1928 the London production of *Her Cardboard Lover* had its first night at the Lyric Theatre. Tallulah Bankhead had the role played by Jeanne Eagles in New York, and Leslie Howard was again the leading man. This production was more successful than its American predecessor, running for 173 performances and—apart from greatly enhancing Miss Bankhead's reputation—proving beyond doubt that Leslie Howard belonged among the elite in his profession.

Plum, meanwhile, was still struggling with *Summer Lightning*. To relieve his feelings about it, he wrote to Townend from Rogate Lodge on 28th September 1928:

> *I have spent the summer writing and rewriting the first thirty thousand words of* Summer Lightning, *and must*

have done—all told—about a hundred
thousand words. It is one of those stories
which one starts without getting the
plot properly fixed and keeps going off
the rails. I think all is well now, but I
am shelving it to do some short stories.

Back at 17 Norfolk Street in October, Plum was able to see more of Denis Mackail and—as Mackail relates—do him a service:

Hob-nobbing at the Garrick Club, to
which they both belonged, Messrs. A. A.
Milne and P. G. Wodehouse had se-
cretly decided that I should belong to
it, too. So Alan had proposed, Plum
had seconded, and as I was neither so
famous as to arouse enmity nor so ut-
terly unknown as to be rejected on
these grounds, the Committee had ap-
proved my candidature almost at once.
Alan broke the news to me a few days
after, and though touched, flattered,
and grateful, I am afraid that for a
moment I was also slightly taken
aback. Almost the next thing that hap-
pened was that Plum had another of
his fits of disgust, and resigned.

During January 1929 Plum and Ian Hay were again collaborating, this time on the dramatisation of one of Hay's stories called *Baa, Baa, Black Sheep.* They enjoyed working together and were apparently highly appreciative of what they were accomplishing, for Leonora recalled that she used to hear gales of laughter penetrating the closed door of Plum's study throughout their writing sessions. Despite this, or perhaps because of it, the play was soon ready and in rehearsal. It opened at the New Theatre in London on 22nd April 1929; and although it made less of an impact than *A Damsel in Distress,* it ran for a respectable 115 performances.

By this time Ethel and Plum were installed in Hunstanton Hall, which they had rented once more, and it was from there that Plum wrote to Townend on 27th April:

> *I would have written before, but I have had a hell of a week. On Sunday I had to condense* Good Morning, Bill *into a sketch for Heather Thatcher. (She opens at the Coliseum on Whit Monday.) From Monday to Thursday night I was writing a Jeeves story in response to an urgent demand from America that I get it off by Saturday's boat, which meant mailing it from here not later than noon on Friday. On Friday and yesterday I was so exhausted I couldn't write.*
>
> *It's wonderful being back at Hunstanton Hall again, though things aren't so frightfully bright at the moment, as host has had a row with butler, who has given notice. The butler is a cheery soul who used to be the life and soul of the party, joining in the conversation at meals and laughing appreciatively if one made a joke, but now he hovers like a spectre, very strong and silent. I'm hoping peace will be declared soon.*
>
> *I think I like Hunstanton Hall as well in winter as in summer, though, of course, I don't get the moat in the winter months. I laid the scene of* Money for Nothing *at Hunstanton Hall.*
>
> *What bloodstained books you seem to read! . . . I don't think any of those books you mention really amount*

to much. It seems to me that at least two-thirds of the stuff published nowadays is by one-book people. You know, A Stirring Revelation of a Young Girl's Soul *by Jane Emmeline Banks, who never writes another damn book in her life. The test is, can you write three?*

On 27th May 1929 Plum's father died at the age of 83. For the past ten years Eleanor and Ernest had been living at Bexhill-on-Sea in Sussex, but now Eleanor went to live with Armine and his wife, Nella.

Towards the end of August, an urgent cable from Ziegfeld had Plum hurrying to New York to write the lyrics for a musical version of the play *East is West* (this version being in no way connected with the one that Plum and Guy had themselves attempted in 1919 under the title of *The Rose of China*). But when he arrived he found himself in the middle of what he called "a usual Ziegfeld experience." Absolutely nothing was happening. Six weeks later, the sum of Plum's work amounted to a few lyrics written in collaboration with a young man named Billy Rose—whose sole claim to fame at that time was that he had written a song entitled "Does Your Chewing Gum Lose its Flavor on the Bedpost Overnight?". The book for *East is West* was in the hands of Bill McGuire, and Vincent Youmans was responsible for the music, but neither of them appeared to be doing the least thing about it.

To fill in the hiatus created by the lack of activity in Ziegfeld's charmed circle, Plum took on the rewriting of a play to be presented by Gilbert Miller. Called *Candlelight,* it had been adapted from Siegfried Geyer's original by Graham John and had already been seen on the London stage, but not to Miller's satisfaction. Plum's version was to star Gertrude Lawrence in her first non-musical acting role, with Reginald Owen and Leslie Howard in support.

During rehearsals for *Candlelight,* and since there was still no sign of life from any of the participants in *East is West,* Plum decided to take a short trip to Hollywood. He had been invited to work there, and he thought it would be a good opportunity to look the place over before making a decision. His only lapse was in forgetting to tell anyone of his intentions, thus adding chaos to confusion when it transpired that both Ziegfeld and Miller wanted him around at that particular time. In each case, when a clue to his whereabouts had been discovered, it was believed that he had deserted and gone to Hollywood to work. Since he'd left no forwarding address, his irate colleagues had no way of contacting him—and Ziegfeld, in particular, was deprived of the chance of sending one of his famous novella-length cables.

Among those most offended by Plum's absence was Gertrude Lawrence who, when he innocently returned to New York nine days later, received him icily. But by the time *Candlelight* opened at the Empire Theatre, New York, on 30th September 1929, all was forgiven and he was welcomed back into the fold. Not without reason. Typical of the reviews the play received was one by John Mason Brown in the *Evening Post* which, among other glowing comments, said: ". . . the most adroit and suave comedy this town has had the chance of laughing at in many months." The fact that *Candlelight* ran for only 128 performances was directly attributable to the Wall Street crash and the consequent Depression.

Writing to Townend on 2nd October 1929 about his most recent experiences, Plum included a few lines about his visit to Hollywood;

> *The only person I knew really well out there was Marion Davies, who was in the show* Oh, Boy! *which Guy, Jerry and I did for the Princess Theatre. She took me out to her house in Santa Monica and worked me into a big lunch at Metro-Goldwyn-Mayer which they were giving for Winston Churchill. All very pleasant. . . . I have reluctantly come to the conclusion that I must have one of those meaningless faces which make no impression whatever on the beholder. This was—I think—the seventh time I had been introduced to Churchill, and I could see that I came upon him as a complete surprise once more.*

The musical version of *East is West* remained in Never-Never land. Nothing more was ever heard of it, and by November 1929 Plum was back at 17 Norfolk Street in London. Ethel, in the meantime, had gone to Hollywood to negotiate a contract for Plum with M-G-M. An astute business-woman, she concluded a deal for a six-month contract at a weekly salary of $2,000 with an option for a further six months at the same salary.

While she was away, Plum was hard at work and having difficulties about which he wrote to Townend:

> *I'm longing to get down and see you all, but I'm in the middle of a story, which I must finish before I can make any move. I've gone and let myself in for one of those stories which lead up to a big comic scene and now I'm faced with writing the scene and it looks as if it was going to be difficult to make funny. It's a village Rugger match, where everybody tries to slay everybody else, described by Bertie Wooster who, of course, knows nothing about Rugger. It's damned hard to describe a game you know backward through the eyes of somebody who doesn't know it. However, I suppose it will come. These things always do. But it isn't easy. . . . What a sweat a novel is till you are sure of your characters. And what a vital thing it is to have plenty of things for a major character to do. That is the test. If they aren't in situations, characters can't be major characters, not even if you have the rest of the troupe talk their heads off about them.*

By the end of 1929 Ethel had returned from Hollywood, and she and

Plum were guests of Le Strange at Hunstanton Hall for Christmas—of which Plum's bitter memory was that he was forced to don the old white tie and tails every evening. Not quite the ideal way of spending a festive season.

8
1930–1938

For the first four months of 1930 Plum remained at his London home, working on his novel and reading the proofs of *Very Good, Jeeves* (the collection of short stories that Doubleday Doran were to publish in the United States on 20th June). But in April he was on the move again, back to America with Leonora as his travelling companion. Denis Mackail and his wife drove them to Southampton to board the *Majestic*, taking Ethel along to see her family off. There was an air of excitement throughout the car journey, but not from the expected quarter. Mackail had to remind himself that it was Plum and Leonora, not Ethel, "who were the real travellers, though you would never have guessed this from Plum's detachment and calm."

Maintaining what would nowadays be called his 'cool,' Plum arrived in Hollywood by train on 8th May 1930 still accompanied by Leonora. They came as strangers, but they soon made new friends and met old acquaintances in the film capital, and at first Plum quite liked it there. This was Hollywood in its heyday—the tinsel town of glamour and overnight fame and fortune that embodied the American dream. Here were assembled the world's most beautiful women, the handsomest of men and, sometimes, the most talented of actors and actresses. The very name Hollywood had a magical quality, and any ordinary mortal might have been expected to write ecstatic letters about the wonderment of it all. But Plum was Plum, and to him Hollywood was just another place in which to work. Being there had hardly any effect on his usual routine; and his first letter to Townend from Hollywood, dated 26th June 1930, made this abundantly clear:

> *I have been meaning to write to you*
> *for ages, but I have been in a tremen-*
> *dous whirl of work ever since I ar-*
> *rived in Hollywood. For some obscure*

reason, after being absolutely dead for months, my brain suddenly started going like a dynamo. I got a new plot for a short story every day for a week. Then I started writing and in well under a month have done three short stories, an act of a play, and all the dialogue for a picture.

There is something about this place that breeds work. We have a delightful house—Norma Shearer's—with a small but lovely garden and a big swimming pool, the whole enclosed in patio form. The three wings of the house occupy three sides, a high wall, looking on to a deserted road, the other. So that one feels quite isolated. I have arranged with the studio to work at home, so often I spend three or four days on end without going out of the garden: I get up, swim, breakfast, work till two, swim again, have a lunch-tea, work till seven, swim for the third time, then dinner, and the day is over. It is wonderful. I have never had such a frenzy of composition.

One of the stories I have written is your cat plot. The story of Webster, do you remember—the artist and the dignified cat? I have added a lot to the plot. It now ends differently. Hero has a row with his girl, flies to whisky bottle, sees cat staring gravely and rebukingly at him, drops bottle, cat laps up whisky, gets tight, springs through window, and cleans up an alley cat which has been saying rude things to

him for weeks. Hero realises cat is one
of the boys after all, and all is well.
It has worked out as one of the best
things I have ever done. . . .

I don't see much of the movie
world. My studio is five miles from
where I live, and I only go there oc-
casionally. If I ever dine out or go to
parties, it is with other exiles—New
York writers, etc. Most of my New
York theatre friends are here.

The pattern of life was to change, however, when Ethel joined her family in July. Hollywood was noted for its spectacular and much-publicised parties, and Ethel was therefore in her element. She was a brilliant organiser and was never happier than when she was running things. Consequently, she began to entertain on a lavish scale, and Plum found himself embroiled in parties galore. One gathering in particular impressed itself upon his memory of those days. "I was seated next to an elderly woman at a dinner party given by Ethel," he recalled, "when she turned and spoke to me. 'This is a great moment for me,' she said. 'I can't tell you how proud I am. I think I have read everything you have ever written. We all love your books. My eldest son reads nothing else. And so do my grandsons. The table in their room is piled high with them. And when I go home tonight,' she added, 'and tell them that I have actually been sitting at dinner next to Edgar Wallace, I don't know what they will say.' " Plum didn't know what to say, either. With a look that might have struck the lady as strangely cold, he nodded his appreciation.

His first studio assignment was on a film called *Those Three French Girls,* starring his old friend and collaborator George Grossmith with Fifi d'Orsay, Reginald Denny and Ukulele Ike (Cliff Edwards), and it initiated him into the vagaries of a screenwriter's work. He had expected to be asked to write the story, but what he was presented with was a script already written by Tottie Harwood and several other scribes (the theory being that if one writer could do a good job a whole lot of writers could do it much better) which seemed to him to be complete and perfect in every respect. Obligingly, however, he added a few lines of dialogue—which apparently made everyone happy—and heard no more from the studio for some time, continuing to draw his weekly salary without being called upon to earn it.

While waiting for something to happen, meanwhile carrying on with his novel at the studio's expense, he was able to do a good turn for another English writer new to Hollywood. Gerard Fairlie had come to write the Bulldog Drummond series following the death of its creator, Herman Cyril McNeile ('Sapper'). Armed with two letters of introduction—one to Arthur Hornblow of M-G-M and the other to Plum—he had booked in at the Ambassadors Hotel on the night of his arrival and sent the letters off. On the following day he had a visit from Plum, who invited him to dinner that evening. During the course of the meal at Plum's Beverly Hills house, it was suggested that Fairlie should stay there for a while until he had met some people and knew his way around. Fairlie, who was naturally delighted to accept the offer, asked when it would be convenient for him to start his visit: and in his autobiography *With Prejudice* he recorded: "I shall never forget Plummy's reply. 'You have already arrived,' he said. 'I had all your things brought to the house some time ago.'" And it was true. Plum had arranged for Fairlie's belongings to be transferred from the hotel and installed in one of his own guest-rooms while they were at dinner. Fairlie had been properly taken under the Wodehouse wing, and Plum and Ethel looked after him for the next couple of weeks. "I met many people through them who have since remained excellent friends," the grateful writer concluded.

The completed act of a play to which Plum had referred in his letter to Townend was part of another collaboration with Ian Hay. This time it was a dramatization of *Leave it to Psmith*. As Hay was still in London, however, the work on it had to be carried on by way of correspondence—an inconvenience but, fortunately, not a hazard. The play opened at the Shaftesbury Theatre in London on 27th September 1930 and showed no signs of its long-distance gestation. It had a comfortable run of 156 performances.

By the end of his first six months in Hollywood, Plum's feelings about the place had undergone a radical change. He now liked it only as long as he didn't have to see it, and the most that he could find in its favour was the weather. But there was to be no escape for the time being, as he confided to Townend in a letter dated 28th October 1930:

> *Well, laddie, it begins to look as*
> *if it would be some time before I re-*
> *turn to England. The Metro people*

*have taken up my option, and I am
with them for another six months and
Ethel has just taken a new house for
a year. Which means that I shall probably stay that long.*

*If you came over here and settled
down, I think I would spend at least
six months in every year here. I like the
place. I think California scenery is the
most loathsome on earth—a cross between Coney Island and the Riviera—
but by sticking in one's garden all the
time and shutting one's eyes when one
goes out, it is possible to get by.*

*As life goes on, though, don't you
find that all you need is a wife, a few
real friends, a regular supply of books,
and a Peke? (Make that two Pekes and
add a swimming pool.)*

*M-G-M bought that musical com-
edy* Rosalie—*the thing Guy Bolton,
Bill McGuire, George Gershwin, Sigmund Romberg, Ira Gershwin and I
did for Ziegfeld for Marilyn Miller—
for Marion Davies. Everyone in the
studio had a go at it, and then they
told me to try.*

. . . I am at last reading The Good
Companions. *I love it. That's the sort
of book I would like to write.*

Plum's work on the *Rosalie* script was his second film assignment, and
it fared even worse than the first. When he had finished it, after three months
of concentration, the studio informed him that there was a slump in the musical-
film market and they would therefore not be going ahead with the production.

At this time, Leslie Howard was filming in Hollywood and had moved
his family there. His daughter, Leslie Ruth Howard, remembered that all the

Howards were hugely entertained by Plum's dogged determination to indulge his love of walking. In a colony where everyone drove everywhere, only Plum put his best foot forward when the studio summoned, briskly striding the not inconsiderable distance—frequently passed by the hilarious Howards, who noticed that he was quite oblivious to the amazed stares of gardeners, maids, and delivery boys driving to their work. As Miss Howard wrote: "No one else was ever seen to walk in Beverly Hills." (There was Garbo, of course. But who ever *saw* her?)

To support Miss Howard's statement, a Los Angeles newspaper had this to say about Plum:

> *In Beverly Hills, he is unique, original, unprecedented—the city's only pedestrian! His home at 1005 Benedict Canyon is six miles from the M-G-M studio in Culver City, yet when the studio calls him up and asks him to run over for a conference, Wodehouse doesn't run, he walks.*

Incredibly, it was not until early in 1931 that Plum was given his next film assignment: and once again he was presented with a completed script. It was called *The Man in Possession,* and he felt that it was as ready as it ever would be. Nevertheless, he tinkered with it a little before returning it and thus earned himself a screen credit for the three lines of his that the movie moguls left in the finished film. No other work was given to him between that time and the expiration of his contract; and to his vast relief, the contract was not renewed. He'd begun to have something of a conscience about drawing his weekly salary for nothing. But he was by no means the only one to have had this sort of experience.

Part of the Hollywood legend was its enormous wealth, for which the cry "Go West, young man" had taken on a new meaning. If there was gold in them thar hills the reference was to Beverly Hills, and you could dig the gold out with your teeth—if they were white and even and photographed well. The studios of the West Coast were being financed by the big banks in the East, and they didn't seem to care how they spent the apparently inexhaustible dollars. Everyone knew about the riches of Hollywood. Fan magazines thrived on perpetuating the stories of million-dollar movies and billion-dollar stars. It was what the public wanted to hear; it was good publicity. But not so much was known about what went on behind the scenes—about the Hollywood where big "names" were bought for fantastic sums and then scrapped; where other creative talents were wooed and then wasted; where the hiring and firing had neither rhyme nor reason but always cost money. Stories would filter through about this lavish and senseless spending and the squandering of colossal amounts of money, but they were spread anonymously and might well have been exaggerations or simply more of that "good publicity." The bankers in the East just didn't know, but they were becoming suspicious and restive. It was as though Hollywood had become a powder keg. The fuse was there. It needed only someone to light it.

In terms of poetic justice, the match was struck by M-G-M and handed to Plum when they asked him—although he was no longer under contract to them—to grant an interview to Alma Whitaker of the *Los Angeles Times.* And the explosion took place on 7th June 1931, when Miss Whitaker faithfully recorded for her readers the candid comments of the world-famous writer:

> *They paid me $2,000 a week—$104,000—and I cannot see what they engaged me for. They were extremely nice to me, but I feel as if I have cheated them. You see, I understood I was engaged to write stories for the screen. After all, I have twenty novels, a score of successful plays, and count-less magazine stories to my credit. Yet apparently they had the greatest diffi-culty in finding anything for me to do. Twice during the year they brought completed scenarios of other people's stories to me and asked me to do some dialogue. Fifteen or sixteen people had tinkered with those stories. The dia-logue was really quite adequate. All I did was to touch it up here and there.*
> *Then they set me to work on a*

> *story called* Rosalie, *which was to have*
> *some musical numbers. It was a pleas-*
> *ant little thing, and I put in three*
> *months on it. When it was finished,*
> *they thanked me politely and remarked*
> *that as musicals didn't seem to be going*
> *so well they guessed they would not use*
> *it.*
>
> *That about sums up what I was*
> *called upon to do for my $104,000.*
> *Isn't it amazing?*
>
> *Personally, I received the most*
> *courteous treatment, but see what hap-*
> *pened to my friend Roland Pertwee at*
> *Warner Brothers. He did a story for*
> *Marilyn Miller, and they slapped him*
> *on the back and said it was great. He*
> *returned to the studio as usual next*
> *morning, and was informed by the*
> *policeman at the gate that he could not*
> *be let in as he was fired.*
>
> *It's so unbelievable, isn't it?*

The interview had far-reaching repercussions. For the very first time, names had been named and the situation had been brought right out into the open. No one could ignore it—least of all the bankers, who were immediately stirred into action and were quick to ring the death knell on Hollywood extravagance . . . for a time, at any rate. Plum, in consequence, became the most talked-of man in America. He had, by simply speaking his mind and turning Hollywood on its tail, done the film industry a great service. And he had done it without malice aforethought. As Rupert Hughes said in the *Saturday Evening Post:*

> *Many authors have been badly treated*
> *in Hollywood, but Hollywood has paid*
> *high for this idiocy. One of the gentlest*
> *and one of the most valuable for Holly-*

wood—P. G. Wodehouse—quietly re-
gretted that he had been paid a hundred
thousand dollars for doing next to noth-
ing. This remark was taken up, and it
stirred the bankers deeply, as it should
have done. But Mr. Wodehouse has
written no ferocious assaults on those
who slighted him.

Mr. Wodehouse, in fact, seemed unperturbed by the furore he had created. There was certainly no guilty flight from the scene. He remained placidly in Hollywood for a few more months.

During his abortive year as a screenwriter, Plum had kept himself busy by working on several short stories and two novels—the first of which, *If I Were You,* was published in America on 3rd September 1931. The second, *Hot Water,* was still at the scenario stage. He had managed 60,000 words of it but was not satisfied and was constantly rewriting. The fact was that he needed a change of scene, and he was soon writing to Townend:

We are toying with the scheme for
going round the world in December on
the Empress of Britain. *Sometimes we*
feel we should like it, and then we ask
ourselves if we really want to see the
ruddy world. I'm darned if I know. I
have never seen any spectacular spot
yet that didn't disappoint me. Notably,
the Grand Canyon, and also Niagara
Falls

Personally, I've always liked wan-
dering around in the background. I
mean, I get much more kick out of a
place like Droitwich, which has no real
merits, than out of something like the
Taj Mahal. . . . I find that I am very
fit, but recently I have been feeling
tired. But then people always tire me,

and I have been in the middle of a
seething mass of people lately.
. . . Have you read A. A. Milne's
serial Two People *in the* Daily Mail?
It's colossal. The sort of book I shall
buy and re-read every six months or so.
What a genius he is at drawing char-
acter. Did you ever see his The Dover
Road? *My favourite play.*

Nothing came of the proposed world tour. Instead, Plum, Ethel and Leonora returned to England in November 1931, when the lease on the Beverly Hills house had expired. Because they had sub-let the Norfolk Street house before going to America, they had to find other accommodation and settled for a mews flat in Mayfair.

Plum immediately picked up the threads of his friendship with Denis Mackail and also made a new friend, mystery-writer E. Phillips Oppenheim, with whom he played golf as often as he could—impressing Oppenheim more with the length of his shots than with the possibility of his ever winning a game. But golfing with Oppenheim at Woking was over by early March 1932, when wanderlust overtook the Wodehouses once more and they were off to France. There they rented a house at Domaine de la Fréyère, Auribeau, Alpes-Maritimes, from whence, on 6th March 1932, Plum was writing to Townend:

The above is our new address. . . .
We have taken it for a year. It is a sort
of Provençal country house, with a hun-
dred acres of hillside and large grounds
and a huge swimming pool. It ought to
be lovely in summer. Just at the mo-
ment it is a bit bleak.

I have written one goodish story
since I got here, and two others which
aren't right. I think I can fix them,
but a comic story which goes off the
rails is worse than any other kind. One
gets the feeling that one's stuff isn't

funny, which is deadly.

. . . I bought Aldous Huxley's Brave World *thing, but simply can't read it. What a bore these stories of the future are. The whole point of Huxley is that he can write better about modern life than anybody else, so of course he goes and writes about the future, blast him. Michael Arlen is down here, writing a novel the scene of which is laid in the future. It's a ruddy epidemic.*

. . . We have settled down here very comfortably. Weather bad so far, but they say from now on we get six months of unbroken sunshine. It's a good place for work. I have written sixty-four pages of Thank You, Jeeves *in seventeen days, and would have done more but I went off the rails and had to rewrite three times. That is the curse of my type of story. Unless I get the construction absolutely smooth, it bores the reader. In this story, for instance, I had Bertie meet the heroine in London, scene, then again in the country, another scene. I found I had to boil all this down to one meeting, as it was talky. By the way, it's not all jam writing a story in the first person. The reader can know nothing except what Bertie tells him, and Bertie can know only a limited amount himself.*

I have just got Denis Mackail's David's Day. *Very good. You ought to read it.*

The scenery is marvellous. But I

*haven't yet got used to being away from
England or America. I can't see any
stuff for stories in this locality, though
you would probably get a dozen out of
the Cannes crowd.*

A different kind of Wodehouse book was published by Faber & Faber
on 10th March 1932. It was called *Louder and Funnier,* and it consisted of
a number of his original *Vanity Fair* articles that Plum had reworked into
essays. His private opinion was that the best thing about the book was its
jacket design by Rex Whistler: and it was to remain the only one of his
volumes to be derived from his light articles.

By now he had finished *Hot Water* and was still working on *Thank You,
Jeeves*—his first full-length Wooster-Jeeves novel—to which he was already
planning a sequel to be called *Right Ho, Jeeves.* And just to ensure that life
wouldn't become dull, he was also writing some short stories about Lord Emsworth and his pig, the Empress of Blandings, and a series concerned with the
adventures of Mr. Mulliner's numerous relatives.

Despite this necessarily solitary activity, there were moments of relaxation.
Neighbours of the Wodehouses on the Riviera were the Oppenheims, with
whom Plum and Ethel spent a good deal of time. They were often guests on the
Oppenheim yacht, and Plum recalled that "Opp was the perfect host." For his
part, E. Phillips Oppenheim remembered in his autobiography the many delightful times he had had in company with the Wodehouses. In particular, he
was reminded of an evening at the Sporting Club in Monte Carlo when he was
seated at the bar with Plum, and Plum leaned towards him and asked, "Who
is that long, sandy gin-and-tonic on the corner stool?" Oppenheim believed it
to be the first time that Plum had used that method of alluding to someone
whose identity was not known to him—and he recognised it with joy a little
later when he read some of Plum's Mulliner stories. The fact is, however, that
the Mulliner stories had started to appear long before this, and Plum had
merely been plagiarising himself.

While Plum and Ethel were in France, Leonora remained in England.
Plum's schoolgirl companion had become a lively young woman with interests
of her own—the most important of which was now Peter Cazalet, the son of
one of Plum's friends. The Cazalet home was a three-thousand-acre estate
called Fairlawne, in Sevenoaks, Kent, which had greater attractions than France

for Leonora since she and Peter had just become engaged and were planning a mid-December wedding.

The Wodehouses would, of course, be returning for the occasion, but in the meantime Plum was still mainly concerned with *Thank You, Jeeves;* and in late April 1932 he was writing gratefully to Townend for having given him a useful idea:

> *The stuff you sent me about the house with monkeys and mice in it is just what I needed for* Thank You, Jeeves. *It fits in perfectly. Bertie's pal Chuffy lives at Chuffnell Hall, Chuffy's aunt and her small son at the Dower House in the park. The son breeds white mice. They smell, and the aunt thinks it's drains, so they shift to the Hall and only a caretaker is in the Dower House. So when Bertie breaks in to get a night's lodging, with his face covered with black boot polish . . . Golly, what rot it sounds when one writes it down! Come, come, Wodehouse, is this the best you can do in the way of carrying on the great tradition of English Literature? Still, I'll bet the plot of Hamlet seemed just as lousy when Shakespeare was trying to tell it to Ben Jonson in the Mermaid Tavern. ('Well, Ben, see what I mean, the central character is this guy, see, who's in love with this girl, see, but her old man doesn't think he's on the level, see, so he tells her— wait a minute, I better start at the beginning. Well, so this guy's in college, see, and he's come home because his mother's gone and married his uncle, see, and he sees a ghost, see. So this*

> *ghost turns out to be the guy's father....')*
>
> *I think we shall open Norfolk Street in March next, when we get back.*

On 20th July 1932 Doubleday Doran published in America a bumper volume which was an anthology of Plum's short stories plus *Leave it to Psmith* in its entirety. The material for the book was selected and edited by verse-humorist Ogden Nash, whose unequivocal Introduction read:

> *P. G. Wodehouse needs no introduction.*

The subject of this pithy preface was, in the meantime, still on the Riviera. And as if such literary companions as E. Phillips Oppenheim and Michael Arlen were not enough for the Wodehouses, H. G. Wells now took a house not far from them. Meetings were inevitable, and towards the end of August Plum was writing to Townend about Wells:

> *I knew him slightly in London, at the time when he had some complicated row on with a man who had worked for him on his* Outline of History. *He asked a bunch of authors to dinner to hear his side of the thing. . . . Arnold Bennett was there and we walked home together. . . .*
>
> *I like Wells. An odd bird, though. The first time I met him, we had·barely finished the initial pip-pippings when he said, apropos of nothing, "My father was a professional cricketer." If there's a good answer to that, you tell me. . . .*
>
> *He lunched here yesterday. . . . I have been seeing him occasionally.*

When Leonora's wedding day was near, Ethel and Plum returned to

London and stayed at the Dorchester Hotel. But Plum did not dawdle long in its plush environment. Almost immediately upon arrival, he dashed off to see a football match at Dulwich. It was one of the things he touched on when he wrote to Townend on 1st December:

> *When I see you I want to talk over an idea for a secret collaboration on a series of sensational stories. I think it would be fun having a shot at these. I don't suppose we shall be able to do anything till I settle in London again, but it now looks as if we should open Norfolk Street in March or earlier.*
>
> *I never in my life experienced such suspense as during that second half of the Sherborne match, culminating in Billy Griffith scoring that superb try. Isn't it strange that one can still be absorbed by Dulwich footer? I never saw such splendid defensive work as we put up. It was easily the best school match I have seen.*
>
> *Don't you find, as you get on in life, that the actual things you really want cost about two thousand a year? I have examined my soul, and I find that my needs are a library subscription and tobacco money, plus an extra bit for holidays.*

Whether or not Plum and Townend ever did get around to discussing the secret collaboration mentioned in the letter is not disclosed, but it is certain that nothing came of it. There were to be no sensational stories—not even by a heavily disguised P. G. Wodehouse.

But there was no question of disguise on 14th December 1932, when Leonora and Peter V. F. Cazalet were married in Shipbourne Parish Church on the Fairlawne estate. Ethel looked on proudly as the radiantly happy Leonora was given away by a beaming and instantly recognisable Plum: and she may have remarked that it was one of the very few social gatherings from which her husband did not do his famous disappearing act.

Immediately after the wedding celebrations, however, Plum and Ethel returned to Domaine de la Fréyère, where Plum finished the first draft of *Heavy Weather*—a sequel to *Summer Lightning*. The headaches it gave him were related to Townend in a letter dated 4th January 1933:

> *I have had a devil of a time with my new one . . . and the first chapters were terribly hard to write because I had to be careful not to assume that people had read S. L. and at the same time not put in yards of explanation which would have bored those who had. In order to get one hundred pages of O.K. stuff, I must have written nearly a hundred thousand words.*

On 17th January 1933 Herbert Jenkins published *Mulliner Nights;* and Plum was still struggling with what now seemed to be aptly titled *Heavy Weather*. Never one to settle for second-best, he was determined to get the story right at all costs. And the lengths to which he was prepared to go were clearly indicated in his letter to Townend on 9th February 1933:

> *I have been sweating at* Heavy Weather, *and must be getting a bit stale, as I simply hadn't any energy left to write a line after a day's work. It's a curious thing about this novel, and probably means that it's going to be good, but I must have written at least 200,000 words so far. For a long time I couldn't get the thing straight. I kept getting dissatisfied with the first 30,000 words and starting again. Today I reached page 254 and have a very*

> *detailed scenario of the rest, and all*
> *up to page 254 now looks all right. It*
> *really reads as if I had written it straight*
> *off without a pause.*

His efforts were rewarded when Little, Brown published *Heavy Weather* on 28th July 1933, for it was an outstanding book by even his own high standards.

By now, Plum and Ethel had returned from France to 17 Norfolk Street; again they rented Hunstanton Hall for the summer. It was there that Plum worked on *Right Ho, Jeeves,* about which he was writing to Townend on 24th September—and including some valuable advice:

> *The story you sent me would, in*
> *my opinion, be much better told in the*
> *first person. It is all right as it stands,*
> *mind you, but could, I think, be im-*
> *proved that way.*
>
> *Only one big criticism. Fatal mis-*
> *take on pg. 5, I think, to risk tipping*
> *the reader off as to the blowout.*
>
> *It's one of the things you've got to*
> *be most careful about, this planting*
> *without telegraphing to the reader. In*
> *the novel I've just finished,* Right Ho,
> Jeeves, *it is vital that the cook shall*
> *not give notice, and in my first version*
> *I planted so strongly that he was a*
> *temperamental Frenchman that no*
> *reader could have helped seeing that*
> *the blowout of Bertie's scheme would*
> *be to make him quit. It ruined the*
> *story, and I had to cut like blazes.*
>
> *Right Ho, Jeeves has come out*
> *splendidly. I have almost finished typ-*
> *ing it out again. Amazing how that im-*
> *proves a book. I've cut out a lot of dead*

> *wood and even so I have added ten*
> *pages. I find that when the labour of*
> *the first draft is off one's mind one is*
> *able to concentrate on small improve-*
> *ments.*

Right Ho, Jeeves was sold to the *Saturday Evening Post,* in which it appeared in December 1933, before it was published in volume form.

On 20th March 1934 *Good Morning, Bill*—the play which had enjoyed only a limited run in 1927—was revived at Daly's Theatre in London with Lawrence Grossmith in his original role but with an otherwise new cast which included Peter Haddon and Winifred Shotter. The *Times* said of it:

> *Altogether a well acted farce, and*
> *a farce worth acting well . . .*

Peter Haddon was himself so taken with it that he, in conjunction with impresario Noel Gay, began to plan a theatre which would be devoted exclusively to Plum's theatrical works.

Not long after the opening of the play, Plum and Ethel were invited to Fairlawne for a very special occasion. Leonora was expecting her first baby, and it was felt that her parents should be on hand for the happy event. Sheran Cazalet was born on 31st March 1934, and Plum's first impression was that "she looked like an old Chinese gangster" who leered at him as she fingered her "gat" beneath her swaddling clothes. But this in no way diminished his pride in Leonora's achievement. After all, old Chinese gangsters were not an everyday occurrence in Kent.

By the end of April the Wodehouses were back on the Riviera, staying at the Carleton Hotel in Cannes, where Plum was again hard at work on a book to be called *The Luck of the Bodkins.* There was also another collaboration with Guy Bolton in the air. Vinton Freedley had asked them to write the book of a musical entitled *Anything Goes,* but it had not yet progressed beyond the discussion stage—which was just as well, for Plum was having difficulties with the novel. So time-consuming had it become that he was completely neglecting his correspondence with Townend; and it was not until he and Ethel had moved to Paris that he at last wrote apologetically on 11th June 1934:

I've been meaning to write for ages, but I've been tied up with The Luck of the Bodkins. *I find that the longer I go on writing, the harder it becomes to get a story right without going over and over it. I have just reached page 180 and I suppose I must have done quite 400 pages! Still, it is in good shape now.*

Paris is fine. I don't go out much, as I am working all the time. I have been here for exactly five weeks, except for one day at Le Touquet. I may be going to Le Touquet again for a few days soon, to talk with Guy Bolton about our play for Vinton Freedley, Anything Goes.

I had an offer from Paramount the other day to go to Hollywood, and had to refuse. But rather gratifying after the way Hollywood took a solemn vow three years ago never to mention my name again. Quite the olive branch!

The necessity of going to Le Touquet to talk with Guy Bolton was occasioned by Guy's insistence that he simply could not work in Paris. As Plum had no intention of going to London, Le Touquet was agreed upon as a sort of halfway house. And by mid-July the Wodehouses had taken up residence there so that Plum and Guy could get started on *Anything Goes*. Staying at the Royal Picardy Hotel, they gradually became aware of the advantages of making Le Touquet a permanent base, and began to look for property there, eventually buying a house called Low Wood, but remaining at the hotel while the place was being redecorated. Townend was to hear about the move in a letter dated 2nd August 1934:

The big item of news is that we

*have bought a house here. . . . At first
I didn't like the place, and then suddenly it began to get me, and it struck
both Ethel and me that as regards
situation it was the one ideal spot in the
world. I can get over to England by
boat in a few hours, and by plane, and
I am within motoring distance of Cherbourg.*

*. . . I'm having a devil of a time
with* Anything Goes. *I can't get hold
of Guy or the composer, Cole Porter.
What has become of Cole, Heaven
knows. Last heard of at Heidelberg.*

But *Anything Goes* wasn't the only problem. While working on it, the two authors had decided to dramatise Plum's novel *If I Were You* at the same time. They were calling it *Who's Who,* and this, too, was in abeyance. If Guy had disappeared and there were no encouraging picture postcards from Cole Porter in Heidelberg, however, there were at least some compensating photographs from Leonora and Peter in England. On 20th August the first pictures of baby Sheran were received, and Plum wrote to Leonora:

*We are deeply enraptured by the
photographs of Sheran. I never saw
such a beautiful baby. You must have
her photographed every year.*

He then went on to give her an account of "The Luck of the Wodehouses":

*The other night I went to the
Casino, had a shot at roulette, won
three mille in two minutes and came
home. At seven a.m. Winky was restless, so I took her out, and we had been
out about ten minutes when Mummie
arrived, having been at the Casino all*

night and lost three mille. So we took
the dogs for a walk and went in and
had breakfast.

"Winky" was the offspring of Susan the Peke, and was formally named Winks.

Somehow and somewhere in between writing *The Luck of the Bodkins,* some short stories, *Anything Goes* and *Who's Who,* Plum had been doing another little odd job. Hutchinson's had asked him to edit a volume of his favourite humorous stories. The result was a volume entitled *A Century of Humour,* and it was published on 1st September 1934.

At about this time, with the Royal Picardy closing at the end of the summer season and Low Wood not yet ready for occupation, the Wodehouses had to find alternative accommodation and eventually moved to the Golf Hotel, where they had rooms on the ground floor. Plum found this a distinct advantage when it came to exercising the Pekes, Winks and Boo, which was accomplished quite simply by "chucking them out of the window."

From the Golf Hotel, Plum wrote to Townend on 13th September 1934:

I have been musing over what you
said at the end of your letter about the
passage of time. I feel just the same.
My particular trouble is that what I feel
I should really like is to vegetate in
one place all my life, and I spend my
whole time whizzing about.

Of course, the trouble is that one
is never quite happy unless one is work-
ing—and by working I don't so much
mean the actual writing as the feeling
that one could write if one wanted to.
It is the in-between times that kill
one. . . .

I am now faced with a difficult job
—a 16,000-word story for the New
York Herald Tribune, *to run in four*
parts. But I can't seem to get the right
idea. A short story of 7,000 words is

> *simple, and a novelette of 30,000, too,*
> *but this in-between length is trying. I*
> *haven't room to build up an elaborate*
> *plot, and yet the story must not be thin*
> *and must have at least a passable cur-*
> *tain for each installment. Oh, well, I*
> *suppose it will come.*

By now, Guy Bolton having eventually reappeared, *Who's Who* had been completed and taken by Guy to London for rehearsals. It opened on 20th September 1934 at the Duke of York's Theatre, and sank with barely a ripple after a mere nineteen performances.

On 5th October Plum finished his 16,000-word story for the *New York Herald Tribune* and mailed it off. But it wasn't to be forgotten. At a much later date it was to become something of a lifesaver.

The Wodehouses were now installed at Low Wood, but the house was apparently not all that Ethel had hoped it would be. Plum didn't entirely share her view, and on 18th October—three days after his fifty-third birthday—he was writing to tell Leonora:

> *Life here is grand. One gets into a*
> *regular routine and the days whizz by.*
> *One excellent thing is that the papers*
> *have to be fetched from the town, which*
> *means a four-mile walk, so there is no*
> *temptation to shirk exercise. I do a*
> *regular forty miles a week, as I exer-*
> *cise the dogs and stroll about as well.*
> *I am tremendously fit.*
>
> *Mummie seems to think this*
> *house won't do, and I must say it has*
> *its drawbacks, but I believe we could*
> *make ourselves awfully comfortable*
> *here. After all, one really only wants*
> *one room to sit in, and the living-room*
> *is just right, as far as I'm concerned.*

But while Plum was making himself comfortable in his living-room in Le Touquet, the man who had commissioned *Anything Goes* was not so comfortable in New York. Vinton Freedley had received and read the Bolton-Wodehouse script and decided that it wouldn't do. He was, he informed Plum and Guy, calling in Howard Lindsay and Russel Crouse to rewrite it. The snag, it seemed, was that the script had reached Freedley on the heels of the *Morro Castle* tragedy—and as Plum and Guy had set their story on a liner in mid-ocean danger, it would have been in dubious taste to have gone ahead with it.

The new version of *Anything Goes,* starring Victor Moore, William Gaxton and Ethel Merman, had its tryout in Boston—where C. B. Cochran saw it and took the unprecedented step of buying it for the London stage without waiting to see how it would be received in New York. But Cochran's judgment proved to be sound. The show opened in New York at the Alvin Theatre on 21st November 1934 and was a smash hit, running for 421 performances. It contained only two of Plum's original lines, but Plum had fulfilled his part of the contract and received his royalty accordingly. Those two lines earned for him £100 a week for as long as the show ran.

To bring 1934 to a successful conclusion, Plum was able to write to Townend in December with the announcement that he had completed *The Luck of the Bodkins,* though not without a struggle:

> *Usually, when I get to the last fifty pages of a story, it begins to write itself. But this time everything went wrong and I had to grope my way through it all at the rate of two pages a day. I began to get superstitious about it and felt that if I could ever get it finished my luck would be in. On November 29th, I was within four pages of the end and suddenly all the lights in the house went out and stayed out! Still, I finished it next day, and it is pretty good, I think. Frightfully long —362 pages of typescript—it must be over the 100,000 words.*

All this, added to the fact that
Ethel has gone to London, and it has
been raining from the moment she left,
has left me pretty limp. I suppose I
shall be all right in a day or so.

Heralding in 1935 on a brighter note, he wrote to Leonora on 1st January:

Darling Snorky,
Happy New Year to you and the
gang, and may 1935 bring Sheran
some hair and eyebrows.
. . . Mummie blew in on Decem-
ber 23 with a six-weeks-old Peke
puppy! ! ! So now we have three Pekes
and are rooted here forever. It is an
angel, a male this time, but Winks and
Boo won't have anything to do with it
at all. Boo sulked for four days after its
arrival, but has now accepted the situa-
tion. We spend all our time spreading
fresh paper. We have named it Wonder.
He sneaks out every now and then and
eats Winky's dinner, with frightful re-
sults.

Wonder was to become the most celebrated, the most photographed, the most travelled and the longest-lived of all the Wodehouse Pekes.

Standing now at the threshold of a new year, with a saga of success behind him, world-famous and wealthy, Plum might well have taken stock of himself and reported "No change." What is remarkable is that his friends and acquaintances could have taken their own long look and come up with the same answer. For it was true that prestige and money had had no effect on Plum's personality. He was as diffident and unassuming as ever, and he certainly had no more money sense that he had had in the days when it was not so plentiful. What he earned from his writings he considered to be in the nature of a professional pat on the back, and he never really gave it serious thought in terms of its buying power. He was as vague about it as he was about other mundane things that existed beyond the perimeter of the private dream-world his work encouraged him to inhabit. Leonora remembered, for instance, that he rarely thought of carrying money with him; when he needed small change for books or tobacco he would sell her a £50 cheque for whatever loose coins she happened to have on her. He wasn't being ostentatious. It was simply a form of barter. Fifty was a nice round figure for cheques—and money, after all, was only money.

The praise that was lavished on him from all quarters was also accepted as a reward for his work rather than something that could be applied to him as a person. He was pleased, but his head wasn't turned, by letters of appreciation like the one he received in February 1935 from Arthur Waugh, chairman of the Chapman & Hall publishing company:

> . . . *it is true that we have never met in the body, but in the spirit we have travelled a good many miles together. There was a time, in Alec's school-days, when we used to read your books together with enormous enjoyment; and, though we are never long enough together nowadays—to read more than a telegram—we have still preserved a sort of freemason's code of Psmithisms, which continually crop up in our letters. Indeed, I can truly say, in emulation of Wolfe, that I would far rather have created Psmith than have stormed Quebec.*

A person completely unaffected by fame is rare indeed; but such a one was Plum. If the world was his oyster, then there must have been a permanent "r" in the month—for he left it alone. He would rise, albeit reluctantly, to the social occasion that couldn't be avoided; but he preferred the company of his "chosen few"—or solitude. And in his solitude he worked harder and more conscientiously than any other writer of the twentieth century.

In March 1935 he was plotting a comedy play set in France, which had been commissioned by actor Ralph Lynn. He had started it in Paris and was continuing with it at Low Wood when he wrote to Leonora:

> *. . . Meanwhile, I am plugging away at my play. It is a maddening thing to work at, and it is on the verge of being really good, but always some little snag crops up. I think now that I am back here I shall get it all right. I found that I couldn't work in Paris.*

A new book, *Blandings Castle and Elsewhere,* was published by Herbert Jenkins on 12th April 1935. It was a collection of short stories including some excellent Lord Emsworth ones and a few featuring Mr. Mulliner, and it also served to introduce the character Bobbie Wickham who was later to plague Bertie Wooster.

Although working on the Ralph Lynn play and turning out several short stories—one of them concerning Ukridge—Plum was beginning to feel uneasy because he didn't have a full-length novel on the go. Even the faintest glimmer of a plot would have been welcome, but inspiration eluded him. In a sort of quiet desperation, he wrote to Townend early in June 1935:

> *I can't get an idea for a novel. Maddening, as except for that I am fixed so solidly for the coming year—for there will be four companies of* Anything Goes *playing, not counting the London one, and I have an original play for Ralph Lynn—*The Inside Stand—*and an adaptation coming on in London, and I am well ahead with short stories. But all is useless unless I can get started on a novel.*

Still bereft of ideas, he took time off to go with his favourite brother, Armine, to visit their mother, who had returned to Bexhill. This gave him something about which to write to Leonora:

Armine and I went down to see Mother.
She seemed a bit frail, but not too bad.
I say, what an enormous size Armine
is. I made him walk from the Dorchester
to Victoria and three times en route he
pleaded for a cab. And when we got
to Bexhill he had a fat lunch at half-
past one, a big tea with some friends of
his at Codden at three-thirty, and an-
other tea at Mother's at four-fifteen. He
told me he thought he had put on a
little weight in front—did I notice it?
I said I thought he had, a little.

On 14th June 1935 the London production of *Anything Goes,* using the original Bolton-Wodehouse script, opened at the Palace Theatre and was rapturously received. As things turned out, it was the last musical on which Plum and Guy collaborated; and it proved a fitting swan-song. It ran for 250 performances.

In the meantime, Plum had invented a new character in a short story and was pondering its future possibilities. He wrote to Townend about it on 12th September 1935:

You remember that story you gave
me, about the woman telling lies about
the girl's relations so that she could
marry the humble suitor? It comes out
in the Christmas Strand, *called "Uncle*
Fred Flits By." Now, in Uncle Fred
I'm sure I have got a character, but at
the moment I simply can't think of an-
other plot for him. I'm just waiting
and hoping that one will come. It's
different if you have got a man with a
definite job—Sherlock Holmes or Raf-
fles. Then you can think of things for
him to do. But I wouldn't sit down and

do a series of Adventures of Psmith, *because there is no definite line that he would take. Uncle Fred is really a sort of elderly Psmith, and I can see in a vague way that he ought to go about helping people—and at the same time getting Pongo into trouble—but it's details that are so hard to think of.*

Here's a rummy thing, Bill. For six months I have been hammering away at a plot, trying to make it come out, with no success. Last night I suddenly said: "Could this be a Ukridge story?" Ten minutes later I had the plot complete. It's the treatment that matters, isn't it?

Treatment mattered in the theatre, too. But there the responsibility was shared. A beautifully written script might be unactable, or badly acted, or wrongly interpreted, or not well produced. There could be so many reasons for the failure of a play. Even a production that was perfect in every respect could flop if its theme didn't suit the mood of the theatregoing public at the time of its presentation. There was therefore no knowing why *The Inside Stand* was less successful than it should have been. Ralph Lynn opened in it at the Saville Theatre on 21st November 1935 and took it off after only fifty performances.

In December 1935 Plum had to face a minor tragedy when his Monarch typewriter finally succumbed to the ceaseless pounding it had received since 1909. Over the years it had received countless transplants and had managed to retain only a few of its original basic component parts, but now it was definitely beyond further repair. A new machine had to replace it, since being able to type his material was essential to Plum, but there was no joy in the occasion. On the contrary, Plum's plaintive query to Townend was, "Don't you find that after you've used a typewriter for a long time you can't get used to the touch of any other?"

But the new typewriter was not to blame for Plum's inability to think of a plot for a novel. Other ideas came in abundance, and the start of 1936 saw a flow of his short stories: but no novel. And then, when he was in a state bordering on despair, he suddenly remembered the story he'd written for the *New York Herald Tribune* to the awkward length of 16,000 words. The more he thought about it the more convinced did he become that here was the nucleus for a full-length book, and he eagerly began to work on it. Its title was to be *Laughing Gas*.

On 3rd April 1936 Herbert Jenkins published a fine collection of Drones Club stories in a volume called *Young Men in Spats*—a title which might have seemed dated and therefore rather off-putting to the general public since spats had gone out of fashion in the mid-twenties. But Wodehouse fans were not affected by that sort of thing. The only style in which they were interested was that of Plum's writing, and they bought *Young Men in Spats* as readily as they bought his other books.

Later that month, Plum and Ethel were again at Fairlawne for a Cazalet blessed event. This time, on 26th April 1936, Leonora gave birth to a boy, Edward. And Plum, perhaps inured by now to the general appearance of newly minted offspring and their aptitude to look like old Chinese gangsters, neglected to make a pithy comment.

Two months later, on 26th June, he was honoured by the receipt of a medallion from the International Mark Twain Society. The covering letter from the Society's president said:

> *Dear Mr. Wodehouse,*
> *In recognition of your outstanding and lasting contribution to the happiness of the world, it gives me much pleasure to offer you the Mark Twain Medal. The list enclosed will show you to whom the Medal has been given in the past.*
> *With all good wishes,*
> *Yours sincerely,*
> *Cyril Clemens.*

Previous recipients included Rudyard Kipling, Marconi and President Roosevelt.

That summer, somewhat to Plum's surprise, he received an offer from

Metro-Goldwyn-Mayer. Since his candid interview in 1931 he had tended to forget about Hollywood, imagining that he would be blacklisted by all the studios for ever more. Indeed, he had been given to understand that for some considerable time the mere mention of his name within the film capital had been considered a crime. But it seemed that Hollywood could forgive and forget. M-G-M wanted him again: and again Ethel negotiated the contract—this time obtaining for him $2,500 a week for six months, with an option for a further six months. By September the contract had been signed and the Wodehouses were on their way to America aboard the *Normandie*.

While they were at sea, on 25th September 1936, *Laughing Gas* was published in London by Herbert Jenkins. And four days later, Plum and Ethel were in New York again for the first time in five years. With time to spare before they were due in Hollywood, they took a trip to Philadelphia and called in at the *Saturday Evening Post* office to see George Lorimer. Plum remembered that "He seemed a little taken aback when I walked in, as he had not seen me since the days when I had thick black hair on my now bald head." Nevertheless, it was a pleasant reunion, and after it the Wodehouses returned to New York for several days, eventually arriving in Hollywood on 10th October.

Ethel immediately started looking for a house and finally settled for Gaylord Hauser's at 1315 Angelo Drive, Beverly Hills, which Mr. Hauser was pleased to rent to the Wodehouses for $1,000 a month. It was a house in the best Hollywood tradition, with two sweeping staircases, huge rooms and enormous windows. There was also a grandiose swimming pool which, together with the comparative isolation of the property, made the whole prospect endearing to Plum. The nearest neighbours—apart from Nelson Eddy, who lived opposite—were half a mile away.

As soon as the Wodehouses had moved in, Ethel began to interview prospective gardeners, housemaids and butlers. There were many applicants for each post, and the constant stream of hopefuls soon had a wearing effect on her. Towards the end of the day, when she was feeling utterly exhausted, a small Japanese presented himself for the position of butler. Accompanying Ethel to the study, he remarked on how tired she looked and suggested that she should sit on the sofa and relax. In other circumstances Ethel, with her propensity for businesslike dealings, might have reflected that this was hardly the way in which an interview should commence: but she *was* weary, and the little man's kindly concern was almost hypnotic. She therefore sank gratefully on to the sofa—whereupon her Oriental visitor proceeded to massage her shoulders and the back of her neck with great skill and efficiency. When he was done, he gave her a respectful bow and informed her that she was now ready to interview him. The revitalised Ethel didn't hesitate. She hired him.

Plum was now given his first studio assignment which, to his astonishment, was the script of *Rosalie*—the selfsame script on which he had laboured, to no good purpose, five years before. It made him wonder if Hollywood in general, and M-G-M in particular, had changed at all. Although the studio itself didn't seem the same since the recent death of thirty-six-year-old Irving Thalberg—top M-G-M executive and husband of Norma Shearer—with whom Plum had had a good relationship.

It wasn't until 7th November 1936 that Plum found time to write to Townend, and then he said:

Well, here we are, settled in a house miles away up at the top of a mountain surrounded by canyons in which I am told rattlesnakes abound, and employing a protection agency to guard the place at nights! We looked at a lot of houses in the valley part of Beverly Hills, where we were before, but couldn't find one we liked, so took this, which is a lovely place with a nice pool, but, as I say, remote. Still, that's an advantage in a way, as we don't get everybody dropping in on us.

Everything is very pleasant and placid here, and I am having a good time. But it doesn't seem as interesting as it was last time. I miss Thalberg very much, though I like Sam Katz, for whom I am working. I am collaborating on a musical picture with a man I last saw twenty years ago, when I was sympathising with him for being chucked out of the cast of one of the Bolton-Wodehouse-Kern musical comedies. He is a wild Irishman named McGowan, who seems to be fighting the heads of the studio all the time. I get on very well with him.

I still swim every morning, but the water is beginning to get a bit chilly. Haven't seen many celebrities yet. We don't see much of anybody except our beloved Maureen O'Sullivan and her husband, John Farrow. I met Clark Gable the other day. Also Fred Astaire. I think Fred is going to do a picture of my A Damsel in Distress, *with music by George Gershwin. I shall know more about that later.*

Some sad news now belatedly disrupted the even tenor of things by way of a letter which had been delayed in transit. It informed Plum that Armine had died suddenly on 9th October, and it distressed him deeply. It seemed awful that this could have happened and he hadn't known about it sooner. But there was nothing he could do about it: Armine was gone. And even had the letter arrived earlier he would have been helpless. Tied up as he was with his commitment to M-G-M, he would have had to go on working. It was left to Ethel to return immediately to England to see what could be done for Armine's widow, Nella.

Towards the end of November, Plum was cheered by the sudden and long-needed inspiration for a novel which he decided to call *Summer Moonshine;* but he was unable to devote much time to it because of his work at the film studio. This didn't mean that he was entirely without news for Townend. On 28th December 1936 he was writing to tell a jubilant tale about one of his short stories:

I have a story coming out in S.E.P. week ending January 30th, which they think is the best I have ever done. It was sent to the Red Book, *and they offered $2,000 for it. Having given me $3,000 for my others, I refused this,*

and on landing in America rang up the
editor and asked him to return my story
—having called on Lorimer the previ-
ous day and, as I believe I told you, got
him to agree that he would pay $4,000
for any stories of mine which he ac-
cepted. The editor of the Red Book
raised the offer to $2,500; but I be-
lieved in the story so much that I turned
it down, and am glad that I did, because
the Post *jumped at it. Title—"All's*
Well With Bingo."

And all was well with Plum, but only for a while. He had been working happily enough on *Rosalie* when he somehow began to get the impression that he was being, as he put it, "edged out." The feeling became a reality when the producer eventually told him that the studio bosses had now decided that they wanted the McGowan half of the collaboration to write the screenplay himself. Plum was to be relieved of the assignment and, at the moment, there was nothing else for him to do. It was the Hollywood mixture as before. Once again he was on the M-G-M payroll without being asked to earn his salary. And once again he could continue with the writing of a novel undisturbed.

Summer Moonshine progressed rapidly at M-G-M's expense, and Plum felt so confident about it that he submitted it to the *Saturday Evening Post* before it was completed. With the first 80,000 words to go on—and knowing that a further 10,000 words had yet to be written—the *Post* bought it for serialisation and paid $40,000 for the privilege and pleasure.

All this activity in America didn't mean that Plum was forgotten in England. On 19th March 1937 Herbert Jenkins followed up the success of *Blandings Castle and Elsewhere* with the publication of *Lord Emsworth and Others,* which was a collection of stories about Blandings Castle, the Drones Club, and the Oldest Member.

Summer Moonshine was finished on 23rd March 1937, shortly after which Plum's contract with M-G-M terminated. His six-month option was not taken up, but this time the studio refrained from asking him to give any interviews. If it had not been for the fact that the lease on the house still had some time to run, he would have been glad to pack up and go. He had had about enough of Hollywood, and even the constant sunshine had lost its charm. As he wrote to Townend:

> *I am getting very fed up with life here—possibly because of the weather. I don't find the people so attractive as last time. I miss Thalberg. And there seems nowhere to go. I mean, when you have a let-down like one always gets after finishing a novel, it seems impossible to get a real change. People say to me that I ought to go to Palm Springs, but I can't see that that would be so very different from this place.*
>
> *What I liked about Le Touquet was that in a few hours I could get to London and be in an entirely new atmosphere, and then back to Le T., feeling that I had had a real holiday.*
>
> *It's largely a question, of course, of people. I want to see you, and I can't, and I want to see Guy Bolton, and I can't, and I have to put up with substitutes.*
>
> *. . . Isn't it difficult to get accustomed to the idea that one is now at the age when most people settle down and don't do a thing? I am now exactly the age my father was when I left Dulwich, and I remember him as tottering to his armchair and settling in it for the day. That's one thing about being a writer—it does keep you young. Do you find you can't walk as far as you used to? I do out here, but I remember last year in Le Touquet I used to do my seven miles without feeling it. I think it's mainly the California climate.*

Things took a turn for the better at the end of May, however, when the R-K-O studio asked Plum to work on the script for *A Damsel in Distress.* Plum's novel had originally been assigned to one of the studio's contracted writers, who had changed the story-line beyond recognition. Not satisfied with it, director George Stevens had had the brilliant idea of sticking to Plum's plot and getting the author himself to adapt it into a screen musical comedy—the music to be supplied by George and Ira Gershwin.

Ernest Pagano and S. K. Lauren collaborated with Plum on the writing of a scenario which provided special material for the unique talents of the crazy comedy team George Burns and Gracie Allen, who were supporting Fred Astaire and his latest partner Joan Fontaine, whose first film this was to be. On the music side, the Gershwins outshone themselves with some wonderfully integrated production numbers which included "I Can't Be Bothered Now," "Stiff Upper Lip," "Things Are Looking Up," "Nice Work If You Can Get It," "The Jolly Tar and the Milkmaid," and "A Foggy Day." It augered well, and it did much to lift Plum's spirits.

On the other side of the continent, in the meantime, another Wodehouse book was published. This was an American edition of *Lord Emsworth and Others,* which Doubleday Doran retitled *Crime Wave at Blandings* when they issued it on 25th June 1937.

The following evening, in Hollywood, Ethel gave one of her spectacular parties. It was held in the garden of the house and it provided entertainment for seventy guests. Like all of her parties, it was a huge success; and it provided a topic of conversation in Hollywood for months afterwards. Looking back on those days and recalling her triumphs as a Hollywood hostess, Ethel pointed out, "Parties were very easy to do if you had the money. We did, because Plum was getting $2,500 a week. I would go down to the supermarkets and buy a big saddle of lamb, vegetables, turkey, ham and chicken livers. We would have seven cases of champagne. Our butler, Arthur, would handle the floral arrangements. He could do the most amazing things with flowers. Then we hired a caterer and barman. He would supply the olives but we had to supply the liquor."

By mid-August 1937 Plum had completed his work on *A Damsel in Distress* and was commenting to Townend:

> *I'm not enjoying life much just now. I*
> *don't like doing pictures.* A Damsel in

> Distress *was fun, because I was work-*
> *ing with the best director here—George*
> *Stevens—and on my own story, but as*
> *a rule pictures are a bore.*

There was nothing to keep Plum in Hollywood now, and he was most anxious to return to Low Wood so that he could get to work on an idea that was germinating for a Wooster-Jeeves novel. Ethel therefore terminated the lease on the Beverly Hills house and booked passages for them on the *Ile de France,* which was sailing on 28th October. On the day before they embarked they read of the death of George Lorimer, who had resigned from the *Saturday Evening Post* not long after the Wodehouses' visit of the previous year. Plum's comment was, "I feel as if a great bit of my life had gone. I think that, outside the family, those who are saddest today are the authors who worked with him."

Ethel and Plum reached their home in Le Touquet on 4th November 1937, and by 22nd November Plum had written the first 50,000 words of the novel he'd been thinking about. He was calling it *The Code of the Woosters.* At a later date he was writing to tell Townend:

> *. . . It looks as if the* Post *are tak-*
> *ing it for granted that they are going*
> *to buy the story—I sent them the first*
> *50,000 words—but they felt that the*
> *early part needed cutting . . . And when*
> *I looked at it, I saw they were right.*
> *Here is the lay-out as I had it.*
> 1. *Bertie goes to see his Aunt Dahlia.*
> 2. *She tells him to go and buy flowers*
>   *for Aunt Agatha, who is ill.*
> 3. *Bertie goes back to his flat and she*
>   *rings up and says she forgot to say*
>   *that she has another job for him—*
>   *which will necessitate a visit to an*
>   *antique shop.*
> 4. *Bertie goes to flower shop and gets*
>   *into trouble.*
> 5. *Bertie goes back to his flat and sobs*

on Jeeves's shoulder.

6. Bertie goes to antique shop and gets into more trouble.

> *Now, can you imagine that I had written that part quite a dozen times and only now spotted that it ought to go thus:*

1. Bertie goes to Aunt Dahlia. She tells him to go to antique shop.

2. Bertie goes to antique shop, then plays the scene which originally took place in flower shop, then plays the antique shop scene.

It cuts off fifteen pages without losing anything of value. And what I am driving at is that isn't it ghastly to think that after earning one's living as a writer for thirty-seven years one can make a blunder like that. Why on earth I kept taking Bertie back to the flat, where nothing whatever happened, I can't think.

> *This necessitated five days of intense work, and I now feel that I might as well get on with the thing . . .*

It is significant that the toil and turmoil that attended the writing of his novels, evidenced in so many of his letters to Townend, is never apparent in Plum's finished work. Each of his books reads as though the words had streamed uninterrupted from an inspired pen, always reflecting the inner world he seemed to inhabit. The real world passed by with scarcely a tremor to disturb his thoughts—except when on one or two rare occasions, usually in a short story, he would take a gentle swipe at the things that irritated him. Phony writers and dilettantes had been among his targets; and in 1937 he found a new provocation. In England, Oswald Mosley and his fascist organisation—known as the Blackshirts—were in full cry, and Plum didn't approve of them or their methods. To show his distaste, and in order to ridicule them, he introduced into *The Code of the Woosters* the unpleasant character Roderick Spode, whose followers were called the Black Shorts. They made an unusually topical intrusion into the world of Wodehouse.

The writing of *The Code of the Woosters* was turning out to be more of an ordeal than was customary, however, and Plum continued his plaint to Townend in a letter dated 4th January 1938:

> *I am finding finishing* The Code of the Woosters *a ghastly sweat. I don't seem to have the drive and command of words I used to. Towards the end of* Thank You, Jeeves *at La Fréyère, I wrote twenty-six pages in one day! Now I find myself quarrying out the stuff.*

Nevertheless, the quarrying was finally accomplished; and it resulted in a book which is now generally considered to be among Plum's very best. One piece of imagery from it will certainly live on in Bartlett's *Familiar Quotations,* thanks to editor Christopher Morley who chose to include the delightful "While he was not exactly disgruntled, he was far from being gruntled."

Plum, with *The Code of the Woosters* behind him, had reason to feel extremely "gruntled" and was almost immediately involved in another novel. This one was called *Uncle Fred in the Springtime*—Uncle Fred being the character he had written to Townend about in the previous September after having introduced him in "Uncle Fred Flits By." The plot was to centre around a visit to Blandings Castle, and again there were the birth pangs about which Plum reported to Townend in a letter dated 15th May 1938:

> *It must be about two months since I wrote you. I have been sweating like blazes getting a new novel started. . . . After writing 150 pages, I now have 40 which are right. Every time I write a book, I swear I'll never write another with a complicated plot. In this one— in the first 40 pages—I have either*

> *brought on to play a scene or men-*
> *tioned heavily each of my principal*
> *characters—ten including Lord Ems-*
> *worth's pig. So the going ought to be*
> *easier now.*

If Plum needed encouragement at this time, it came in a letter dated 1st June 1938 from Malcolm Johnson, editor of Doubleday Doran, to whom he had sent the manuscript of *The Code of the Woosters.* Johnson wrote:

> *The new novel is extraordinarily*
> *fine, a statement which I can make with*
> *complete honesty. I don't know how*
> *you manage to make each new book so*
> *fresh and so good. Good isn't the word,*
> *but there isn't any exact word for the*
> *quality which makes a reader, on com-*
> *pleting the first paragraph of the book,*
> *sit back with confidence and a pleasure*
> *uncontrolled by any fear that the story*
> *may be in any degree disappointing.*
> *As for the projected novel,* Uncle
> Fred in the Springtime *is an ideal*
> *Wodehouse title and Uncle Fred is an*
> *equally ideal Wodehouse character. I*
> *hope we will be able to read the manu-*
> *script soon.*

Plum doubtless shared Johnson's hope; but as the summer months sped by, he found it increasingly difficult to make headway. Reporting to Townend on his progress, he wrote:

> *Isn't writing in the summer a sweat! I*
> *find that my output slows down to*
> *about half, and if I can average three*
> *pages a day I think I am doing well. I*
> *started* Uncle Fred in the Springtime

*on May the first and have only got up
to near half-way—i.e. about a month
behind my schedule. Still, I think the
stuff is good. I find it so hard to write
in the afternoons. If I go for an exercise
walk, I'm too tired to write, and if I
don't get any exercise, my brain won't
work!*

By October, however, *Uncle Fred in the Springtime* was finished and on
its way to the *Saturday Evening Post* for consideration. But the feeling of relief
and release that normally followed the completion of a full-length work was
to be denied Plum. There were soul-destroying complications, about which he
wrote to Townend on 13th November 1938:

*Two weeks ago I got a cable from
Reynolds saying: "Saturday Evening
Post will buy* Uncle Fred in the Springtime *provided you make certain changes.
They like story but think at present it
is difficult to follow week by week.
They suggest you might want to elimi-
nate a character or two and clarify rela-
tionships."*

*You can imagine what it's like,
taking two characters out of my sort of
story, where a character is put in only
because he is needed for at least two
big scenes later on in the book! However, I cabled that I would do it, and
for these last two weeks I have been
hard at work.*

*I found that I could simplify the
story enormously by dropping the whole
of one motive and the two characters
it involved, but this meant rewriting
practically the whole book. Whenever*

I came to a spot where I had been hop-
ing to be able just to rip a dozen pages
out of the original version and pin them
together, I found they were studded
with allusions to the vanished charac-
ters.

Plum's struggles with this revision were eventually rewarded when the *Saturday Evening Post* accepted *Uncle Fred in the Springtime;* and in due course the book was welcomed by his publishers in both England and America. But much was to happen before its publication in volume form.

1939

By 1939 the popularity of P. G. Wodehouse, which had become worldwide during the early twenties, was at its peak. Readers and critics alike recognised that here was no mere humorist. The quality and quantity of his work proved him to be nothing less than a master of his art. He had developed a unique style of writing with which to create characters and situations intended to provoke laughter, and he had effortlessly achieved his object time and time again. Effortlessly, that is, as far as the reader was concerned. Certainly there was no hardship in following the author's happily inventive phrases from page to page, and the even flow gave not the slightest indication that any of the hilarious episodes might have resulted from hours of toil, torment and sometimes despair.

But if the general public accepted the facile humour at its face value, the critics and columnists were beginning to dig beneath the surface in an effort to analyse and explain its ingredients. One such attempt by an unnamed reporter at this time concluded that:

Mr. Wodehouse is pre-eminent as our
leading English humorous novelist—
because his art conceals his art; he has
a creative quality; he suggests sponta-
neity, yet his action is carefully planned

and controlled; he has a real gift for
dialogue, for verbal fun, for realising
the exact description value of slang so
that he expands our vocabulary and en-
larges our expression phraseology; and
to all these literary arts and graces he
brings the great gift of ingenuity in
comic situations which is the foundation
on which the humorist builds.

What bothered most reviewers, however, was not how to dissect Plum's work but how to find new ways of singing his praises. His books maintained such a high standard that even the most eloquent of reporters were running out of words. As one of them wrote:

Mr. Wodehouse's own fertility is ap-
parently inexhaustible, but he is begin-
ning to exhaust the superlatives of his
critics.

Between 1902, when he made his professional debut, and 1939 Plum had written twelve plays, thirty musical comedies and innumerable song lyrics, two hundred and forty-seven short stories, and forty-two novels in which he had established seven major literary sagas (those of Psmith, Lord Emsworth and Blandings Castle, Bertie Wooster and Jeeves, Ukridge, the Oldest Member, Mr. Mulliner, and Uncle Fred). It was a staggering record, and it prompted one overawed critic to comment:

Not one author in ten even tries to
write a funny book. Not one in fifty
ever succeeds. The number of those
who turn out volume after volume of
comedy burlesque, each as filled with
inanely delightful mirth as a physician
is with polysyllables, is a simple and
chaste 'one'—and his name is Pelham
Grenville Wodehouse.

That his output over thirty-seven years should have been so prodigious was somehow less surprising than the fact that it was generally of such unimpeachable quality, the consensus of opinion being that prolific writers could not be expected to turn out anything really worthwhile. Somerset Maugham once tried to explode this theory by pointing out that all the greatest authors had been prolific and that, although not all their works were of value, it was the fact that they had written so much that had enabled them to now and then produce great works. This was certainly true of Plum, except that even his not-so-great works were never entirely without merit. Part of his art was in knowing what he could do best. He had found his métier and had stuck to it, telling the kind of story he enjoyed telling in the manner he had made his own, choosing his words with precision for their picturesque and rhythmic value and placing them carefully in crisp, clean and properly balanced sentences. As the *Times Literary Supplement* put it: "Mr. Wodehouse has mastered a technique which is fearless of its kind and unapproached by anybody else."

Written humour has always been the most precarious of commodities. It has for generations been the bugbear of editors and publishers, the majority of whom were quick to discover that it was no laughing matter. In other categories they knew where they stood: a romance called for star-crossed lovers; a thriller needed crime and excitement; a Western had to have wide-open spaces, good men and bad men, and perhaps an Indian or two; science fiction required beings from other planets or rocket-trips to the stars. But humour . . . Who was to say what was funny? One man's joke could be another man's yawn of boredom. And what seemed topically uproarious today could soon be as dated as yesterday's news. To be successful, therefore, the humorous writer needed a special kind of magic—and Plum had it. Mainly, it was a gift of phraseology that transcended time, place and situation. He was not concerned with the changing fashions of the years, nor was he a slave to literary customs. No one could have accused him of being a profound thinker, so not for him the novel with a 'message.' There was no propensity for exposing the evils or otherwise of the age in which he lived, and he was not preoccupied with the desire to right wrongs. He was simply a man who had a talent to amuse—and that was all he wanted to do. His good fortune in the dubious branch of the literary market in which he had chosen to trade was that he had the remarkable ability to amuse most of the people most of the time.

William Lyon Phelps, distinguished teacher and critic of English literature at Yale University, got to the very root of the matter when he wrote of Plum:

. . . With him humour is not a means but an end. His intention is pure diversion; he wishes to make us laugh. There are no teeth in his genial humour; he is just downright funny. That is, outside of supreme creative genius, perhaps the most difficult thing to accomplish in literary composition; many try, but few succeed.

I regard Mr. Wodehouse as a public benefactor, because I think he has given thousands of men and women real happiness; he cheers us all up by making us roar with laughter. We forget our problems of life while we read his pages. I am sure Mr. Wodehouse must enjoy writing, for his books reveal creative enjoyment.

But it was not only the critics who felt that a debt of gratitude was owed to Plum. He was also a writers' writer, admired and looked up to by his fellow authors. And they made no secret of the fact. Sheila Kaye-Smith, for instance, wrote glowingly of Plum in her autobiography *All the Books of My Life* and finished by saying, "It is true that he has a deep-set dislike of aunts and lady novelists, both of whom I am, but I hope that will only increase the value of this tribute." In that tribute, Miss Kaye-Smith delightedly pointed out that Plum did more than merely create characters and situations: "he opens the frontier of another world." This was echoed by an anonymous critic, who wrote:

There is the world we live in, and there is the world of Wodehouse, and it is good that man should be able to escape for brief periods from the one into the other.

The wonderful world of Wodehouse into which one escapes is an elaborate but perfectly constructed, romanticised, idealistic conception which is gleefully detached from reality. And the manner in which it is evoked—with extravagant phrases, outrageous similes, highly embroidered descriptions, original metaphors, intricate situations meticulously well-defined, and some of the most endearing characters in the history of literary humour—amounts to little short of genius. Indeed, *The New York Times* was not bashful about using the word "genius" when it stated:

> *If P. G. Wodehouse has ever written a dull story, we have not come across it. He is not merely a writer with a keen sense of humour: he is a genius in the formulation of a thoroughly good tale, first-rate characterisation and sparkling dialogue. He is without doubt one of the greatest living humorists of the day, and he never lets his readers down.*

This seemed to apply even to a reader such as James Agate, who could be the most astringent of critics yet was able to talk kindly of "P. G. Wodehouse, whose works I place a little below Shakespeare's and any distance you like above anybody else's."

One of the most perceptive comments at this time came from music and literary critic Ernest Newman, who wrote:

> *Mr. Wodehouse's strength is not in invention but in treatment, which accounts for the fact that though we have met with all these people twenty times before in his novels we are still not yet tired of them, and will not be tired of them so long as Mr. Wodehouse can keep it up, though we should meet with them twenty times more. It accounts for the further fact that we can always re-read with gusto the old Wodehouse books, while nothing on earth would induce us to re-read the yesteryear nov-*

els of Mr. X or Mr. Z, though these gentlemen present us with a different set of characters and a different plot and a different series of actions in each of their books.

As with all great gifts, the unique style of writing that won such unstinted praise from critics and public alike came naturally to Plum. There was no conscious effort there. What worried him, and what he constantly talked about, were his plots. It was with them that the headaches started. And he remembered that Kipling had had the same problem, saying to him once, "But tell me, Wodehouse, how do you finish your stories? I can never think how to end mine." Plum, when in the greatest of difficulties, usually wrote to William Townend. Sometimes he received useful tips in return, but often it was enough to have someone to whom he could sound off. It was Townend, therefore, who learned most about Plum's tactics and soul-searchings in a variety of letters over a long period of time. In one way or another, almost every aspect of Plum's work was touched upon:

In writing a novel, I always imagine I am writing for a cast of actors. Some actors are natural minor actors and some are natural major ones. It is a matter of personality. Same in a book. Psmith, for instance, is a major character. If I am going to have Psmith in a story, he must be in the big situations. One big character is worth two small ones. Don't diffuse the interest. Generally, the trouble is that you can't switch Character B's stuff so that it fits Character A.

The absolute cast-iron good rule, I'm sure, in writing a story, is to introduce all your characters as early as possible especially if they are going to play important parts later. I think the suc-

cess of every novel depends largely on one or two high spots. The thing to do is to say to yourself, "Which are my big scenes?" and then get every drop of juice out of them. I believe that when one has really got a bit of action going, it can extend as long as you like.

. . . What a problem it is to get a novel started just right. That business of introducing your characters and trying not to have them jostle one another and get in each other's way, and at the same time trying to make the damned thing readable. Particularly when you reflect that an editor probably makes up his mind about a story after reading page one. Guy Bolton says the great thing in writing plays is never let your characters sit down—i.e. keep the characters buzzing about without a pause. He also thinks that it's a mistake to give the audience too much to think about at any one time. In other words, in a play one mustn't try to develop two threads simultaneously, and this applies equally to stories. My besetting sin is a tendency to do all the exposition in one chunk on the first two pages instead of taking my time and spreading it out, and it generally takes me about six shots before I get the first five hundred words right.

. . . I think one has to be ruthless with one's books. I find I have a tendency to write a funny line and then add an-

other, elaborating it where there is no necessity for the second bit. I keep coming on such bits in the thing I'm doing now. I go through the story every day and hack them out. Do you find you write more slowly than you used to? I remember I used to do eight pages a day regularly. This present thing is growing like a coral reef. I am only up to page 130 after months of work. Still, the consolation is that the stuff seems good, and there is no hurry, as I am so much ahead of the game. But I wish now and then that I could strike one of those spots where the thing really flows.

. . . It's a funny thing about writing. If you are a writer by nature, I don't believe you write for money, for fame, or even for publication, but simply for the pleasure of turning out the stuff. Personally, I love rewriting and polishing. Directly I have got something down on paper, however rough it is, I feel the thing is in the bag. A. A. Milne says much the same thing in Two People. *He says that books ought not to be published. They ought to be written and then one copy ought to be beautifully printed for the author to read.*

. . . How can *anybody dictate? Could you? I should be feeling shy and apologetic all the time. The nearest I ever got to it was when Ethel bought me one of those machines Edgar Wallace used to use, where you talk on to a wax*

cylinder and then turn back to the be-
ginning to hear how it sounds. I started
Thank You, Jeeves *on it, and when I*
played it back I was appalled how un-
funny the stuff sounded. I hadn't known
it till then but apparently I have a voice
like a very pompous clergyman inton-
ing. Either that or the instrument was
pulling my leg. Anyway, I sold the
damned thing next day.

Plum's talent for making people laugh may never have seemed more necessary to the British people than in 1939, the year of the false peace. After the war scare of the previous year, tensions found their release in laughter— and Plum was one of the prime laughter-makers. It may therefore be no coincidence that it was in 1939 that he was given an honorary degree at Oxford University in recognition of his services to literature.

To be made a doctor of letters was naturally pleasing to Plum, but he looked forward to the actual ceremony with little relish. He had been told that it would entail walking through the streets of Oxford in a cap and gown. Horrifying as the prospect was, however, he knew that he would be in good company. Also to be so honoured at the same time were two of the world's greatest authorities on English literature—Sir Edmund Chambers and Sir Herbert Grierson. On balance, it would be worth the trip from Le Touquet.

Thus, on 21st June 1939, Plum was in the academic procession from Magdalen College to the Sheldonian Theatre in the Encaenia at Oxford University, there to receive his honorary D.Litt. degree. It was the first to be given to a humorous writer since Mark Twain had received his in 1907.

In introducing Plum to the University, Dr. Cyril Bailey, the Public Orator, excelled himself in a speech which not only extolled the virtues of the author's work but also managed to touch upon Bertie Wooster and Jeeves, Mr. Mulliner, Lord Emsworth and the Empress of Blandings, Psmith, the Honourable Augustus Fink-Nottle, and the love life of the newts . . . in Latin. Not to be outdone, the Vice-Chancellor of the University, George Stuart Gordon, presented the degree to Plum with these words:

Vir lepidissime, facetissime, venustis-

sime, iocosissime, ridibundissime te cum turba tua Leporum, Facetinarum, Venustatum, Iocorum, Risuum, ego auctoritate mea et totius Universitatis admitto ad gradum Doctoris in Litteris honoris causa.

Which meant:

O Sir, of all men most polished, facetious, graceful, whimsical and uproarious, I hereby admit you and your whole crowd of ditto creations to the degree of honorary Doctor of Letters.

And the *Times* reported on 22nd June:

. . . there is no question that in making P. -G. Wodehouse a doctor of letters the University has done the right and popular thing. Everyone knows at least some of his many works and has felt all the better for the gaiety of his wit and the freshness of his style. Style goes a long way in Oxford; indeed the purity of Mr. Wodehouse's style was singled out for particular praise in the Public Orator's happy Horatian summing up of Mr. Wodehouse's qualities and achievements.

It was in truth fitting that Plum's enormous contribution to literature should be formally recognised by the academic world—and most particularly that it should have been in the exalted company of Sir Edmund Chambers and Sir Herbert Grierson. No award could have been more justly deserved.

Plum wasted no time in returning to Le Touquet when the ceremony was over, and he was busily writing at Low Wood when *Uncle Fred in the Spring-*

time was published in volume form—first in America by Doubleday Doran on 18th August and then in England by Herbert Jenkins on 25th August 1939. He was still in Le Touquet when Britain declared war on Germany on 3rd September 1939.

It was the end of an era, remembered with great affection by Denis Mackail, whose happiest memories were of the days when the Wodehouses lived in London:

> *We were constantly going there and they were constantly coming to us. Or Plum and I would be off on our own somewhere, until the usual moment when I suddenly found that I was walking along the street by myself. He was soaring now. For almost everything that he wrote was first serialised in two countries and then rushed by eager publishers into another book. His strange world—which if it ever existed at all must have passed away before the first great war—struck no one, apparently, as out of date; while his amazing and entirely individual gift of language was lapped up not only by magazine-readers but by the loftiest highbrows in every land. Something here, it would seem, for everyone, in the way of amusement and admiration, as he tapped away on the almost primeval typewriter from which nothing would separate him; and did this in a bedroom, because he felt easier there than in the glorious, book-lined, panelled study which his wife had provided for him on a lower floor. It was in this room that he talked and relaxed, and polished his spectacles, and beamed,*

and was covered with Pekes. I can still
see it, and can still hear him beginning
again: "I say, with regard to this busi-
ness of plots . . ."

But September 1939 marked the close of that particular chapter, and the real-life plot was about to thicken.

10

1940–1946

After the first shock of the declaration of war, life in England quickly settled down to a new kind of normalcy in which total blackouts, the carrying of gas masks and a knowledge of the whereabouts of public air-raid shelters were accepted as a way of life. The initial anxieties were gradually minimised and places of entertainment reopened as the expected horrors of warfare failed to materialise. If there had been a tendency to fearfully scan the sky, it was soon dropped as the sky remained encouragingly empty of anything but barrage balloons. Maybe the war hadn't been over by Christmas after all: but surely by *next* Christmas . . . So speedily did life in these circumstances find its own level that in January 1940 the first All-England Jitterbug Championship was held at the Paramount Dance Hall in London, which was packed to overflowing for the occasion. Oh, what a lovely war!

In Le Touquet, too, there was little immediate change. Some of the foreign residents returned to their own countries, but there were still many Britons and other non-French people living there and in the surrounding area; and an RAF squadron was stationed there. It wasn't until early May that these people became aware of the danger of a German invasion; but the official warning of its imminence was inexplicably delayed. By the time it reached this little colony, it was too late. By now the RAF squadron had departed and only one fighter plane remained, the pilot of which offered its single vacant seat to Plum. But there was naturally no question of Plum abandoning Ethel. Instead, he bundled Ethel and Wonder, the Peke, into his car and set out towards the coast. To his frustration, the car broke down after they had travelled a mere two miles. It seemed that all was not lost, however, when they were invited to clamber aboard the truck of a neighbour who was also making for the coast. False hope. All was very much lost indeed. The truck jerked along for a distance of one hundred yards and then stopped, never to start again. There was no alternative but for the would-be refugees to return on foot to Le Touquet, where the Wodehouses opened Low Wood to their fellow unfortunates while waiting to see what would happen. And at first it seemed that nothing would.

The Germans occupied Le Touquet on 22nd May 1940 and were apparently content to do no more than keep Low Wood under strict surveillance. Every morning at nine o'clock Plum had to report to the Kommandatur in Paris Plage but was otherwise left to his own devices. There was no immediate feeling of restriction, and the Wodehouses and their companions were lulled into a sense of false security.

But events were moving rapidly. On 26th May the evacuation of Dunkirk began; and by 14th June the Germans were in Paris. Pétain was asking the Germans for armistice terms on 17th June; and on 22nd June the Franco-German armistice was signed in the same railway coach that had seen the signing of the 1919 armistice. Britain was on her own, and the people of Britain were soon to learn that they were in the front line.

The Wodehouses, on the other hand, were to know only what their German watchdogs chose to tell them. They were completely cut off from the outside world. Nevertheless, they had come to terms with their lot and realised that they could be much worse off. It was therefore something of a shock when, on 21st July 1940, Plum's morning call at the Kommandatur did not follow the usual pattern. Instead of being summarily dismissed, he was informed that an internment order had come through for all the male aliens in Le Touquet. He would be escorted to Low Wood, where he was to pack only the barest necessities, and would then be brought back to the Kommandatur for transportation to an internment camp.

Ironically, the day was one of those perfect summer days that are wont to crop up so frequently in a Wodehouse novel. The sun beamed brightly, the scent of flowers filled the air, and the birds twittered and chirruped merrily in the trees: but somehow Plum seriously doubted that all could possibly be for the best in the best of all possible worlds. Apart from anything else, what on earth should he pack? He'd never been a prisoner before.

The packing was undertaken in the presence of the German corporal who had escorted him home and a stunned Ethel. Pulling out a small suit-case, Plum—with no precedent to guide him and therefore acting purely on instinct—threw into it some pipes, tobacco, pencils, pads of paper, a pair of shoes, six pairs of socks, a razor, soap, underclothes, a woollen pullover, a couple of cardigans, a volume of Tennyson's poems, the *Complete Works of Shakespeare,* and half a pound of tea. Ethel, struggling to keep a tight rein on her emotions, added to this a cold mutton chop and a chunk of chocolate. In the attendant haste, neither of them thought to include Plum's passport.

As the guard started to hustle him out, Plum kissed his wife and grabbed his raincoat. Then he was on his way back to the Kommandatur where, with twelve fellow internees, he sat and waited until the transport arrived at two o'clock in the afternoon. The thirteen men were herded into a bus and driven off without a clue as to their final destination, the bus stopping several times en route to pick up other internees. In all, the frequently inter-rupted journey took seven hours; and it terminated at the prison in Loos, a suburb of Lille, some seventy miles from Le Touquet.

Upon entering the prison, Plum's name—"Widhorse," followed by "Crime . . . Anglais"—was recorded in a large book, after which he and two others were led to their cell. Access to the cell—number 44, on the ground floor—was by way of an iron-studded door into which was set a small panel of a size to allow food to be passed through. In the centre of the panel was a peephole, covered on the outside by a flap of steel.

The interior of the cell measured twelve feet by eight feet. A barred window was set in the wall opposite the door, and beneath it stood a solitary bed. Against one wall there was a small table with an equally small chair chained to it, and in the corner by the door there was a water-tap with a tiny basin beneath it. Near this was the toilet. An oak shelf into which was set a wooden hook completed the furnishings. It was a cell that had obvi-ously been designed for only one inmate, and in the sharing of it age was given preference. The Oldest Member, so to speak, was granted the bed. Plum and the other man had to make themselves as comfortable as they could on the granite floor.

Their daily routine began at seven a.m., when a resonant bell woke them from their slumbers in order that they might receive the three mugs of thin, lukewarm soup and three hunks of bread that were thrust through the now open panel in the door. The panel was then closed and they were left undisturbed until eight-thirty, at which time they were led from their cell to join other internees in an enclosure with high brick walls, partially open to the sky, for exercise and recreation. After half an hour of this, all the prisoners were led back to their cells. At midday and again at five p.m. they were given more soup and bread, but there were no further excursions from the cells. Two or three days later, however, the Kommandant relaxed a little and allowed the men the freedom of their cell blocks.

Within a week it was made known that prisoners aged sixty years and over were to be released and that the remainder would be transferred to a new camp. Plum, a mere youth of fifty-eight-and-three-quarters, was among those who had to prepare to move.

When the time came, forty-four men from Loos Prison were taken to a railway station where, with something like eight hundred internees from other places, they were bundled on to a train composed of fully enclosed cattle trucks. The allotment was fifty men to a truck, which meant an extremely tight squeeze for the nineteen hours that their journey took. Most of the internees were middle-aged men, but the mode of travel and its duration had remarkably little ill effect on any of them. They had been given no idea of where they were being taken and could see nothing of the countryside through which they were passing. It was therefore not until the train made its final halt that they discovered they were at Liège, in Belgium.

A group of S.S. men assembled the cramped and weary prisoners as they stumbled from their trucks and immediately marched them for several miles through undulating countryside to their destination at the top of a hill. It was a barracks that had once housed Belgian soldiers; but the soldiers had clearly left in something of a hurry and without thought to the comfort of future occupants. The place was utterly neglected and absolutely filthy. There was about it what Plum was later to describe as "an atmosphere of unpreparedness." Everything was in confusion, not least the feeding arrangements. True, there were bubbling cauldrons of what passed for soup—but there was nothing on hand in which it could be served to the tired eight-hundred-odd. Consequently, they had to root around for something themselves and were fortunate enough to find an enormous rubbish heap which contained a miscellany of old and rusty mess tins, chipped and broken cups, empty bottles, battered kettles and old motor-oil containers. These were quickly dug out, given a hasty wash and brush-up and pressed into service. Plum managed to secure for himself one of the oil containers, which he felt gave to the soup that little extra something it might otherwise have lacked.

In most respects, the camp was like a rehearsal for the real thing. The Germans in charge seemed to be feeling their way with something of which they hadn't quite got the hang, and there was only the most rudimentary kind of organisation. They managed to get as far as assigning so many men to a dormitory and appointing a Room Warden for each dormitory, and then they appeared to give up. What, after all, was one supposed to do with such a large and motley collection of middle-aged civilians?

To begin with, the internees were not idle. For their own sakes, they started straight away to clean the barracks, using whatever scraps of rag they were able to beg, borrow or steal. It was no mean task. The dormitories, the corridors, and particularly the latrines were in an appalling state. But when the unpleasant labour had been completed, Plum had to admit that Liège was a material improvement on Loos. Here, at least, every man had a bed; there were no restrictions on walking about in the fresh air; and the food, if not much better, was slightly more varied. Breakfast consisted of two ladlefuls of ersatz coffee and a slab of black bread; lunch, at eleven-thirty a.m., was two ladlefuls of soup with rice or potatoes in it; and supper, at seven p.m., was again coffee and black bread.

There were two parades a day—one at eight in the morning and the other at eight in the evening—and each took almost an hour, entirely due to the fact that the Germans found it extremely difficult to do an accurate count of their prisoners. It seemed that the internees just didn't have the knack of parading. When they were ordered to form fives, some of them would form fours, some would form sixes and others would form eights. At the same time, a man in one group might catch sight of a pal in another group and decide to go and have a chat with him, thus getting himself counted twice or not at all. The constantly changing patterns as the prisoners obligingly did their best to form themselves out of their fours, sixes or eights and into the required fives added further to the confusion; the bewildered Germans had to keep starting again when they found that they were eight men short or had twelve men too many. After several abortive attempts, the Germans would huddle together for a short conference before trying yet again. Eventually, they would be satisfied—or pretend that they were satisfied—that all the men were present and correct and the parade would be dismissed. The prisoners never tired of this diversion.

By the end of the week they had established themselves as comfortably as they could, only to be told that they were to pack their things and be ready to move again. There was a certain sinking of hearts at this news although there was little about the Liège barracks to endear the place to them. It was really a matter of the devil they knew. They had no idea where they were being sent, and there was every possibility that it could be even worse than the barracks.

On 3rd August 1940 they were once more taken to a railway station and wedged into cattle trucks; but this time the journey took only six and a half hours. It ended at Huy, where they were marched along a winding path—there being no proper road—out of the town to the Citadel.

The Citadel of Huy was built entirely of stone and had outer walls that were fourteen feet thick. It had been intended to accommodate something like two hundred people—but here were eight hundred, for whom the Germans had made no special provision. Beds were at a premium, and of bedding there was virtually none. In fact, there were blankets for only twenty men: and Plum was not one of the fortunate twenty. For the first three weeks he had to make do with his raincoat; but he was permitted to write to Ethel (as all the internees were permitted to write to wives or other nearest relatives), and she sent him a suitcase full of blankets.

As at Liège, the days soon fell into an unvarying pattern. Everyone was woken at six a.m., and an hour later the Room Warden would collect the breakfast ration for his particular charges—one mugful of black coffee per person, and one loaf of bread for every eight men. At one p.m. there was a watery vegetable soup, and at six p.m. another mugful of coffee. It was a meagre diet. To supplement it, once a day two of the internees would be taken into the town by a guard to buy whatever extra provisions were available. What these two men were able to carry had to be shared among the eight hundred. There was therefore little in the way of luxuries. But if Plum was missing his regular meals, he missed even more his tobacco. Like other pipe-smokers, he was forced to resort to mixtures of straw and tea.

After almost five weeks of this, on 3rd September 1940 the men were again peremptorily herded to the railway station to be carried off to an unknown destination. On this occasion they were put on board a regular train, eight to a compartment, and each man was given a ration of half a loaf of bread and half a sausage. Thirty-two hours later they were given another half a loaf and some soup, but there were no further issues of food on a journey which eventually took three days and three nights. Throughout it, no one was allowed to leave his compartment at any time for any reason.

When this gruelling trip was over, the internees found themselves in the village of Tost in Upper Silesia (now part of Poland); and their new home was the local lunatic asylum. Contrary to their dismal expectations, it proved to be a haven. After Liège and Huy, it seemed almost luxurious.

The asylum consisted of three buildings of which one was capable of accommodating thirteen hundred and the other two, though smaller, were reasonably spacious. Sleeping quarters were in the large building, and part of one of the others was used as a mess hall—the other part being the camp hospital. The third building was designated the social centre, and it was here that those with musical or other talents practised and gave concerts. Here, too, church services were held on Sundays; and here, after he had been given a padded cell to himself in which to work, Plum eventually wrote the novel *Money in the Bank.*

Whereas Liège and Huy had had nothing to commend them in the way of local scenery, the asylum had its own small park filled with trees and was not in itself of unpleasant aspect. It was, in fact, a properly organised civilian internment camp: and it is significant, in view of Plum's later conduct, that this type of camp was the sum total of his experience of German camps. It was no place of confinement for political prisoners. Plum's companions were, in the main, middle-aged men whose only crime was that they were non-Germans who happened to be in German-held territory during a time of war. They were of no personal consequence to the Germans, other than as a liability, and they posed no threat. No brutalities were practised against them, and they were left more or less to their own devices. The two roll-calls a day—one in the morning and one in the evening—were a mere formality.

So mild was the way of life at Tost that men aged fifty and over were not expected to do any of the heavier tasks like hauling coal and clearing the roads of snow—about which Plum was later to say, "I don't know anything that so braces one up on a cold winter's morning, with an Upper Silesian blizzard doing its stuff, as to light one's pipe and look out of the window and watch a gang of younger men shovelling snow."

On 26th December 1940 an Associated Press correspondent, Angus Thuermer, was allowed to visit the camp at Tost, and there he met and talked with Plum. The article he wrote about it mentioned how Plum steadfastly refused to accept any special privileges from the Germans, who had offered him, among other things, a private bedroom. It was the first news that the outside world had had of Plum since the fall of France, and it caused a furore in America. Now that they knew where he was, his American friends—authors, editors and theatrical producers—plagued the German authorities in Washington with requests for his release. And Guy Bolton drew up a petition, signed by many influential people, asking the Germans to send Plum back to America. Since America was not yet in the war, it might have been hoped that the Germans would be glad to let him go as a placatory gesture. But in fact they did no more than announce that he was "quite comfortable."

It was not until 21st June that Plum was released from Tost, and then it was solely because he was verging on sixty—the age at which internees were given conditional freedom. He was brought to Berlin where, in a statement to American correspondents, he said:

> *It is a curious experience, being completely shut off from the outer world, as one is in an internment camp. One lives on potatoes and rumours. One of my friends used to keep a notebook in which he would jot down all the rumours that spread through the corridors, and they made curious reading. To military prisoners, I believe, rumours are known for some reason as 'Blue Pigeons.' We used to call them bedtime stories. They never turned out true, but a rumour a day kept depression away, so they served their purpose. Certainly, whether owing to bedtime stories or simply the feeling that if one was in one was in and it was no use making heavy weather about it, the morale of the men at Tost was wonderful. I never met a more cheerful crowd, and I loved them like brothers.*

He also mentioned that he had found it difficult to be belligerent in the camp—meaning that he had felt ineffectual as a prisoner—and this was later to be completely misinterpreted.

During Plum's internment, Ethel had been living with friends in Hesdin, Pas de Calais. She now sold all her jewellery and borrowed money from these friends so that she could join Plum in Berlin where, on German orders, the reunited Wodehouses occupied a suite at the Hotel Adlon under surveillance.

Five days after his release, on 26th June 1941, Plum agreed to do a broadcast to America from a script written and prepared by Harry W. Flannery, an American correspondent with the Columbia Broadcasting System. He had already given interviews, but it struck him that this would be a perfect way of letting his friends and fans have firsthand news of where he was and how he was. The result of it was that the German Foreign Office asked him if he would like to do a series of broadcasts over the short-wave radio to America, for which he would be permitted to write his own scripts. It seemed like a generous offer with no obvious ulterior motive, and Plum accepted it. He hoped that his friends and followers in America would hear him and he therefore wrote five humorous talks about his experiences as British Civilian Prisoner Number 796. That the Germans allowed him to broadcast those talks exactly as he had written them leaves their motive very much in doubt. It is difficult to see what they could have hoped to gain from them, for Plum did not gloss over the miseries of internment. If they were intended merely as a sop to the many important Americans who had urged for Plum's release and were therefore regarded as just so much worthless nonsense, then the Germans obviously did not understand the subtleties of the Wodehouse brand of humour. For Plum, in his inimitable way, made the Nazis look particularly stupid in their handling of the internment camps.

In doing these broadcasts to America, however, Plum—perhaps foolishly, certainly naively—did not anticipate the hornets' nest he would be stirring up for himself in his own country. Comparatively few people actually heard the talks, but the mere knowledge that they had been given on the German radio was enough to whip the British press into a frenzy of hate and vituperation. Without checking the facts and without giving the astonished public a hint of what Plum had said in his broadcasts, the papers reviled him and accused him—placing him on a par with the arch-traitor known as Lord Haw-Haw.

At first, and in the climate of the times, this was understandable and even excusable. That one of the most famous and most loved of Englishmen was apparently broadcasting propaganda for the Germans while England stood alone and bombs rained down on London was almost too much to comprehend. And the public knew only what it was told, not only in the newspapers but also through the medium of the British Broadcasting Corporation. For on 15th July 1941 what was possibly the bitterest and most vehement attack on Plum was made to the largest of audiences in a post-script to the nine P.M. news on the BBC Home Service. It was written and read by William Connor, better known and often feared as the outspoken columnist "Cassandra" of the *Daily Mirror,* and it was unsparing in its fury, venom and condemnation. In its way, it was a masterpiece of invective, well calculated to strike a responsive chord in the hearts of angry, bomb-weary Britons. But it had one flaw: it failed to give the true facts.

"I have come to tell you tonight of the story of a rich man trying to make his last and greatest sale—that of his own country," the broadcast began. "It is a sombre story of honour pawned to the Nazis for the price of a soft bed." Stating that the "elderly playboy" was "throwing a cocktail party when the storm-troopers clumped in on his shallow life," Connor went on to fantasize about how Dr. Goebbels had groomed Plum for "the most disreputable stardom in the world—the limelight of Quislings" and had then offered him his liberty. According to Connor, Dr. Goebbels "said unto him: 'All this power will I give thee if thou wilt worship the Fuehrer.' Pelham Wodehouse fell on his knees." There followed a reminder of the fifty thousand Britons behind barbed wire in Germany who would not give in or sell out. "Between the terrible choice of betrayal of one's country and the abomination of the Gestapo, they have only one answer. . . . But they have something that Wodehouse can never regain. Something that thirty pieces of silver could never buy." The journalist ended with an account of an air-raid on Dulwich—"the suburb of London where you went to school"—telling of the dead and dying lying under the rubble. "*You* should have been there, Mr. Wodehouse," he emphasised, "—you with your impartiality, your reasonableness and perhaps even one of your famous little jokes."

In all of this there was not the slightest hint of what Plum had said in his talks. Connor's listeners were left with the firm impression that he had indeed been broadcasting Nazi propaganda in the manner of Lord Haw-Haw.

That the BBC should have warranted an attack of this nature on a man who was in no position to defend himself against the charges seems very much out of character. But the truth is that the BBC's Board of Governors was strongly opposed to it. The Board was overruled, however, by the then Minister of Information, Mr. Duff Cooper, on whose insistence Connor went on the air.

In contrast, the Americans took a quite different view of what Plum had done. Throughout the war, the United States War Department used recordings of his broadcasts in its Intelligence School at Camp Ritchie as models of anti-Nazi propaganda.

The backlash of the British reaction was to be felt by Plum a little later. In the meantime, and in all innocence of the private war being waged over him in his homeland—with old friends like A. A. Milne, Denis Mackail and Sax Rohmer springing to his defence—he and Ethel were on the move again. On the completion of the recording of his five broadcasts—entitled "How To Be An Internee In Your Spare Time Without Previous Experience"—they were permitted to go to the Bavarian Alps to stay on the estate of a cousin of Raven Barnikow, a friend from their Hollywood days, their hosts having undertaken to be responsible for them. The fact was that the Wodehouses were not political prisoners and the Germans didn't really care where they were provided that someone was willing to keep an eye on them. They may even have been glad to have the English couple out of their capital, but with the approach of winter, Plum and Ethel were back in Berlin. The country house had had to be closed for lack of fuel.

All of this travel and accommodation had to be paid for, and the wherewithal came from *Money in the Bank.* Long before America's entry into the war in December 1941, Plum had been permitted to send the manuscript to the *Saturday Evening Post* and receive a monthly payment from its sale. The Germans had no intention of giving free board to someone capable of earning his keep. (*Money in the Bank* was published in volume form in America by Doubleday Doran on 19th January 1942—a measure, perhaps, of the faith the publishers had in Plum.)

In Berlin, that winter of 1941, Plum was staggered to learn of the effect his broadcasts had had in Britain. He had, after all, given the talks in good faith to the noncombatant United States. It had never even occurred to him that they might be picked up in Britain. Not that it really made any difference. He had said nothing to which any reasonable person could take objection. What could it all be about? Puzzled and disturbed, he appealed to the Swiss Embassy to get word to the British Government explaining what had happened and reaffirming his loyalty. He also applied for permission to leave Germany and return to England to defend himself in person, but this was not granted. Frustrated, but maintaining his fatalistic outlook that whatever happens happens, he realised that he would have to put the matter out of his mind until the war was over.

During the summers of 1942 and 1943 the Wodehouses were again given permission to live in the country as paying guests, returning to Berlin for the winter months. With no other diversions, Plum spent most of his time writing and managed to complete two novels, *Full Moon* and *Spring Fever*.

In September 1943 the Germans decided that they definitely did not want the Wodehouses in Berlin any longer. Heavy air-raids on the city had made accommodation scarcer than ever, and there was a need for the rooms occupied by Plum and Ethel. Furthermore, there were more urgent duties for the men assigned to keeping them under surveillance. The paying but unwelcome guests were therefore sent to Paris.

Paris, even under occupation, was a good deal nearer home, and the Wodehouses were glad to be there. In effect, though, it was not that much different from Berlin. Staying at the Hotel Bristol, just behind the Champs Elysées, they found that their movements were every bit as restricted as they had been before. But Plum used the time to his advantage, writing and rewriting.

When Paris was liberated, on 25th August 1944, the Wodehouses joined in the general rejoicing: but their happiness was marred by the cloud hanging over Plum's head. It was imperative to get the matter cleared up. On the following day, therefore, Plum reported to an American officer in charge of advance troops and asked that his whereabouts be made known to the British authorities in order that an enquiry could be made. As a result of this, a Home Office official flew to Paris and began an investigation which was carried on for the next two weeks. In the course of it, Plum made a full statement and every aspect of his case was gone into in the minutest detail. He expressed a wish to return to England and speak for himself, but he was advised to remain in France for the time being. There was nothing more he could do.

It was a trying time made worse by more unhappy news of a personal nature. Eleanor Wodehouse, Plum's mother, had died at the age of eighty-eight in a Maidenhead, Surrey, nursing home on 21st February 1941; and Leonora Cazalet had died in a London hospital on 16th May 1944 at the age of thirty-nine. Plum had never seen very much of his mother anyway, but his attachment to Leonora had been extremely deep, and it seemed incredible that her wonderful companionship was lost to him for ever. He and Ethel grieved together. But their tribulations were by no means over.

Two months after the liberation of Paris, the Hotel Bristol was requisitioned by the French Government to provide accommodation for De Gaulle's diplomats, and the Wodehouses moved to the Hotel Lincoln in the Rue Bayard. There, on 20th November 1944, at one o'clock in the morning, they were roused from their sleep by the French police and taken to the Palais de Justice. Seated on wooden chairs in a draughty corridor, they were held there for sixteen hours without food or drink. They knew only that they had been brought in on the orders of the Prefect of Police, M. Levitre, but they were not told why.

As soon as the British Government was informed of the situation, a Home Office representative was rushed to Paris to look after the interests of the Wodehouses—the assumption being that they were being held for some offence against the French laws. The French, on the other hand, seemed to think that they were doing the British a favour by apprehending Plum and Ethel, although there had been no request for them to do so.

While the tangle was being sorted out, sleeping quarters were arranged for the bewildered couple and provisions were procured for them by Malcolm Muggeridge, who happened to be serving with the British Forces in Paris.

Ethel was released the next day; but Plum was detained at the police headquarters for a further four days. Apparently unperturbed and still taking everything as it came, he simply continued with the writing of his latest novel, *Uncle Dynamite,* encouraged by the watchful interest of a number of Inspecteurs who appeared to be entranced by this glimpse of a literary master at work. The Inspecteurs were deprived of this mild divertissement on the fourth night, however, when it was decided that Plum should be removed to a local hospital—not because he was showing any ill effects but because it would be more convenient to keep him under surveillance there . . . and perhaps because the Inspecteurs would then give more concentration to their own work.

Plum still didn't know why he was being held, but it began to matter less as he settled comfortably in the best place of internment he had known in years. The hospital provided him with a private room, good food and—best of all—plenty of tobacco. Ethel and friends were allowed to visit him daily, and he had writing materials.

As with previous internments, the days followed a pattern. He would awaken at four a.m. and remain in bed until breakfast was served at six. At nine a.m. mail would arrive, and an orderly would start to clean the room. The cleaning had to be finished by nine-thirty and lunch was not until twelve-thirty, so he had three undisturbed hours in which to write. After lunch, he would continue writing until visiting time at three p.m. At four p.m., or later if he had guests, he would take his regular afternoon walk in the hospital gardens. Dinner was at six p.m., and by eight p.m. he was in bed and ready for sleep. He said of it at the time, "It isn't a bad sort of life if you have a novel to write."

Nevertheless, it couldn't go on indefinitely. The matter of Plum's mysterious detention by the French was not being overlooked in England. It raised once again the whole question of his wartime broadcasts and what interpretation should be placed on them, leading eventually to an enquiry in the House of Commons. The complete discussions are recorded in the fifth series of *Parliamentary Debates in the House of Commons.* They began on 6th December 1944 with Major Sir Jocelyn Lucas asking the Secretary of State for Foreign Affairs, the Rt. Hon. Anthony Eden, if his attention had been called to the case of "Mr. P. G. Wodehouse, a British subject formerly interned in Germany and now in France." Captain Gammans then asked why Mr. P. G. Wodehouse had not been brought to Britain for internment or for trial. Mr. Eden replied that the case was being closely watched, that Mr. Wodehouse had been arrested in Paris on the ground that he had broadcast from Berlin and that he had been released on condition that he would reside in a hospital. He added that Mr. Wodehouse had expressed no wish to go to England and that he, Mr. Eden, was asking the French Government to state the legal grounds upon which the surveillance was being maintained. In answer to a further question about whether a British subject could be tried by Great Britain or France for an offence in Germany, Mr. Eden said that there was no question of a trial or of a charge. And after more questions, he remarked that the Home Office had advised that there were no grounds upon which action could be taken.

The debate then began to revolve around the degree of Plum's guilt, if indeed he was guilty of anything. Mr. Quintin Hogg asked if it was not obvious that anyone broadcasting on the enemy wireless and receiving a fee, either in kind or money, was trading with the enemy and was therefore punishable by law. He felt that, since a serious legal principle was involved Mr. Eden should consult with the appropriate authorities; and Mr. Eden suggested that if Mr. Hogg was sure there were legal points involved he should himself put a question to the appropriate Minister.

Reference was again made to this by Mr. Quintin Hogg on 15th December 1944, when he stated that he had learned that speaking on the enemy wireless during wartime was not considered an offence. If this was so, he said, "it very soon ought to be made one." Later in what was to be a very long speech, he remarked, "I have no personal feelings about this matter at all. . . . I have derived considerable amusement and pleasure from his (Plum's) contribution to English literature. I could wish that there were other personalities involved, but the law must be impartial as between persons, and if it is the misfortune of a gentleman to have incurred its penalties, one cannot be deterred by any feeling of predilection which one might entertain for his person." After pointing out that the Members of Parliament present were not concerned with penalties and that he was not calling for blood, Mr. Hogg returned to the question of law.

In his opinion Plum's offence was covered by the Treason Act, which named it treason if a person tended to act in a way which "strengthens the King's enemies, and has tended to weaken the country." It did not matter, he said, whether or not the broadcasts were tendentious; "the purpose of the enemy in broadcasting to this country is fundamentally the same as his purpose in sending over flying bombs. It is to weaken the morale of the country, and a person who happens to clown on the enemy wireless, instead of producing directly anti-British propaganda, is committing just as much an act of treason towards this country as Lord Haw-Haw himself, although the punishment might well be less."

Mr. Hogg went on to say that he was aware that in order to commit the crime of high treason, or any other crime, there had to be guilty intention. "A man, according to the law of England," he stated, "is presumed to intend the consequences of his own action, and nobody, short of a lunatic, who broadcasts on the enemy wireless would fail to realise that the consequences would be to strengthen the King's enemies, and it follows that he should be condemned as having intended the inevitable result." He then turned to the Trading with the Enemy Act of 1939, under the provisions of which he felt that Plum might be held answerable, his only doubt being that its terms might not apply to acts committed outside its jurisdiction. In conclusion, he drew attention to what he considered the laxities in the criminal law as it stood.

The debate continued with the pros and cons of the law and the extent to which it could be applied to the broadcasts, the Attorney-General stating that the Wodehouse case had been thoroughly investigated and that it had been agreed that there was not sufficient evidence of intent to assist the enemy to justify proceedings. In his final summing up, he said, "To take an extreme case, if a man has had a gun and been in the German Forces it is no use for him to say, 'I did not intend to assist the enemy.' If he has done propaganda of the kind which some of us have heard over the wireless, it is no use his saying, 'I did not intend to assist the enemy.' If he tried to persuade people to join the German Forces it is no use his saying that he did not intend to assist the enemy. The problem and the difficulty for those who have to consider these matters only arises in cases where one cannot say that that ends the argument."

If it did nothing else, the debate at least made clear the official view that Plum had broken no laws and would therefore face no charges. But it wasn't until 17th January 1945—when it was absolutely certain that the British intended taking no action against him—that Plum was released from what the French authorities now called his "preventive detention" in hospital. Malcolm Muggeridge was on hand to drive him and Ethel and Wonder to Barbizon, thirty miles from Paris, where the Wodehouses stayed at a hotel which was normally open only during the summer months. It had no running water, no heating and no carpeting—but they were free and together and were not much concerned with creature comforts.

Talking of Plum's detention period, Muggeridge said, "Plum and Ethel displayed the most tremendous courage. Ethel knew that this was a hot spot but she was absolutely plucky. She never cried. She has a true love for Plum." And Plum was later to write to William Townend:

> *Aren't women wonderful? Ethel took the whole thing in her stride without a word of complaint. She was simply magnificent and the love and admira-*

tion on which she has inspired me for
the last thirty years hit a new high.

Three weeks after their arrival at Barbizon the hotel was commandeered by SHAEF, so Plum, Ethel and Wonder returned to Paris and stayed once more at the Hotel Lincoln until, on 23rd April 1945, they were able to move into a furnished apartment at 78 Avenue Paul Doumer. Paris was comparatively quiet at this time and they were very happy in their new home.

With the lifting of postal restrictions, Plum had begun to receive a volume of encouraging mail from friends and fans. He had not yet been given an opportunity of defending himself publicly in the matter of the broadcasts, but he could not help unburdening himself privately. When Townend sent him copies of letters written to the *Daily Telegraph* by the anti-Wodehouse element after William Connor's inflammatory broadcast, Plum responded:

> *Those letters in the* Daily Tele-
> graph *about my having found intern-*
> *ment so terrible that I bought my re-*
> *lease by making a bargain with the*
> *German Government were all wrong.*
> *I was released because I was on the*
> *verge of sixty. When I was in Loos*
> *Prison the first week, a dozen of our*
> *crowd were released because they were*
> *sixty, including my cellmate William*
> *Cartmell, the Étaples piano tuner. Of*
> *course, he may have made a bargain*
> *with the German Government, offer-*
> *ing, if set free, to tune its piano half-*
> *price, but I don't think so. It all looked*
> *pretty genuine to me.*
>
> *As for finding internment terrible,*
> *I didn't at all after the first few months.*
> *Loos Prison, Liège Barracks and the*
> *Citadel of Huy were on the tough side,*
> *but Tost was fine. One thing that*
> *helped us enormously there was the*

presence of the internees from Holland. A good many of them were language teachers, lecturers and musicians, so we were able to have concerts, shows and so on and brush up on our Beowulf. We also played cricket all through the summer.

In another letter to Townend, he wrote:

Did you see a book called—I forget what, but something by Harry Flannery, one of the American correspondents in Berlin? If so, I hope you didn't believe the bilge he wrote about me—e.g. that some sinister German had come to the camp to see me and arrange about my being released and speaking on the radio. Nobody ever came near the camp. Also, all the talks he reports as taking place between him and me are pure inventions. I only saw him twice, but from his book you would think that we were always together. I wish, by the way, when people invent conversations with one, they wouldn't give one such rotten dialogue. But writers on daily and weekly papers always will go all out for the picturesque. When they interview you, they invariably alter and embroider. As a rule, this does not matter much, but when a war is in progress it is kinder to the interviewee not to indulge the imagination. . . .

When I arrived in Berlin, I told an interviewer that I had found it diffi-

cult to be belligerent in camp, a mild
pleasantry by which I intended to con-
vey the feeling of helplessness—of having to be just a number and a well-
behaved number at that, which comes
over you when you find yourself on the
wrong side of the barbed wire. But it
did not get over. It was too subtle. The
interviewer sniffed at it, patted it with
his paws, wrinkled his forehead over
it. Then he thought he saw what I was
driving at, and penned the following:

"I have never been able to work
up a belligerent feeling," said Mr.
Wodehouse. "Just as I am about
to feel belligerent about some
country, I meet some nice fellow
from it and lose my belligerency."

(Have you ever heard me talk like
that?) With the result that I was accused of expressing unpatriotic sentiments and being indifferent to the outcome of the war....

When I was interned, a man from
Time Magazine, sitting down to write
something picturesque and amusing
about me, produced the following:

"When the German army was
sweeping toward Paris last Spring
'Plum' (to his friends) was throwing a cocktail-party in the jolly old
pine woods at Le Touquet. Suddenly a motorcycle Gendarme tore
up, shouted 'The Germans will be
here in an hour', and tore off. The
guests, thoroughly familiar with
this sort of drollery from Wode-

house novels, continued to toss down cocktails. The Germans arrived punctually, first having taken care to block all the roads. They arrested the Wodehouses and guests, later permitting Mrs. Wodehouse and celebrants to depart southward."

You wouldn't think anyone would have believed such an idiotic story, but apparently everyone did. In 1941 someone wrote in the Daily Express:

"He lived in Le Touquet. He was drinking a cocktail when the Germans arrived, and he was led away quite happily into captivity."

And someone else thus in the Daily Mail:

"He was, in fact, just sinking a cocktail when, in 1940, someone dashed in and cried that the Germans would be there in an hour or less. The party stayed put with a phlegm worthy of Drake's game of bowls."

I wonder where I am supposed to have collected these light-hearted guests whom I am described as entertaining. By the time the Germans were threatening Paris, the resident population of Le Touquet had shrunk so considerably that the most determined host would have found it impossible to assemble even the nucleus of a cocktail-party, and the few of us who had been unable to get away were not at all in the mood for revelry. We were pensive and pre-

occupied, starting at sudden noises and trying to overcome the illusion of having swallowed a heaping teaspoonful of butterflies. Odd, too, that a motorcycle Gendarme should have torn up and shouted: "The Germans will be here in an hour," when they had been there two months. They entered Le Touquet on May 22nd. At the time when the incident is supposed to have taken place we were all confined to our houses except when we went to Paris Plage to report at the Kommandatur to a German Kommandant who had a glass eye.

But it seemed that the fantasies woven around Plum's internment, and the non-clarification of the broadcasts, would continue to plague him despite the good friends who sprang to his defence. George Orwell's essay "In Defence of P. G. Wodehouse," in his book *Dickens, Dali and Others,* attempted to show how Plum's internment had placed him out of touch with events, having started before the war had really got under way. "He had missed the turning-point of the war," wrote Orwell, "and in 1941 he was still reacting in terms of 1939." Admitting that in the circumstances then prevailing it was excusable to be angry at what Plum had done, Orwell concluded by saying that to go on denouncing him three or four years later "—and more, to let an impression remain that he acted with conscious treachery—is not excusable."

Denis Mackail also had something to tell the public about the broadcasts in his autobiography *Life With Topsy:*

And the next time I heard those mild and familiar tones was . . . when Diana suddenly roused me from sleep and rushed me to the radio. She had been twiddling knobs, and Plum's voice— doubly removed, for it was a record that was being played over—was ad-

dressing us from Germany, where he had recently emerged from forty-nine weeks of internment. I was much moved, but I can't say that I was indignant. He was being funny; I thought he was being remarkably courageous; he seemed to be making a quiet and almost casual plea against intolerance. But this didn't stop a Minister of Information from overriding the authorities of the B.B.C. and putting up a journalist to blackguard him in another broadcast, to sneer at his Christian names, and to describe him as a "playboy." Plum! The most industrious author that I had ever known. But the war couldn't go on without hatred, and Plum hated no one. That was his crime.

In response to a well-wishing letter from a young writer named Scott Meredith, who was then in the American Air Force, Plum wrote:

The whole thing is an example of what a blunder it is to let your feelings get the better of your prudence. I had no other motive in doing the talks than to make some return for the great number of letters which I had received from American readers during my internment —your card among them. It never occurred to me that there was anything different between using the German radio to tell my friends in America how I had been getting on and using the German postal system to send that article, "My War With Germany," to the S.E.P. The main trouble, of course, was that practically nobody heard the talks, and so people jumped to the conclusion that I had been doing German propaganda.

I think this view is gradually being changed. The fact that the Attorney-General made that announcement in the House of Commons that the government had absolutely nothing against me must have helped. But it always takes a long time to change people's opinions, and I shall have to be patient. It is so difficult to impress the fact on the public that I was not living at the Adlon from choice but because the authorities made me live there—and though I have stated on several occasions that I paid all my own expenses (my wife selling her jewellery), there must still be thousands who think I was being supported by the German Government. It was only for a very short time, during the winter months, that I was ever in Berlin. Nine months of each year I spent with friends in the country.

Among the first to have written to Plum was Guy Bolton, who had kept in constant touch with the Cazalets for whatever news they could give him and who was now anxious to assure Plum of all possible support. Plum's appreciation was expressed in a letter dated 30th May 1945, which reached Guy at the end of June:

I was very bucked when I got your letter wanting me to come and visit the old home and resume the old collaboration. There is nothing I would like better, but I wonder how soon it can be done. I'm afraid it won't be possible for civilians to travel for at least a year or so.

I have had no new book published in England since 1940, but my London agent tells me that half a million copies of my cheap editions have sold over there in the last three years, so that the feeling against me can't be so very solid. From the fact that without exception all the English and Americans I have met in Paris—about a hundred in all—have been friendly I imagine that the anti party is principally made up of newspaper people. Anyway, my friends have been wonderful, thank God. Every one of the people whose friendship I value has written to me sympathising. You can imagine how glad I was to get your letter, and I can only hope that my reply reached you, as I wouldn't want you to think I had ignored a letter like that.

Having dispensed with what might have been termed the formalities, Plum then launched into his favourite topic:

After finishing my last novel, I had a two and a half months spell of absolute inactivity, with no ideas of any kind, until it suddenly struck me that there was a play in the novel which I had written in 1943, and I am now working happily on it. It has been a frightful sweat, as I have had to re-write the first scene of act one nine times, each time getting it a little more simplified. I hear your voice saying "Never give the audience too much to think of at one time," which I believe is the whole secret of play writing, and I keep shedding things from the novel which I started by believing essential. In the novel, for instance, the hero knew the heroine when she was fifteen and has been in love with her ever since, and I thought this was the whole nub of the story. I now see that the story can be told just as well, in fact better, if he met and fell in love with her a month or so before the play begins, and of course it cuts out pages of exposition. But how much more difficult a play is to write than a novel.

I know exactly the formula for writing a sure-fire play, but unfortunately I can't think of the details! What never fails is the strongly marked, eccentric character who attaches great value to the services of the hero or heroine and strains every nerve to bust up his or her romance in order to prevent him or her leaving him. Thus: In The Front Page *the editor has a pet reporter whom he needs. The reporter wants to marry and quit, and the editor sets himself to bust up the marriage. In* The Man Who Came to Dinner *Sheridan Whiteside has an invaluable secretary (female) who wants to quit him and marry a small-town newspaper man, so he sets himself to block the thing. All one wants is something equiv-*

alent, but I am unfortunately barren of ideas!

Are you beginning to feel at all old nowadays? I am now on the verge of sixty-four and for the first time am starting to abandon the illusion that I am really a sprightly young fellow in the early forties. The way it affects me as regards my work is to make it increasingly difficult to write quick. I used to rattle off the stuff on my machine, but now I have to do each paragraph in pencil first and it is only after about half a dozen shots that I get the thing right.

If Guy had required proof that Plum was still Plum, this letter must have reassured him.

With the nip of autumn in the air, Ethel began to hunt for a heated apartment—of which there was a scarcity in the Paris of 1945. But she was an expert where such things were concerned and, back in form again, she eventually found one at 36 Boulevard Suchet. It had not only hot water but also a number of electric heaters in working order, and she was able to turn the place into a comfortable winter home.

By this time, Scott Meredith had received Plum's letter and was reacting to it in his own way. He was determined that Plum's name should be finally and irrevocably cleared and was so aroused by the lack of information being given to the press that he wrote to Watson Washburn, Plum's lawyer in the States:

I am aware that there is a school of thought which states that the best way to restore Wodehouse to his former position is to say absolutely nothing about him at all in the public press until the whole thing dies down of its own accord. I hope you are not of this school. I certainly am not.

The thing will never die down of its own accord—not enough to matter, at any rate. There are far too many people who read hurriedly about the Wodehouse broadcasts—hurriedly because they were anxious to turn to the stories of men who had cut their wives into six neat pieces, and of Explosions Which Kill Ten—and now think of Wodehouse only as a Nazi collaborationist. If you delve into it you learn that they remember so little of what they read that they can't quite tell you why they think so: but they remember that they think of Wodehouse as a collaborationist because he broadcast for the Germans—but who do not know that the broadcasts were light, non-political talks about his experiences. It is amazing how many of them are positive that they read somewhere that the Wodehouse talks were certainly political, and that, in fact, he advised the British and Americans to give up. (Ridiculous, of course, when you know that he did not broadcast to the British, and the Americans were not then at war with the Germans: but so very, very many people have told it to me that way.) Then there are the people who are somewhat better informed, and who know that the broadcasts were non-political, but who believe he is guilty because he was warned after each broadcast of the furor he was causing in England and America, and still con-

tinued with the series.

These people must be told the facts of the case—the actual facts. They must be told that the broadcasts were non-political; that he was not warned between broadcasts because the airings were recorded and he therefore did not stay around Berlin, making them in person and talking to American correspondents all the time; and that he has been labelled by the British government itself as merely "injudicious, but obviously not a German collaborationist."

Plum was himself becoming restless about the way things were going. In maintaining the dignified silence advised by his publishers and literary agents, he felt that he was being unfair to himself. Everyone else, it seemed, was having a go. Why not he? Acting on his own initiative, therefore, he wrote to Abel Green, the editor of *Variety*—*the* American showbusiness paper—detailing his case. *Variety's* only reference to Plum's adventures had been a short paragraph on the front page of the issue for 24th April 1946:

FRENCH LIFT NAZI CLOUD FROM P. G. WODEHOUSE

Paris, April 23

Writer P. G. Wodehouse has received notice from the French Government that he's been completely cleared of any charge of collaboration resulting from his broadcasts from Berlin in 1940 (sic). Wodehouse had previously been vindicated by the English government and is now free to return to England at any time.

But on 8th May 1946 *Variety* printed his letter:

Editor, Variety:

I can't tell you what pleasure it was to get your letter this afternoon and how grateful I am for your offer to give me some of your space for my story. I have been one of Variety's *most assiduous and enthusiastic readers for more than 30 years, and there is no paper in the world in which I would rather put my case. Yours is just the public whose opinion I most value.*

When I came out of camp I wrote a book about my experiences as an internee, the second chapter of which dealt with the broadcasts. I had hoped to publish this as my first postwar production, but Doubleday, my publishers, advised putting it off for a while and are bringing out a "Jeeves" novel in the early fall.

I think the trouble all along has been that nobody in the United States heard the broadcasts and this uproar in England gave to the American public the impression that they were in some way pro-German, if not actual German propaganda. In fact, they were merely a humorous description of camp life, designed purely to amuse my American readers and could have been printed as they stood in any American or English paper.

In support of this statement I should like to quote a letter I received this morning from a man in England, a stranger to me, who said that he had been a prisoner-of-war for two and a half years and that it was reading my books that kept up the spirits of the men in his camp. He says:

"I would like to tell you that having read your broadcasts I cannot see how anyone could possibly see anything in the slightest pro-German or anti-British in them. But I will not give you my own opinion, I will tell you that of the late Air Marshal Boyd. I was his personal assistant and we were prisoners together in Italy. He read your broadcasts and gave them to me saying, 'Why the Germans ever let him say all this I cannot think. They have either got more sense of humour than I credited them with or it has just slipped past the censor. There is some stuff about being packed in cattle trucks and a thing about Loos jail that you would think would send a Hun crazy. Wodehouse has probably been shot by now.' "

I think the opinion of a British Air Marshal who knew what was in the talks ought to carry more weight than that of British newspaper men who didn't. But unfortunately it was the views of the latter that reached the public.

When, after the liberation of Paris, I notified the British authorities of my address and my desire for an investigation, they sent over a Home Office official to whom I made a long statement. It was after examining this statement carefully that first Mr. Anthony Eden and later Sir Donald Somervell, *the Attorney-General, stated in the House of Commons that the Government had nothing against me. Unfortunately, in addition to my statement, the Home Office official took back to London with him my only copy of the broadcasts with the exception of the second talk, the one that deals with Loos prison (where I spent the first week of my internment), and it seems impossible to get hold of them. On Feb. 22 this official wrote to me that he was making enquiries of the appropriate authorities, but no dice as yet. But I do have the second talk, and I propose to give it to Mr. de Beix (Variety's Paris correspondent) to forward to you, in the hope that you will see your way to print it. The other talks were exactly similar in tone. My internment took the form of a week in Loos prison, a week at Liège barracks, five weeks at the Citadel of Huy in Belgium, and about 10 months at Tost in Upper Silesia, and I gave one talk to cover each phase, starting with a description of my arrest and journey to Loos. I think when you see this Loos prison talk you will agree with Air Marshal Boyd that it is pretty harmless stuff. Will you please consider yourself free to use anything from the book that you think would interest and amuse readers of* Variety.

He had, at last, said his piece publicly, if only to a limited audience.

On 27th May 1946 Herbert Jenkins published *Money in the Bank,* which

David Low's famous caricature of Plum in 1933.

Party at Denis Mackail's (third from left standing) in 1928 with Plum standing at left.

Plum at the wheel of Ian Hay's car in 1928.

Ed Wynn, Ethel Wodehouse, musical comedy performers,
and Plum standing in the center at Great Neck in 1924.

Plum's hit songs from those history-making musicals.

Ian Hay and Plum on a golfing trip in Scotland.

The famed Princess Theatre where the trio of
Bolton-Wodehouse-Kern established the idea of integrating
the elements of book, lyrics-music, and dance in musical comedy form.

Morris Gest, Plum, Guy Bolton, Ray Comstock and Jerome Kern
rehearsing the 1924 production in Sitting Pretty in Detroit.

The World's Fair cover of Saturday Evening Post featuring

Redbook's all-star issue featuring Plum with his
1935 short-story masterpiece, Uncle Fred Flits By.

Plum, E. Phillips Oppenheim, Ethel Wodehouse
and Elsie Oppenheim aboard Opp's yacht at Cannes in 1934.

Above: Plum and Leonora arriving in Hollywood in 1930.
Below: Sir Herbert Grierson (left) and Plum receiving
honorary doctorates from Oxford University in June 1939.

Plum Wodehouse and David Jasen on Remsenburg grounds in April, 1963.

was the first of Plum's books written during internment. No Wodehouse book had been published in Britain since 1940. Jenkins had issued a volume of short stories about members of the Drones Club, called *Eggs, Beans and Crumpets*, on 26th April 1940; and on 4th October 1940 they had published what was to become Plum's own favourite novel, *Quick Service*. In America a collection of golf stories, *Wodehouse on Golf*, had been published by Doubleday Doran on 23rd August 1940; and *Quick Service* had been brought out by the same company on 11th November 1940. *Money in the Bank* had first been serialised in the *Saturday Evening Post* and then published in volume form by Double-day Doran on 19th January 1942: but it was its fate in Britain in 1946 that now concerned Plum. Would the adverse personal publicity he had received affect its sales? And if so, wouldn't that be an indication that the British public had neither forgotten nor forgiven?

He needn't have worried about the sales. In the first month of its publication, Herbert Jenkins sold 26,000 copies of *Money in the Bank*. But that didn't, after all, answer Plum's second question. The fact that people were prepared to read his books didn't necessarily mean that they were no longer concerned about the broadcasts. He still had the feeling that the matter would never be resolved until everyone in Britain had been given the opportunity of hearing his own explanation. But again he was advised to say nothing.

Writing to Townend about *Money in the Bank*, Plum mentioned that his main character, Lord Uffenham, had been drawn from a man in his dormitory at Tost. "It isn't often," he commented drily, "that one has the luck to be in daily contact with the model for one's principal character."

At about this time, in the spring of 1946, a flash of inspiration had Plum writing excitedly to Guy Bolton:

> *Listen. I've suddenly got the most*
> *terrific idea—a book of theatrical remi-*
> *niscences by you and me to be called*
> **BOOK AND LYRICS**
> *by*
> *Guy Bolton and P. G. Wodehouse*
> *I only got the idea an hour ago, so*
> *haven't thought out anything about the*
> *shape of the thing, but I believe we*
> *could make a big thing out of it. You*

have an enormous stock of theatrical stories and I have a few myself. My idea would be to make it a sort of loose saga of our adventures in the theatre from 1915 onwards, studded with anecdotes. Think of all the stuff we could put into it! I remember you telling me a priceless story about Bill McGuire, but I've forgotten the details, and between us we must have a hundred unpublished yarns about Erlanger, Savage, etc. Do you think in your spare time you could dictate a few to a stenographer—quite in the rough, just the main points for me to work up? Meanwhile, I'll be trying to shape the vehicle. Don't give away the title to a soul, as it seems to me a winner and somebody might pinch it. A book like this would be a cinch for serial publication.

I was very bucked by that "Show Boat" programme and immediately wrote a grateful letter to Oscar thanking him for being such a sportsman. He really is a good chap. It would have been quite easy for him to have confined himself to putting my name after the number in the programme. Well, one thing you and I have never wavered on, and that is that he is a splendid fellow.

Plum was referring to Oscar Hammerstein II and the credit he had given to Plum for the "Bill" lyric in *Show Boat*. As for Plum's bright idea about a theatre book, it was to bear fruit later.

In the meantime, *Joy in the Morning*—the Jeeves novel he had written at Le Touquet during the German occupation—was published by his American publishers, now known simply as Doubleday, on 22nd August 1946. It was the first of his books to be published in the United States since the end of the war in Europe, and the 15,000 copies ordered in advance of publication left no doubt that his popularity remained unimpaired there.

During the summer of 1946, Ethel and Plum returned to Le Touquet to inspect Low Wood for the first time since Plum's internment. The house had fallen into such disrepair that they would have had to spend several thousand dollars on it to make it habitable again, so—since they were planning to return to America at the end of October anyway, in connection with the dramatisation of a Psmith novel—Ethel decided to sell it. They still had a housing problem, however, because their lease at 36 Boulevard Suchet was due to expire at the beginning of October. But Ethel saved the day once again by securing accommodation at the Pavillon Henri Quatre in St. Germain-en-Laye, only nine miles from Paris. They thus had the joys of the countryside with easy access to the city.

Plum enjoyed the peace and quiet of the historic country town and was happy in Ethel's company, with Wonder to provide both exercise and amusement. It was a far cry from the turbulence of the past six years, and he was gratefully aware of the contrast. "It's curious," he wrote to Townend, "how life nowadays has got down to simplicities. All that matters is three meals a day and light and warmth."

As it transpired, the Wodehouses didn't leave France as planned after all. Plum explained why in a letter to publisher Nelson Doubleday dated 2nd December 1946:

> I'll tell you what caused my change of plan as regards coming to America at the end of October (which I shouldn't have been able to do, anyway, as the America, on which my passage was booked, didn't sail from Havre till towards the end of November, owing to the strike). My main idea in planning to be in New York before Christmas was to be on hand to help in the production of the Psmith play. When I found that the production wouldn't take place for quite a while, probably not

> *till next season, I thought it would be wise to dig in in some quiet spot and finish the Jeeves novel,* The Mating Season, *because once I was over in N.Y. I might not have had time to concentrate on it. Also, I hated the idea of leaving my wife all alone here, and she refuses to sail till she has got some clothes.*

Wasn't that just like a woman!

Since his letter to *Variety,* Plum had resumed his silence about the Berlin broadcasts in accordance with the wishes of his well-meaning but possibly injudicious advisers. But he still felt a pressing desire to present his case to at least one British publication with a wide circulation, and he therefore independently decided to grant an interview to the magazine *Illustrated.* Hubert Cole travelled to St. Germain-en-Laye to talk with him, and on 7th December 1946 *Illustrated* published an exclusive story in which every facet of Plum's case was fully explored. After a preamble in which he set the scene, Mr. Cole put before the public his own very pertinent questions and Plum's frank and open answers, at the end of which he said, "Whether you believe that a man of such genius could have acted so foolishly and yet innocently, I do not know. After having gone over the story with him for many hours, I do believe him. . . . My impression of Wodehouse is that he is that rare creature—a man completely without guile or suspicion. . . ."

Plum felt much better for having had this opportunity of explaining himself to British readers. The newspapers had certainly not done him justice. They had found space enough for the sensational accusations against him, but by the time he had been cleared it was old news to them and they barely mentioned the fact. Perhaps that was a punishment in itself.

If it could be said that Plum was guilty at all, then he was guilty of political naivety. As Malcolm Muggeridge so succinctly put it: "He'd been extremely imprudent and foolish. It was an act of folly. But it was a product of his peculiar temperament. It wasn't that he was other-worldly, or un-worldly, as much as that he was a-worldly; a born neutral in relation to the conflicts, individual and collective, which afflict mankind."

11

1947–1955

It apparently took Ethel some little time to acquire what she considered a suitable wardrobe for a return to the United States, for it was not until well into 1947 that the delayed trip was finally undertaken. By then, overtures concerning work had been reaching Plum and he had accepted a commission to do an adaptation of Molnar's romantic comedy *Arthur.* When he, Ethel and Wonder boarded the S.S. *America* at Cherbourg on 18th April 1947, there was therefore no question of him having an idle voyage. In fact, by the time the crossing had been made he had finished the job.

Anxious to get ashore, Plum was surprised at being asked to attend a press conference in the ship's saloon before landing. It was rather more of a reception than had ever been accorded him before, and he had reason to feel apprehensive about the course it might take; but the reporters were pleasant and it turned out to be an enjoyable occasion—so much so that by the time it was over and all the usual formalities had been gone through it was evening.

Thus the Wodehouses set foot on American soil for the first time in ten years at 7:15 P.M. on 26th April 1947 and were taken to the Weylin Hotel in New York, where Watson Washburn had booked temporary accommodation for them. They had both known New York well, but they now had to acclimatise themselves all over again after the austerity of their life in Europe. Everything seemed bigger and better than before, and they found it somewhat overwhelming.

Plum's literary affairs were now in the hands of Scott Meredith, Paul Reynolds having died in 1944. Meredith, upon his demobilisation in late 1946, had bought a dying literary agency and breathed new life into it. Since he had striven so hard to clear Plum's name during the darker days, it was Plum's pleasure to be represented by him. And Meredith hadn't wasted time. Shortly before the arrival of the Wodehouses, he had sold two of Plum's short stories to *Cosmopolitan.* That sale took care of the immediate financial problem of the couple, whose money was tied up in England and France.

Those first few days in New York were hectic. Doubleday, who were planning to publish *Full Moon* the following month, had lined up an impressive series of newspaper, radio and television interviews which plunged their author into the centre of a whirl of activity. Plum had never sought this kind of thing but he had also never failed to co-operate, and so he let it all eddy around him while he observed it with mild wonder. It really seemed to him to be much ado about nothing, as he made clear to Townend in a letter dated 15th May 1947 which chronicled the events so far:

> *. . . It's quite a business arriving in New York now. In the old days the only newspaper man one saw was the ship reporter of the* N.Y. Times, *who sauntered up as one was seeing one's stuff through the Customs and asked if one had had a pleasant voyage, but now a whole gang of reporters flock aboard at Quarantine and a steward comes to you and tells you that the gentlemen of the press are in the saloon and request your presence. It's like being summoned before a Senate Committee.*
>
> *I always get on well with report- ers, and I found them very pleasant, especially the man from* P.M., *one of the evening papers. We became insepa- rable, and last Monday he gave a big dinner for Ethel and me at his home down in Greenwich Village.*
>
> *My second morning I held a formal "Press Conference" at the Dou- bleday offices, with a candid cameraman taking surreptitious photographs all the time. These were the literary columnists. I am going to a cocktail party at the house of one of them next week.*
>
> *Next day I was interviewed on the radio, reaching three hundred and fifty stations, and the day after that on tele- vision. All this sounds as if I were a*

hell of a celebrity, but the explanation is that Doubleday's publicity hound arranges it all in the hope that it will lead to the sale of a copy or two of Full Moon. *I don't suppose it helps a bit, really. I don't imagine the great public sits listening spellbound while I answer questions from the interlocutor, and says: "My God! So that's Wodehouse! How intelligent he looks! What a noble brow! I must certainly buy that last book of his!" Much more probably they reach out and twiddle the knob and get another station.*

. . . New York is simply incredible. About five times larger than when I last saw it. I said in my radio talk that every time I came back to New York it was like meeting an old sweetheart and finding she had put on a lot of weight. The prosperity stuns one after being in France so long. There is nothing in the way of food and drink you can't get here.

Full Moon was duly published on 22nd May 1947 and the public bought it, but there was no way of knowing if the publicity had indeed affected the sales.

Not long after their arrival, the Wodehouses and Wonder moved from the Weylin to a penthouse apartment in the East Sixties, just off Madison Avenue, where Plum was all set to start working. He was particularly anxious to resume his collaboration with Guy Bolton, but Guy and his wife had gone to Europe at the time that Plum and Ethel were on their way to the States. It was a frustrating coincidence as far as Plum was concerned, for he discovered that he needed Guy's advice more than ever before. If nothing else had changed, the world of Broadway certainly had. Its methods now seemed completely different from those he had known; and though he was being offered work for the theatre, he didn't know how to cope with it. Some of his confusion was relayed to Guy in a letter dated 6th July 1947:

> *The theatre here has me absolutely
> squiggle-eyed. I keep getting things of-
> fered to me, but I can't make out if
> they're real solid propositions or not. I
> have adapted a Molnar play and am to
> adapt his new one when he gets it fin-
> ished, but as far as I can make out noth-
> ing is settled about the production of
> either. Now a manager wants Ogden
> Nash and me to make a musical of
> Enter Madame. I believe the money end
> is all right, but he doesn't seem able to
> get a composer and I'm darned if I can
> see how you can make that play into a
> musical.*
>
> *I can't get used to the new Broad-
> way. Apparently you have to write your
> show and get it composed and then give
> a series of auditions to backers, instead
> of having the management line up a
> couple of stars and then get a show
> written for them. It's so damned diffi-
> cult to write a show without knowing
> who you are writing it for. It's like try-
> ing to write lyrics without a book. I feel
> lost without you.*

The eight-year gulf that had separated Plum and Guy was bridged, however, when the Boltons returned from Europe at the end of September and
carried Plum off to stay at their home at Remsenburg, Long Island. Ethel remained in New York, not because she knew that the men would have a lot of
reminiscing to do but because she was looking for a new apartment. She
eventually decided on a suite of rooms at the Hotel Adams, at 2 East 86th
Street, with which Plum was quite pleased when he arrived back from Remsenburg. He mentioned the advantages in a thank-you letter to Guy dated 11th

November 1947:

> It really was wonderful of you to entertain me in such princely fashion for so long, and I loved every minute of my stay at the Bolton Arms. I only wish Ethel could have been with us. She found this hotel and I have just discovered a marvellous roof six floors above us, which will be a great place for me to stroll. And I ought to be able to do a lot of work in my bedroom. It is quite big, and Ethel has bought me a really superb desk. Also, there are French windows opening on a small terrace, so I don't feel closed in.
>
> The only catch is that I am being driven into a corner where I can't escape from starting work on the adaptation of Molnar's new play, and I can't see any chance for it. It's right out of my line, being about a man with heart disease and frightfully medical. It ends with a scene where they do a blood test, and the mere thought of a blood test always gives me the creeps.

But Plum soon found himself involved in something far less chilling. Towards the end of November the longed-for opportunity to again collaborate with Guy presented itself, and the two of them started on an adaptation of a Sacha Guitry play that Guy had brought back from Paris and which they entitled *Don't Listen, Ladies*. When they were half way through it, Plum was delighted to hear from Gilbert Miller that he was going to revive Plum's version of Molnar's *The Play's the Thing*, with Louis Calhern in the lead. It meant that Plum's work would be established on Broadway again in what he considered to be the best possible way. "There's no getting away from it that a Gilbert Miller production is different from any other," he said. "Nobody else gives you that feeling of perfect safety."

He was less enthusiastic, however, about a proposed revival of *Sally* by another management, for which it was planned to include a selection of Kern-Wodehouse songs from various Bolton-Wodehouse-Kern shows. For this production Plum was asked to make some script changes and rewrite the lyrics—which he did, with much scepticism about its chances.

The Play's the Thing opened at the Booth Theatre, New York, on 18th April 1948, and it lived up to all of Plum's expectations. Considering that it was a revival, it had an unusually long run of 244 performances. *Sally,* on the other hand, having opened shortly after *The Play's the Thing,* survived for only thirty-six performances, again fulfilling his prophecy.

There was no doubt now that, despite the war years, Plum was still in fashion. And on 20th May 1948 his steadfast public was rewarded with the simultaneous publication in America by Doubleday and in England by Jenkins of *Spring Fever,* which he had written in Germany.

At this time Guy was in England to supervise the London production of *Don't Listen, Ladies,* but he was not left in the dark about what was going on in New York. His friend and partner kept him in touch with events which, in a letter dated 17th June 1948, proved to be quite varied:

> *Not much news. Milton Schubert, having acquired all Puccini's music, is doing a sort of* Song of Norway *about the life of Puccini, using all his best music. Sounds good, but what about the comedy? That's always the snag. He wants me to do the lyrics.*
>
> *Talking of lyrics, I am simply lost in admiration of Dietz's in* Inside U.S.A. *I had no idea he was such a wizard.*
>
> *. . . Did I tell you that Ethel was in a stick-up? I don't think I did. She was being fitted at her dressmaker's on Madison Avenue and a young man came in with a knife and threw his weight about, collecting fifteen bucks from Ethel and twenty from the dress-*

maker. The big laugh was that Ethel had put her diamond clips on the table and the dressmaker officiously had taken them and put them in Ethel's bag. So when Ethel gaily produced her bag, thinking it contained only $15, she nearly fainted when she saw the clips. Luckily the man overlooked them, so all was well.

I hope you are enjoying yourself in London. By now you must be up to your eyes in theatre rehearsals.

Guy was certainly fully occupied, but his toil was rewarded when *Don't Listen, Ladies* opened at the St. James's Theatre on 2nd September 1948. It was acclaimed by the critics, and it enjoyed a run of 219 performances.

On 22nd October 1948 Herbert Jenkins published the last of the backlog of novels written by Plum during the war, *Uncle Dynamite.* This was the book that had started out under the scrutiny of the French police officers, and it featured Lord Ickenham—more familiarly known as Uncle Fred. One reviewer welcomed it by touching upon the essence of Plum's work:

Now it may be that with the war and the recent experiment in socialism the old environment has dissolved, and is not to be found in the England of today any more than in the United States. But we don't care, we old P. G. Wodehouse fans. His stories are not dated. Considerations of war don't come in, and we don't really know the period depicted. We are off on a Wodehouse binge, and we're not interested in whether he describes England of today or yesterday or just a fantastic England which is a burlesque. We're back where our author is at home.

The reviewer was absolutely right: the whole world knew where "our author" was "at home" in the literary sense. But practically speaking, it was less easy to pin Plum down. The nomadic Wodehouses never seemed to stay very long in one place, and at this time they had just moved again. Their new abode was a duplex apartment at 1000 Park Avenue, and it offered the best kind of outdoor life a thriving and frenetic city could provide. Plum's workroom was on the lower floor of the apartment, but it was the upper floor that had the greatest attraction. It consisted of a long gallery with French windows which gave access to a terrace the size of a suburban garden. There were no high buildings in the vicinity to obstruct a magnificent panoramic view which included Central Park, and Ethel wasted no time in planting a hedge, trees and flowers to give the rooftop paradise a down-to-earth atmosphere. It was on this terrace that she and Plum ate their meals, and they would sit there in the evenings reading and relaxing. But they were not the only ones to benefit from it. Wonder was able to scamper about freely, far above the city's traffic, and even played host there when Guy Bolton's Peke came to the apartment as a temporary guest.

Guy had returned to America as soon as *Don't Listen, Ladies* was safely launched in London, and having spent some months at Remsenburg he was now—at the beginning of May 1949—taking his wife back to England for a while, leaving their Peke, Squeaky, with the Wodehouses. If there had been any anxiety about how Wonder and Squeaky would hit it off together, Plum was able to reassure Guy in a letter dated 12th May 1949:

> *Well, first of all, Squeaky has been a stupendous success. I thought Wonder would have thrown her weight about, but they get on together like Klaw and Erlanger. She really is the most angelic dog in existence. She loves everybody. Her tail never stops wagging, and she is a universal pet. Her passion for me, which one noticed at Remsenburg, is now stronger than ever, and she won't let me out of her sight. If I sneak down to my study and start working, I hear yells of agony on the*

stairs and have to go and open the door, and then she rushes in and I have to nurse her on my lap for about ten minutes before she will settle down on her armchair (where she sleeps at night). Yesterday she insisted on lying on my desk when I was writing. The wonderful thing is that Wonder isn't a bit jealous of her.

With that said, Plum then turned to his favourite topic:

I am very busy now, making a 25,000-word novelette (which will later become a full-length novel) out of that play of mine, Spring Fever. *I wish you would get hold of it and read it and, if possible, give me some plot suggestions. I can see that the start of the play is wrong. It needs a prologue. I start my novelette with a scene showing the heroine turning down the hero because he's too crazy, then go to Hollywood, where "Bill" (whom I have now turned into a woman of the Marie Dressler type) springs on the hero a scheme for buying a literary agency (so that he and she will both be involved in the venture). I think it is an improvement. At present, the venture on which getting the money depends is too casually introduced. I think I can make an adequate book of the thing, but I am doubtful if it is strong enough for a play. I wish I could get something more Hollywoody than that Button Gwynnett autograph. It ought*

> *to be a star's diary or something, which*
> *people are after. I have now made the*
> *B. Gwynnett stuff more plausible by*
> *planting Smedley as a man who is al-*
> *ways buying up second-hand books etc.*
> *in the hope of finding something val-*
> *uable, but I haven't got anything that*
> *really justifies laying the story in Holly-*
> *wood.*

The play to which Plum referred was based on his novel *Spring Fever* but was later retitled *Phipps.*

On 9th September 1949 Herbert Jenkins published *The Mating Season.* This was the Jeeves novel that Plum had completed at St. Germain-en-Laye early in 1947, before returning to America. It had had to wait its turn for publication, but it proved well worth waiting for. The reviewers raved about it, one of them making his point by stating:

> *To Wodehouse fans, there are only*
> *three classifications of his books: good,*
> *better and best.*

The Mating Season, it was felt, was one of the very best.

At this time, Plum was commissioned by a London management to rewrite a play called *Keep Your Head.* Assured that he would not have to bother with rehearsals and tryouts, he was pleased to do it. But its main attraction for him was that it was a thriller. As a confirmed detective-story addict, he would have enjoyed doing it no matter what the conditions. His delight in it was conveyed to Guy in a letter which also gave other theatre news:

> *Vast activity prevailing chez Wode-*
> *house. A man named E. P. Conkle—*
> *quite celebrated, they tell me, as an*
> *American "folk" playwright—has writ-*
> *ten a thriller which is no earthly good*
> *as it stands but has a fine central idea,*

and I am turning it into a comedy thriller. I have had an advance so it looks like a cert for production. It is coming out extraordinarily well. Meanwhile, John Schubert and Romberg have formed a company and want me to do a musical with Arnold Horwitt, the chap who wrote Make Mine Manhattan, *for early production. No advance or contract yet on this one, but I think it will be all right. Horwitt is one of those revue men, very bright and full of ideas for scenes but not so hot at plot, and I have had to do a lot of solid thinking. Something seemed to emerge this morning, and I am feeling more hopeful. But I hate working on a musical unless it's with you. When you and I talk a plot over, we diverge into all sorts of outside topics and the old brain, rested, comes up with something. But with Horwitt I feel that if I talk of anything except the play he will think I'm slacking.*

Far from slacking, Plum was as busy as he had ever been; and he was reminded of his early days of ceaseless productivity when he read that the *Strand* was coming to an end and would be publishing its final number in March of the following year. Commenting on this passing from the scene of yet another magazine, he wrote to Townend:

> *. . . As practically everything I have written since July 1905 appeared in the* Strand, *I drop a silent tear, but I can't say I'm much surprised, for anything sicker-looking than the little midget it had shrunk to I never saw.*

Inevitable, I suppose, because of the paper shortage. And in my opinion never anything worth reading in it, either, the last year or two.

How on earth does a young writer of light fiction get going these days? Where can he sell his stories? When you and I were breaking in, we might get turned down by the Strand *and* Pearson's, *but there was always the hope of landing with* Nash's, *the* Storyteller, *the* Royal, *the* Novel, *the* Grand, *the* Pall Mall, *and the* Windsor . . . *and probably about a dozen more I've forgotten.*

What, indeed, had happened to the magazine market? The decline was as marked in America as it was in England: and the cause was television. Writers were turning to this new and more lucrative medium, which gobbled up their output and cried for more, and they had no time for the magazines. The magazines, in consequence, cut down on their content until they had reduced themselves out of existence. But the threat of television to all other forms of entertainment was in its infancy. Books were also to suffer.

The time was now drawing near for Plum and Ethel to renew their American visas—something unheard of in the days of Plum's constant transatlantic scurryings. As things were now, he would have to apply for a visitor's visa every six months. But there was a way around this. It meant spending a night on Canadian soil and re-entering the United States on the Canadian quota. The Wodehouses therefore went to Niagara Falls on 16th December 1949, stayed overnight and reported next morning for the necessary medical examination before returning to the States. Plum had no worries on this score, having always kept himself in good physical condition, and he was not surprised that his chest X-ray showed him to be in perfect health. But he found it disquieting to be told that there were indications of approaching deafness in his left ear. He had not been aware of any deficiency in his hearing. It was something for him to think about, but it did not materially affect his medical record and he was permitted to enter the United States on a permanent visa. Writing to Townend about it the day following his return, he neglected to mention the ear trouble:

> . . . *Next day the Consul drove me in his car to Buffalo, which saved me some tedious travelling, and I am now back home on the quota, so unless I plot to upset the American Government by violence—which I doubt if I shall do; you know how busy one is—I can't be taken by the seat of the trousers and slung out.*
>
> *But, gosh, what a lot of red tape, as the man said when they tried him for murdering his wife. I remember the time when I would be strolling along Piccadilly on a Tuesday morning and suddenly say to myself: "I think I'll go to America," and at noon on the Wednesday I would be on the boat en route for New York. No passports, no visas, nothing. Just like that.*

Secure now as far as staying in America was concerned, Plum spent the first half of 1950 working on two plays—one of which was his own, based on the novel *Spring Fever*. The other was someone else's original piece, called *The House on the Cliff*, which had been produced with disastrous results the previous season and which he had been asked to rewrite. There was some urgency about this one, for the management had already contracted Fay Bainter and Ian Keith to appear in it and were anxious to get it into rehearsal. It meant that Plum had to go with the company to Skowhegan, Maine, where rehearsals were begun on 17th July prior to the first tryout, and continue his rewriting, readjusting and polishing while the pre-Broadway tour was in progress. There were ten days of rehearsals at Skowhegan followed by eight performances, and then the company moved on to Watkins Glen in the state of New York—a distance of six hundred and fifty miles.

Plum made the journey by road, rising at five-thirty a.m. and travelling all day and most of the night. He was not unused to moving around, of course, but he preferred doing it in easy stages and at a more leisurely pace. As he wrote to Townend:

> I enjoy my little bit of motoring as a rule, but it's a pretty gruesome experience to realise, after you have gone three hundred miles, that you have scarcely scratched the surface, so to speak, and there are still another four hundred to go. Even assuming, mind you, that there was such a place as Watkins Glen. We had only the management's word for it, and they might easily have made a mistake.
>
> . . . Well, sir, it turned out that there really was a place called Watkins Glen, and we reached it at four in the morning. We stayed there a week, playing in the High School Auditorium with an enormous basketball arena behind the stage. This rendered the show completely inaudible.

Whatever the shortcomings of Watkins Glen, they were more than compensated for by the unexpected arrival of Ethel. Plum had reluctantly left her in New York at the start of the tour, but a sudden impulse had prompted her to join him. She had acted on that impulse by going to a car showroom, selecting a Nash, buying it on the spot and immediately driving the two hundred miles from New York to Watkins Glen. Plum was delighted. He had just been thinking that if Watkins Glen needed anything it was Ethel. And it must have been her presence that inspired him there and then to complete his work on the play—for which, although he had done his best with it, he held out little hope. He was therefore happy to be free to return to New York with Ethel when the company moved on to Chicago. It was enough for him to be able to follow the play's progress by means of newspaper accounts, all of which confirmed his forebodings. He was moved to express his feelings about it, he wrote to Townend, by echoing the sentiments of James Thurber who, when asked what he thought was wrong with his latest play, said, "It had only one fault. It was kind of lousy."

All was not gloomy, however. On the credit side, while he had been working on the ill-fated play, Herbert Jenkins had published a collection of his short stories under the title *Nothing Serious.* The book came out on 21st July 1950.

Recovered from the exhaustions of the tour, Plum turned his attention once again to his own play. After writing six versions of it, he realised that it had become so far removed from *Spring Fever,* upon which it had originally been based, that it would now provide the material for an entirely new novel. No further thought was necessary. He started writing the book without delay, calling it *The Old Reliable.*

No sooner was *The Old Reliable* completed, in mid February 1951, than Plum had what he described to Townend as "a giddy attack. (At least, it's not exactly giddiness. The scenery doesn't get blurred or jump about. It's just that I lose control of my legs)." It seemed serious enough, though, to warrant the seeking of medical advice; and the conclusion drawn from an initial series of tests was far from encouraging. He had, it appeared, a brain tumour. Other opinions were sought and further examinations and tests, including a spinal tap, reversed this terrifying diagnosis but produced nothing specific to put in its place. The doctors confessed themselves baffled. One school of thought had it that his eyes were the cause of the attacks; another put the blame on his ears. But through it all, the subject of these clinical ponderings remained philosophically calm and—on the surface, at least—cheerful. Giving Townend a run-down on his general state of health, he wrote:

> *The score, then, to date is that I am deaf in the left ear, bald, subject to mysterious giddy fits, and practically cockeyed. I suppose the moral of the whole thing is that I have simply got to realise that I am a few months off being seventy. I had been going along as if I were in the forties, eating and drinking everything I wanted to*

and smoking far too much. I had al-
ways looked on myself as a sort of
freak whom age could not touch, which
was where I made my ruddy error, be-
cause I'm really a senile wreck with
about one and a half feet in the grave.

(My doctor, by the way, summing
up on the subject of the giddy fits and
confessing his inability to explain them,
said, "Well, if you have any more, you'd
better just have them." I said I would.)

By the time *The Old Reliable* was published by Herbert Jenkins, on 18th April 1951, Plum was feeling better and was back at work on the play from which it had sprung. Doing the one from the other had been a complicated business, and there were still problems concerning the play which Plum would have liked to discuss at first hand with Guy Bolton. But Guy was again in England, and his comments could be obtained only by way of correspondence. Plum therefore wrote to him on 11th May 1951 and, in seeking advice about the play, detailed some of the difficulties that had attended the writing of *The Old Reliable:*

I am writing to Jenkins to send you
a copy of the novel [The Old Reli-
able], *as it has stuff in it which is not*
in the play. What happened—and it
has been an experience that has made
my head swim—was that I started off,
as you know, by making a play out
of my novel Spring Fever, *using all*
that stuff about the stamp. Then bit by
bit in the course of writing six new
versions, I shoved in every good line
I could find in my other books, so that
when I came to write the novel from
the play, I had to concentrate like the
dickens in order to cut out these lines.

> *There are still some of them in, dam-*
> *mit, notably "Do the police want you?"*
> *"No, they don't." "How I sympathise*
> *with the police. I know exactly how*
> *they feel," which is from a novel*
> *called* Full Moon. *When you read* The
> Old Reliable, *you will see that I am*
> *making Bill (the "Jane" of the play)*
> *trying to get money to start a literary*
> *agency. This was because I had used*
> *the stuff about the country club in* Full
> Moon. *Maybe the literary agency idea*
> *is better than the country club. Any-*
> *way, glance through* The Old Reliable,
> *if you think it will help you at all. I*
> *think the characters come out better*
> *in the book than in the play, as I could*
> *take so much more room in the book.*

The fact that turning the play into a book had given him more scope with the characters was something that remained in Plum's mind. He could see possibilities in it that, later that spring, while he waited for Guy's thoughts on the play, he began to explore. A play that had appealed to him immensely was George S. Kaufman's comedy *The Butter and Egg Man,* which had been one of the Broadway successes of 1925. The more he thought about it the more certain he became that it would make a good novel, and he was soon writing to Kaufman about it. To his delight, Kaufman responded to the suggestion with great enthusiasm.

George S. Kaufman had started his career as a drama critic and had ended up as one of the greatest of American playwrights. His comedies were pure Americana, their plots woven around situations which were unique to the United States in their commentary on politics, the economy and society: and *The Butter and Egg Man* bore his unmistakable stamp. Since its humour was so typically Kaufman, it may seem surprising that Plum should have chosen to adapt it to his own particular style; but he set to work on it with a will and at a rate that he hadn't matched for some time. By 12th August, the book—called *Barmy in Wonderland*—was finished. It had taken just three months, making it the fastest time for the writing of one of Plum's books since before the war. But to what extent the endeavour had been successful remained to be seen.

At the beginning of October, Plum started working on a new Blandings Castle novel to be called *Pigs Have Wings*. It progressed well, with only one major interruption when Guy Bolton's version of the *Spring Fever* play was received. Writing to Guy on 12th December 1951, Plum said:

> *I have just finished reading the play, which arrived this morning, and I think it's terrific. I propose to change the title to* Phipps *as I don't think* Spring Fever *gives the right idea of the play. Glutz is a wonderful character. Until nearly the end I thought he led the field. But Phipps comes out very strong at the finish. I like your ending.*
>
> *You know I always regard your stuff as sacred writ, but as a butler is involved and butlers are my specialty, I have taken the lib of touching up Phipps's dialogue a little. I thought once or twice you made him too colloquial and lost the butler flavour— just little things like him saying "I don't think" when it seemed to me that "I am not aware" would be better. And I shoved in a lot of "sirs" and "madams."*

It is a sad consequence that, despite the hard labour that went into it, *Phipps* was never produced.

At about this time Herbert Jenkins reissued an anthology called *Week-end Wodehouse*, which they had originally published in 1939 but which had been out of print for many years. One old friend who was glad to see it was Ian Hay, who wrote:

> *I have just been reading* Weekend
> Wodehouse, *which has recently been
> published here, with intense enjoy-
> ment. Most of the stories, of course,
> are old friends, especially "Lord Ems-
> worth and his Girl Friend," which Rud-
> yard Kipling once told me was one of
> the most perfect short stories he had
> ever read.*

If Plum blushed with pleasure at the compliment, no one was on hand to record it.

Having worked on *Pigs Have Wings* every day without fail for sixteen weeks, he was putting the finishing touches to it in March 1952 when Guy suggested a collaboration on a play to feature Jeeves. Plum was all for it, and he and Ethel left their Park Avenue apartment to stay with the Boltons at Remsenburg so that the work could proceed undisturbed. While the two men were mapping out the proposed play, Mrs. Bolton took Ethel on a sightseeing tour of the small village. And Ethel liked what she saw. She was taken not only with the peaceful surroundings but also with a ten-room furnished house that stood enticingly vacant in the attractively named Basket Neck Lane, just three-quarters of a mile from the Bolton residence. The house was isolated enough to be reminiscent of Low Wood, and yet was in close enough proximity to the Boltons to recall the days at Great Neck when the Wodehouses and the Boltons were neighbours. It was something to think about. . . .

A few evenings later, Ethel—having so far kept her own counsel— mildly announced to her husband and friends that she had just acted on one of her impulses and purchased a nearby house. Plum, accustomed as he was to Ethel's impulses, was surprised and also delighted. He could have wished for nothing better than to live near Guy again, in addition to which he was already convinced that the atmosphere of Remsenburg was conducive to work. Some alterations would have to be made to the house before he and Ethel could move in, but the prospect was pleasant to contemplate.

Meanwhile, on 21st April 1952 Herbert Jenkins published *Barmy in Wonderland,* and on 8th May 1952 it was published in America by Double-day under the title *Angel Cake.* In both countries it was a great success in the Wodehouse tradition. There was nothing about it, apart from the dedication in the American edition, to suggest that it was not pure Wodehouse. And it remains probably the best example of what Plum meant by his oft-repeated maxim that the treatment of a novel is more vital than the plot. Indeed, when talking about how he turned Kaufman's play into a book, he prefaced his remarks with the statement that "it isn't the plot that's important but the treatment, which is everything. In the play, the hero is a guileless young American from the Middle West who is talked by a tough Broadway manager into putting money into a production. I made him a guileless young Englishman, added several characters, and changed the heroine a good deal. George and I split the proceeds fifty-fifty. The book was published under my name and the reviewer of *The New York Times* was very nice about it, but he clicked his tongue in the final paragraph. He wrote, 'After all these years, by the way, Wodehouse has not learned to imitate colloquial American. His Broadway characters talk like Aaron Slick of Punkin Crick, which rather tends to spoil the effect.' " But Plum was not too deeply wounded by this criticism because, as he gleefully pointed out, "Every single line of the Broadway characters' dialogue was Kaufman's, that recognised master of Broadway slang."

On 1st June, Ethel moved into the Basket Neck Lane house to supervise the reconstruction work. She was mainly concerned with a working area for Plum, knowing by now that his taste didn't run to exquisitely elegant libraries. There was a sun-porch running the entire length of the house, and this she had bisected by a soundproof wall—on one side of which was constructed a bedroom, with adjoining bathroom, from which there was access through an open archway to a cosy study. It seemed ideal.

By July the house was ready and the Wodehouses were in occupation, together with an odd assortment of unexpected permanent guests about whom Plum wrote to Townend in some detail on 5th July 1952:

> *The above is where we have just bought a house. When writing, address the letter "Remsenburg, L.I." because it's one of those primitive hamlets where you don't have a postman, but go and fetch your mail from the post office.*

I went up to New York for a few days while Ethel stayed here to see the furniture put in. I rang her up one night and asked how things were going, and she said everything looked pretty smooth. "But," she added in a melancholy voice, "a foxhound has turned up." It seems that she was just warming to her work when she looked round and there was this foxhound. It came into the garden and sat down, looking on. It was in an advanced state of starvation, and so covered with ticks that it took two hours to get them off. These beastly ticks get on the dogs and swell to the size of marbles. The poor animal had hardly any blood left in him, and had to be taken to the vet for transfusions. When I came down, he was quite restored and full of beans. We can't imagine where he came from.

The next thing that happened was that we went to a man's birthday party in Quogue and somebody had given him two guinea hens as a present. Ethel asked him what he was going to do with them, and he said "Eat 'em." Ethel was horrified, and asked if she could have them. So we took them away and built a large run for them in the garden; and they settled down very happily.

A few nights later we heard something crying in the dark and went out and there was a tiny white kitten. This was added to the strength.

About a week after that I was

walking to get the mail when I saw a car ahead of me suddenly swerve and it seemed to me that there was a small dark object in the middle of the road. I went up, and it was a black kitten. I picked it up and put it on my shoulder, and it sang to me all the way to the post office and back, shoving its nose against my face. It, too, has been added to the menagerie, so the score now is one foxhound, two guinea hens, Squeaky, our Peke, and two kittens, and we are hourly expecting more cats and dogs to arrive. I think the word must have gone round the animal kingdom that if you want a home just drop in at Basket Neck Lane, where the Wodehouses keep open house.

The bright side is that all our animals get along together like sailors on shore leave. Bill, the foxhound, has the most angelic disposition and lets the kittens run all over him, while Squeaky, of course, would never dream of hurting anything. A very united family, thank goodness.

With peace prevailing on all fronts, Plum and Guy finished their play later that summer. Its plot centred around the efforts of Jeeves to help an impecunious young peer to become a Silver Ring bookie, and they had aptly called it *Derby Day.* When they learned that there was already a film of that title, however, they had to think again; and their eventual choice was *Come On, Jeeves.* The play was bought by a London management for presentation the following year, but Plum's interest in it didn't stop there. He was by now an old hand at turning plays into novels, and he had never been one to waste a potentially good plot. So without giving the idea time to cool off, he started writing the book of the play: and he finished it quite quickly. It was his sixth Jeeves novel, and he called it *Ring For Jeeves.*

At the beginning of September, Plum found himself faced with the task of editing his own writing in a manuscript that had been prepared by William Townend. Throughout the thirty-two years of their correspondence to date, Townend had kept all of Plum's letters; and it had occurred to him that a selection of them would make an autobiographical type of book which would be not only fascinating to Wodehouse fans but also of instructional value to aspiring young writers. The manuscript contained Townend's selection, together with his Introduction to the book and his personal asides that would link the letters. To give the book pace and interest, it was left to Plum to rework the material—cutting and, where necessary, rephrasing. It was a formidable undertaking, as Plum made clear in a letter to J. Derek Grimsdick, managing director of Herbert Jenkins Limited:

> *. . . When Townend sent me the letters, they must have run to about 200,-000 words, and I cut 70,000 right away. After that I was continually cutting, but also adding, so that now it must be about 120,000. I think we ought to cut a lot more.*

But before Plum could more than scratch the surface of this project, which was to bear the title *Performing Flea,* he and Guy were commissioned by Simon & Schuster (Plum's new American publishers) to write the book that Plum had first excitedly proposed to Guy in 1946—the story of their theatrical experiences, which Plum had then intended to call *Book and Lyrics.* There had been a change of heart about the title and it was now going to be *Bring on the Girls,* but in essence it would be the book that Plum had originally envisaged: a mixture of fact and fiction; largely autobiographical but with no strictures on embroidering the truth where it would serve to add humour to a situation. The prospect appealed immensely to the co-authors and they gave it their immediate attention, working on it until November—when Plum and Ethel went back to their New York apartment for the winter.

With the writing of *Bring on the Girls* completed, it was left to Plum to give the book its final polish: and Simon & Schuster were unequivocally delighted with the result. Enthusiasm on the other side of the Atlantic was cautious, however. Mr. Grimsdick of Jenkins liked the book in principle, but he felt that it was too strongly slanted towards the interests of an American audience to have equal appeal in Britain. There followed a flood of correspondence between Plum, Mr. Grimsdick and Peter Schwed of Simon & Schuster, the outcome being that there would be a revised version of the book for the British market. In the final analysis, both versions contained a fine sense of theatre and were considered a valuable contribution to theatre history. So everyone was happy.

Plum was now able to concentrate on *Performing Flea* which, like *Bring on the Girls,* needed to be taken with a grain of salt as far as some of the incidents described were concerned but which nevertheless contained an honest expression of his opinions and feelings in addition to much invaluable advice.

The new year was to see a return to the field of Plum's initial literary endeavours. Many years had passed since he had written for the magazine market; but at the beginning of 1953 Malcolm Muggeridge was appointed editor of *Punch,* and one of his first actions was to invite Plum to become a regular contributor. The magazine, one of the most famous of humorous journals, had lost much of its lustre in recent years and was more or less in the doldrums when Muggeridge took charge. But Muggeridge had vigorous ideas for revitalising it and was intent upon securing the services of the world's leading humorous writers. It was natural that Plum's name should be at the head of his list. The consequence was that Plum's first humorous article for *Punch* in forty-six years appeared on 15th July 1953.

October of that year saw the publication of the two semi-autobiographical books, one in America and one in England. On 5th October 1953 Simon & Schuster published *Bring on the Girls,* and on 9th October 1953 Herbert Jenkins published *Performing Flea.* It was undeniably a good month for almost-true stories. But with them behind him, Plum was already at work on a new Wooster-Jeeves story which was a continuation of the saga that had commenced with *The Code of the Woosters* and *Joy in the Morning.* He called it *Jeeves and the Feudal Spirit* and had finished it by April 1954.

The ideas were flowing again, and there was scarcely a pause between the completion of *Jeeves and the Feudal Spirit* and the start of preliminary work on a novel to be called *French Leave.* This one, as its title implied, was set in France—the first book to depart from the customary England/

America backgrounds since *Hot Water* in 1932. It took Plum the best part of a year to write it, and it was not finished to his satisfaction until March 1955.

Since buying the house in Basket Neck Lane, Plum and Ethel had been using it only as a summer residence. On 1st May 1955, however, they gave up their New York apartment and settled permanently in Remsenburg. New York had become altogether too noisy and frenetic for Plum, and he no longer wished to see quite so many people. All he really wanted was to be left alone with Ethel, the animals, his pipe, his books, and the thoughts that would evolve into new stories. Ethel, for her part, was content with the move. With the knowledge that this was to be their permanent home, she brought all of her organising ability into play in the arranging of the environment in which they would live. She had a large lawn laid in front of the house, replete with flowers, plants and trees decorating its sides, and she also devised a breathtaking garden behind the house which, especially in the summer, was not only picturesque but also a perfect haven for rest and meditation.

The driveway, which curved to the left of the house, came to rest at a two-car garage—for although Plum didn't drive, he started out by keeping two cars. (He eventually gave his to the housemaid so that she could commute between Basket Neck Lane and her own home; but Ethel retained her 1950 Nash.) To the right of the driveway was woodland—seven acres of it—into which Plum would delve daily with his dogs, Debby, a boxer, and Jed, a dachshund. While giving them their exercise, he would think out the complications of whichever plot he was working on; and as an aid to thought he would take with him a pipe with an extra-large bowl, into which he would cram tobacco derived from crushed cigars.

A river ran past the property, at the far end of the woodland, but it had become unsuitable for swimming and boating as the result of a hurricane which had deposited an enormous amount of debris in it several years before. That was only a minor disappointment in a situation which was otherwise ideal. In Remsenburg, Plum and Ethel felt that they had come home. The days of aimless wandering were over.

Plans for Plum's next novel were unusually ambitious. It was hoped that he would write a story involving all of his major established characters— what Simon & Schuster described as "an all-star Wodehouse novel." When it came to it, however, he was unable to evolve a plot of sufficient strength and the idea had to be abandoned. Instead, he began toying with the possibility of utilising some of his *Punch* articles for a volume. He didn't think that a straightforward collection of articles would have great appeal, but he felt that if he worked on the pieces and put them into an autobiographical framework the result could be an amusing book. At the very least, an amusing autobiography should be a welcome relief from the spate of "frank confession" books that were then passing as autobiographies. It seemed worth a try.

He started working on the book in July 1955, calling it *America, I Like You*—taken from the title of a popular song by Bert Kalmar and Harry Ruby. Like *Bring on the Girls* and *Performing Flea,* it was a mixture of fact and fiction, and it gave him a great deal of trouble right from the start. He felt that he was too close to the material to trust his own judgment, and he really needed the advice of an outsider who would be unbiased. For one thing, he thought he had a tendency to drag out his funny stories—over-elaborating in an effort to drain the last drop of humour from each situation. He was therefore constantly cutting them and endeavouring to give them a snap finish.

It would have been unusual if Plum had been working on only one project at a time, so even the difficulties that were arising out of *America, I Like You* couldn't prevent him from starting another novel. This time it was a book which did not fit into any of his series categories. Called *Something Fishy,* its only familiar character was Keggs—now an ex-butler and, having lost the rough manner he had sported in *The Good Angel,* a lovable old man. The plot was more than customarily complex and full of suspense, making the book really something of a mystery story.

On 8th September 1955, while very much involved with the two books —and perhaps not a little influenced by *America, I Like You*—Plum took a step he had been contemplating for some time. He went to Riverhead, Long Island, and filed naturalisation papers, having been in the United States a little over the required five years. And on 16th December 1955 Justice D. Ormonde Ritchie of the Supreme Court in Suffolk County administered the oath of allegiance to ninety-one petitioners, one of whom was Pelham Grenville Wodehouse. At the age of seventy-four, he had become an American citizen.

After the ceremony, Plum told an enquiring newspaper reporter that he had no intention of returning to England, that he hadn't lived there since

1934 and that the last time he had been there was in 1939, when Oxford University had awarded him the honorary degree of Doctor of Literature. Quoting Kipling, Plum said, "You can't cross old trails. . . . After all, I've lived over here for many years now. I just wanted to make it official. It's like being asked to join a very good club."

Among the congratulatory letters he received was one from the famous American humorist Frank Sullivan:

December 17, 1955.

Dear Plum,

The happy news that you had joined our club met my eye in this morning's Herald Tribune *and I hasten to offer congratulations to you. Also, to this country, as I consider you one of the most valuable acquisitions we have made in a long time. I have given it careful thought and my opinion is that your becoming an American citizen makes up for our loss of T.S. Eliot and Henry James combined. I think you'll like the club, although the dues often seem heavy, payable on March 15 and quarterly thereafter. But there are no meetings to attend and there is no house committee except the House Committee on Appropriations, so-called because it appropriates your money and mine and uses it to build dams and other public works, usually in parts of the country to which you and I are indifferent. (They haven't built a damn dam in Saratoga within my memory.) I have been a member of the club for sixty-three years now and I think I'll stay. I was sort of born into it because my mother and father, with admirable foresight, left the Counties Limerick and Kerry, respectively, in the 1870s and settled here on a spot three blocks from the best racetrack in the country. That was my father's idea, I'm sure. But it is no great transition for you, you having been a kind of honorary member of the club for a long time and have contributed more to its general well-being and high spirits than any citizen since Samuel Langhorne Clemens.*

As you know, having formally become a citizen, you now have the inalienable right to abuse the Government. I hope you will take full advantage of this pleasant privilege, when feeling logy and out of sorts. It is wonderful as a pepper-upper and my psychoanalyst says it rids you of all that repressed bile and libido and old pieces of orange peel that accumulate in the ego and curdle the milk of human kindness. If you don't know how to abuse the Guv'mint I will be glad to teach you in six easy lessons.

My hearty wishes to Mrs. Wodehouse and you for the happiest sort of Christmas and for a prosperous and happy 1956!

Yours cordially,
Frank Sullivan.

Telling William Townend of his naturalisation, Plum wrote: "Thank God for being an American (I don't mean God is, I mean I am)."

12 1956 on

On 2nd January 1956 Plum sent a congratulatory cable to Professor Gilbert Murray, the Greek scholar and authority on Homer, whose ninetieth birthday it was. He greatly admired and respected the professor and was therefore particularly pleased to receive a letter of thanks from him in which he said:

> *The first three telegrams I received were from the Prime Minister of this country, the Prime Minister of Australia, and you, an illustrious trio. As a matter of fact, I had been on the point of sending you a reproachful letter because I want a new volume from you. When I turn from more worldly matters to refresh my spirit with some book of yours, my secretary complains, "But you know this one by heart"— which is generally the case. True, my collection is incomplete. I have only eighteen volumes under my hand because so many people borrow and don't return, which I recognise as not your fault except indirectly that you tempt them.*

There was one thing about which the professor need have had no fear: a new volume was indeed in the offing. It was only Plum who had any anxiety about it, having spent what had seemed like an extraordinarily long fifteen months in completing it. By the time copies of the typescript of *Something Fishy* were on the way to J. Derek Grimsdick in London and Peter Schwed in New York he had, in fact, lost his initial enthusiasm for the story and was more than usually apprehensive about its reception. It was consequently with vast relief that he received Peter Schwed's letter of 31st July 1956, which told him:

Something Fishy seems to be just about a perfect work of art and I am about to send it to press for spring publication. I would have only one editorial suggestion. On page 21 when Keggs brings out his piece of chicanery in the pub, it would seem to me to point out the winning of the bet more effectively if the following small addition were made.

Your text reads, " 'Oh, that Jack Dempsey?' he said with one of those faint tolerant smiles. 'I was not referring to him. Naturally, I meant the original Jack Dempsey, the Nonpareil.' " I would suggest that the beginning of the incident read, " 'Oh, that Jack Dempsey?' he said with one of those faint tolerant smiles. 'His name was William Harrison Dempsey. I was not referring to him. Naturally, I meant the original Jack Dempsey, the Nonpareil.' "

Do you agree?

The only other point which seems to be worthy of discussion is whether or not the title Something Fishy *is the ideal title. I am very sympathetic to anyone who says "You don't like that title. Suggest a better one," and I will put my giant brain to work on it. But you might do the same. There is still plenty of time on this in any case.*

Never averse to constructive criticism and always ready to act on what he considered to be good advice, Plum immediately replied:

It's wonderful that you think S.

Fishy is so good. I don't think I have ever put in so much work on a book. I took eight months thinking it out and seven for writing it. Snags kept coming up all the time, and when I started in on the final version I had three *scripts on the desk in front of me, each about 200 pages long and all different.*

Of course that suggestion of yours about William Harrison Dempsey is genius. I had grave doubts all along whether the landlord would have given the stakes to Keggs and not returned them to the various punters because there had been a misunderstanding in the terms of the wager. Will you alter the script as in your letter.

As regards the title. Grimsdick liked it as *a title but thought there might be some confusion because forty years ago I had a book published in England called* Something Fresh. *I pointed out to him that the damn thing only sold 35 copies last year and it is forgotten except in a very small circle of fans, and so we are calling it S.F. in England. But I have a feeling that you are right about this title for American publication. "Fishy" has rather an English ring. Originally I called the story* Close on a Million, *which I subsequently changed to* The Jackpot, *but finally settled on* Something Fishy *as I thought it a lucky title, the first serial I ever sold to the* Saturday Evening Post *being called* Something New (*changed to* Fresh *in England, I don't know why*).

If you think either of the above
titles would do, we'll go ahead. If not,
we shall have to dig up something.

Neither of Plum's suggested titles caused his American publishers to throw their hats in the air and declare a public holiday, and there was further cogitation before they finally decided on *The Butler Did It*—which proved to be as lucky a title as *Something Fishy* when the book became Plum's biggest seller in America since the end of World War II.

By now, Mr. Grimsdick was interested in taking the autobiographical *America, I Like You* for the Herbert Jenkins list, but felt that it should be rewritten with the British public in mind. Coincidentally, Plum had himself been mulling over such a possibility for some time and needed only the encouragement to go ahead with the idea. Using the American volume as a working draft, he gave the book an entirely new slant by turning it into reflections on various topics, drawn from his *Punch* articles, and adding more about his early life. The result, called *Over Seventy,* was a great improvement on *America, I Like You*—a comparison of the two books showing how meticulous and painstaking Plum could be in adapting his own work.

While engaged on this major rewrite, he was struck with an idea for a new Uncle Fred novel and immediately began to get it down on paper. His biggest private worry at this time was his slowness in formulating ideas and developing them, and the progress of the work of fiction gave him no cause to think that the situation was improving. Called *Cocktail Time*—a title suggested by Ethel, as others had been in the past—it was the source of constant trouble and frustration. But it was finished by October 1957, at which time Peter Schwed began urging for an American version of *Performing Flea.* Since in publication by Jenkins in 1953, Schwed had been hoping to do an edition of it in America and had frequently mentioned it in a tentative way. In a letter to Plum dated 17th October 1957, however, he was more specific:

Have you given serious thought to
my proposal that you do a major re-
vision and rewriting job on Performing Flea *for the American audience? I*
think if you jazzed it up with real and
fictitious letters, bringing it up to date

but concentrating on advice, chit-chat and other matters relating to the writing craft, you might have one of the great textbooks of the writing trade. Really, Plum, I think you could make a winner out of this but it would require a complete rewrite. I've never known whether you were politely enthusiastic or rather cool to the idea and I wish you'd set me straight. . . .

P.S. What is Over Seventy *which I see listed as a forthcoming publication in the* London Times *Literary Supplement?*

In his reply of 21st October, Plum showed an encouraging interest in Schwed's proposition—but not before he'd unburdened himself about his latest novel:

I hope you will like Cocktail Time. *For some reason it was a difficult one to write, as my scenario let me down. I suddenly found the middle of the story was all wrong and that what I had been relying on as big scenes wouldn't write. The character of old Mr. Saxby wasn't in the scenario at all; but I think it all worked out well in the end.*

Over Seventy *is the English equivalent of* America, I Like You. *It has at least 40,000 words of new stuff. I am sending you a copy. I have an idea that we can get a good book by combining this new stuff with some of the* Performing Flea *material. I am not very keen on P. F.'s letter form, and this would make a good switch.*

> *As you will see when you get the*
> *book,* Over Seventy *is much more firmly*
> *based than* America, I Like You. *It has*
> *a framework into which one can insert*
> *anything. As, for instance, the advice*
> *to writers which you mention. But no*
> *good talking much about it till you*
> *have read the book.*
>
> *As you say, P. F. would have to*
> *have a complete rewrite for America,*
> *and this might be the way to do it.*

But despite his obvious interest in rewriting *Performing Flea,* it was to be some time before Plum would get around to it. Early in 1958 he was taken with an idea for a Wooster-Jeeves novel, and this took precedence over all else. If he imagined that he was going to be able to dash the book off quickly, however, he was due for a disappointment. The months dragged by and progress was maddeningly slow. At times it seemed that the plot would never fall into place, and his growing frustration only made matters worse. He therefore gave himself a break by putting the novel aside and writing several short stories which later appeared in a volume called *A Few Quick Ones.* Of these, the tale entitled "Jeeves Makes an Omelette" was an adaptation of the original Reggie Pepper story "Doing Clarence a Bit of Good"—the new treatment of a plot first conceived forty-six years earlier, making it a prime example of how Plum's style had changed and developed.

Towards the end of April 1959, having returned to his tussle with the novel, Plum suddenly had one of his inexplicable giddy attacks. It was the first since 1951 and it was more severe than its forerunners. This time, in addition to losing control of his legs, he developed a fever and became too weak to get out of bed. Not unnaturally, his condition caused him some concern; but he remembered his doctor saying of the attacks "if you have any more, you'd better just have them," and he also remembered lightly agreeing that he'd do just that. There seemed little alternative anyway. So he stayed in bed and, remaining reasonably calm, let the attack run its course. Within two weeks he was on his feet again, and shortly afterwards he was enjoying his customary good health as if nothing had happened. He was no nearer knowing what the attacks were all about, but he was prepared to take any further ones in his philosophical stride.

Not long after his recovery, there was a reminder of a past success in the theatre with an off-Broadway revival of the Bolton-Wodehouse-Kern musical *Leave it to Jane*. Opening on 25th May 1959 with Kathleen Murray and Art Matthews in the leading roles, the show started out as just one of hundreds of similar off-Broadway offerings. Only seven reviewers deigned to notice it. Three of them liked it, two didn't, and two were of divided opinion. But its audiences appeared to have no doubts at all, and business began to pick up quite suddenly as appreciation of the show was spread by word of mouth. So effective was this that it soon became clear that the production was in for a long run.

On the evening of the hundredth performance of *Leave it to Jane*, on 18th December 1959, Guy Bolton, Plum, and the three surviving members of the original 1917 cast were invited to see the show and attend a party in their honour afterwards. It was Plum's first sight of the revival, and also his first visit to a theatre in four years, and newspaper reporters present were avid for his reactions. They were especially interested in his views on current musicals and were later able to quote him as saying:

> My Fair Lady *was the last musical production I saw in New York City. I hated it. It seemed to me dull. I may have been awfully tired because I motored up and had dinner at Sardi's and went on to the show. I probably wasn't in the mood for it, because I seem the only fellow in existence who didn't like it. I hardly ever go to the theatre— didn't even when I was in New York. I saw* Guys *and* Dolls. *I rather liked that. But I'm not frightfully keen on the modern musicals today. They seem long and heavy. They always seem to be a quarter of an hour too long. I do think, though, that the lyrics of today's musicals are fine.*

Leave it to Jane went on to achieve 928 performances, thus establishing itself among the five longest-running off-Broadway shows in American theatre history.

A heart-warming compliment from England saw 1960 away to a promising start when, on 27th January, Plum was notified that he had been elected to the *Punch* Table—a privilege reserved for the magazine's most illustrious contributors and editors. The Table, a relic of the founding of *Punch* in 1841, stood in the centre of a room at 10 Bouverie Street, London, overlooked by oil-paintings of the carefully selected members. Traditionally, a new member was expected not only to sit for his portrait but also to carve his initials in the Table: but Plum did neither. Apart from the fact that he felt sure he would be unable to bring himself to deface the furniture, his oft-suggested return to England failed to materialise and the occasion never arose. In lieu of an oil-painting, however, he sent *Punch* a photograph with which to adorn the room, and this was hung above the doorway.

At this time, too, there was further cause for rejoicing on the completion of the troublesome Wooster-Jeeves book. It had taken him a year and a half to write, and it was with great relief that he eventually saw it published on 4th April 1960 by Simon & Schuster under the title *How Right You Are, Jeeves*.

There was less difficulty with his next book, which had already been started in odd moments during the past year. It was the first full-length novel to feature Freddie Widgeon of the Drones Club, and it was tentatively titled *Hot Ice*. Everything about it appealed to Peter Schwed except the title, as he mentioned in a letter to Plum dated 3rd May 1960:

> *I like* Hot Ice *a great deal. . . . This seems to me one of the best of your novels which involve a number of American underworld characters, and the plot and situations fairly crackle.*
>
> *I have only a couple of thoughts to toss out in casual conversation, as it were. I think the title* Hot Ice *really does sound like "another Wodehouse." What would you think of giving it a title like* The Ice in the Bedroom? *It just seems to me to be more distinctive and to differentiate this book from*

others, such as Hot Water. . . .

Amiably, Plum accepted *The Ice in the Bedroom* as the title and wrote to Schwed confirming it on 7th May, adding:

> . . . *I am now going through that hor-*
> *rible between-books phase, when I feel*
> *as if I would never get another plot.*
> *But as I remember feeling like that in*
> *1922, I'm not discouraged. Something*
> *is bound to emerge eventually.*

Peter Schwed was sympathetic but unperturbed. Like all of Plum's friends, he was accustomed to the author's sense of let-down at the finish of a novel and knew that it would not be too long before he was engrossed in another. And he was right. Almost as soon as he had written those plaintive words to Schwed, Plum was launched into a book which would bring together his fictional Lords—Lord Emsworth and Lord Ickenham reunited for the first time since *Uncle Fred in the Springtime* and joined by publishing tycoon Lord Tilbury of *Bill the Conqueror, Sam the Sudden* and *Heavy Weather*. He was calling the novel *Service with a Smile*. What he couldn't know, of course, was that he was writing what would later be acclaimed as one of his masterpieces.

Plum's British and American publishers didn't always see eye to eye about titles, and it was not unusual for one of his books to have a different title in each country. So it was that when Herbert Jenkins were presented with *How Right You Are, Jeeves* they had no compunction about scrapping that title and publishing the book on 12th August 1960 as *Jeeves in the Offing*. Hard lines on the travelling Wodehouse fan who, on crossing the Atlantic in which-ever direction, might joyfully buy himself what appeared to be a new novel by his favourite author only to discover that it was the book he'd just read at home under another title.

By the beginning of 1961 *Service with a Smile* was finished and in the hands of Peter Schwed, who again started urging Plum to work on an American version of *Performing Flea*. And this time, Plum began to give the project his serious consideration.

Significantly, the pressures on Plum to continue writing to publication schedules appeared to take no account of his advancing years. It was as though the timelessness of his novels had extended itself to the author—and he would have been the last person to dispel the illusion. On the contrary, he fostered it without conscious effort. He seemed, indeed, to believe that time stood still for him and that it was only other people who actually grew older—although that did not prevent him from being mildly surprised when any of them showed signs of it. "I remember some years ago a grey-haired matron accosting me in a restaurant," he reminisced at this time, "and she turned out to be a girl who had been in the chorus of one of the Princess shows. My, how she had aged." The fact that she'd had forty-five years in which to do it didn't seem to weigh with Plum at all.

But time is no respecter of persons, and in 1961 Plum was not to be allowed to ignore it. When 15th October dawned, it appeared that the whole world intended to remind him that it was his eightieth birthday. Congratulatory telegrams came pouring in to Basket Neck Lane in the thousands, one of the most highly prized reading:

> ON THIS HAPPY DAY I WISH TO
> THANK YOU ON BEHALF OF
> LARRY HART OSCAR HAMMER-
> STEIN AND MYSELF FOR ALL
> YOU TAUGHT US THROUGH THE
> YEARS PLEASE STAY WELL AND
> HAPPY
>
> AFFECTIONATELY
> RICHARD RODGERS

Plum's British and American publishers celebrated the occasion by making his latest books available to their respective ever-eager publics. For Herbert Jenkins it was a field-day with the publication of not only *Ice in the Bedroom* (the "The" having been dropped from the American title) but also Richard Usborne's analytical study *Wodehouse at Work;* and Simon & Schuster published *Service with a Smile,* having brought out an anthology, *The Most of P. G. Wodehouse,* the previous year.

There was no possibility of the press overlooking the eightieth birthday of a writer who seemed to be in no way diminishing, either in style or output, and Plum therefore found himself besieged by reporters to whom he was affable and unflappable. Whatever the journalists might have expected, they could see no evidence of senile decay in the man who told them:

From my earliest years I had always wanted to be a writer. It was not that I had any particular message for humanity. I am still plugging away and not the ghost of one so far, so it begins to look as though, unless I suddenly hit mid-season form in my eighties, humanity will remain a message short. The curious thing about those early days is that, in spite of the blizzard of rejection slips, I had the most complete confidence in myself. I knew I was good. It was only later that doubts on this point began to creep in and to burgeon as the time went by. Today I am a mass of diffidence and I-wonder-if-this-is-going-to-be-all-right-ness, and I envy those tough authors, square-jawed and spitting out of the side of their mouths, who are perfectly sure, every time they start a new book, that it will be a masterpiece. But with each new book of mine I have always the feeling that this time I have picked a lemon in the garden of literature. A good thing, really, I suppose. Keeps one up on one's toes and makes one write every sentence ten times. Or in many cases twenty times. My books may not be the sort of books the cognoscenti feel justified in blowing the three [dollars] seventy-five on, but I do work at them. When in due course Charon ferries me across the Styx and everyone is telling everyone else what a rotten writer I

*was, I hope at least one voice will be
heard piping up: "But he did take
trouble."*

For all his talk of being ferried across the Styx, there was a twinkle in Plum's
eyes, and none of his interviewers had the impression that he was in any way
feeling the burden of his years.

Perhaps the most notable thing about Plum at eighty was his air of contentment. At Remsenburg he had found the peace and tranquility so essential
to him, and he had no desire to leave the place—although there had been some
hope that he might make the long-deferred visit to London to celebrate his
birthday. Only those close to him knew how small that hope was, for he always
tried to ensure that no commitment would necessitate him spending a night
away from Basket Neck Lane; and even his one-day trips to New York had
been cut to an absolute minimum. The truth was that the outside world had
less allure for him than ever before.

When asked how he filled his time in what amounted to a virtual retreat,
he replied cheerily, "I get up at eight in the morning and then take three-
quarters of an hour doing my exercises. The thing I read in *Collier's* in 1919
called 'The Daily Dozen,' by Walter Camp, is the basis for these exercises. I've
added a lot more than his dozen, over the years. I think it has been an awfully
good thing. I've never missed a day of it and it has kept me fit all my life. I always
found what I liked about them was that you didn't have to lie down on the
floor, which is usually the basis for all those exercises of that type. In mine,
you just stand up and wave your arms about and breathe deeply. I still touch
my toes fifty times and sort of twist the body while standing up. I suppose one
of these days I'll just come apart." He added that he made his own breakfast,
consisting of toasted black bread, jam, honey and five cups of tea, and then
worked on his stories for the rest of the morning. At noon he would join Ethel
in her room, where they would watch a soap opera on television; and at one
o'clock they would have lunch.

"Fairly soon after lunch," Plum continued, "I've got to take the dogs out.
So I take them to the post office and get the mail. Then I work again from
three till about five, when I take my bath. Ethel joins me for cocktails, usually
martinis. We have dinner generally at about six or a quarter past six. It's got
earlier and earlier because the maids don't live in and they like to get off. That
gives you a very long evening. We used to play double-dummy bridge but we

were never very keen on it, so now we generally read. From eight to about nine, I might go and write letters. I correspond a bit with Evelyn Waugh. At ten o'clock I take the dogs out to get exercise. I think the secret is that as a writer you're never really not writing. If you aren't actually at the typewriter, you're trying to think out something. Going for a walk with the dogs helps me to think.

"Ethel loves feeding the birds and looking after the dogs and cats. I'm not as crazy about birds as Ethel is. I do my duty by them, like filling their bowls, but Ethel is very sentimental about them. She's always huffing about the house. In the early part of the evening she goes into the kitchen and messes about, cleaning up.

"I love it here. It's so quiet. I hated the big parties in Hollywood. Funnily enough, we don't go to bed early. I go to bed at about half-past twelve and Ethel stays up till half-past one. It sounds extraordinarily monotonous, but it doesn't to me. I'm frightfully happy. I find that I get into a routine of work and walks and reading which makes the time fly. I never want to see anyone, and I never want to go anywhere or do anything. I just want to write."

Plum then talked of his married life, pointing out that he and Ethel had been together for forty-seven years. "We are like one person really," he said. "After you are happily married for such a long time, you get like that. At the beginning it was wonderful. I think it's not so much doing things together but that you are absolutely at your ease together. There is never a sense of strain or anything. Of course, we are both devoted to animals, which is a terrific bond."

When the clamour and excitement surrounding his eightieth birthday had begun to die down, Plum was reminded of it in a letter from Evelyn Waugh, dated 12th November 1961, which said:

> *Your birthday was much celebrated in England both in the papers and in private. Your position as defined by Belloc long ago is pre-eminent and undisputed.*

The hectic comings and goings that had surrounded the highly publicised birthday had been permitted to make only the smallest of dents in the Wodehouse working day. For Plum was, at last, expending his energies on the American version of *Performing Flea*, already retitled *Author! Author!* And it was no mean task. Retaining the format of the original—a series of letters from him to Townend, punctuated by Townend's explanatory notes—he added comments of his own in support of or expanding what Townend had to say. Most of the comments were reworkings of his *Punch* articles, but he also included material of a personal nature that had never before appeared in print. The result was a book both entertaining and of practical value, and Peter Schwed had cause to congratulate himself on having been so persistent. It was precisely the volume that he had envisaged; and his faith in it was borne out by the response of Ogden Nash who, after receiving an advance copy, wrote to Plum:

> *Dear Masterissimo—*
>   *Once again I break into your morning, this time to thank you for* Author! Author! *I read it with joy and humility, undergoing the same experience of watching the transformation of craftsmanship into art as I followed you through the years. I wish I could put it in the hands of every young writer whose alphabet runs to five or more letters. Meanwhile, I return to Bertie, Jeeves and Ukridge with added appreciation.*
>   *Gratefully yours——*
>   *Ogden Nash*

Author! Author! was published on 20th June 1962, by which time Plum was engrossed in a plot involving Bertie Wooster and Jeeves. He had never been much taken with the business of rewriting one of his already published works for either British or American consumption and was glad to be working on a novel again. For this one, he was developing a segment of the plot of *The Code of the Woosters;* he was calling it *Stiff Upper Lip, Jeeves.*

New York City was in the midst of a newspaper strike when, on 22nd March 1963, *Stiff Upper Lip, Jeeves* was published. The strike was serious enough to ring the death knell on one major newspaper, but it didn't prevent the new Wodehouse novel from getting away to a good start. And it had no apparent effect on the way of life at Basket Neck Lane. If Plum missed his daily paper, it was only in passing. He was already well under way with a book called *Biffen's Millions* which was to occupy him for the rest of the year.

The following year was to see the most famous Wodehouse characters entering a new medium when Caedmon Records issued a long-playing record uncompromisingly entitled *Jeeves*. Issued on 24th May 1964, the disc was made up of two short stories—"Indian Summer of an Uncle" and "Jeeves Takes Charge"—presented in play form with Terry-Thomas as Bertie Wooster and Roger Livesey as Jeeves. But there was no new Jeeves novel. Instead, *Biffen's Millions*—a novel that had no connection with any of the sagas—was published by Simon & Schuster on 14th July 1964. A month later, when Herbert Jenkins published the same book on 14th August, it had undergone one of those increasingly familiar title changes and was called *Frozen Assets.*

But it wasn't only titles that were changing. The old-established firm of Herbert Jenkins Limited was itself due for a change. On 6th April 1965 it was taken over by Barrie & Rockcliff, who at first retained the well-known imprint and the company's successful policy. The new owners' greatest acquisition was Plum; and so closely was Plum indentified with the firm that had been publishing him in Britain for forty-seven years that the newspapers announced the take-over under headlines stating "Wodehouse Publishers Are Sold." It was not a bad time for Barrie & Rockcliff to be taking Plum under their wing, for an enormous amount of valuable free publicity was about to be focused on him and, more particularly, Jeeves. This was thanks to the BBC who, on 27th May 1965, launched a television series called *The World of Wooster,* based on the Jeeves short stories, with Ian Carmichael as Bertie Wooster and Dennis Price as Jeeves. From the very first transmission, it was clear that the BBC had a resounding hit on their hands. The transference from the printed page to the television screen had been effected with great skill, and the living-room public was quick to express its approval and appreciation. This was family viewing supreme, and it was no surprise that the Guild of Television Producers and Directors named *The World of Wooster* as the best comedy series of 1965. Writers Richard Waring and Michael Mills received the "best script" award for their masterly adaptations.

But even this did not provoke a new Jeeves novel. With *Biffen's Millions* (or *Frozen Assets*) behind him, Plum was hard at work on a Blandings Castle book which in its theme related directly to *Full Moon* and which would be the ninth in the saga. It was called *The Brinkmanship of Galahad Threepwood* by

Simon & Schuster when they published it on 13th January 1965; but by the time it was published under the Herbert Jenkins imprint on 26th August 1965 it had become *Galahad at Blandings.*

While working on the last two novels, Plum had also been writing a number of short stories for magazine publication. There was nothing new in that; but there was little short of a sensation when it became known that the magazine they were to appear in was *Playboy.* Somehow, Plum didn't quite fit into the *Playboy* image. Could it mean that the customary good clean fun was going to become neither good nor clean? Or were the *Playboy* models going to keep their clothes on during the Wodehouse season? As it turned out, the fans of Plum had no more cause for worry than those of *Playboy.* The stories —one of them featuring Jeeves—remained pure (in every sense of the word) Wodehouse; and they sat comfortably and unblushingly between *Playboy*'s naked ladies. So untainted were the stories, indeed, that they were published in volume form by Barrie & Rockcliff—still using the Herbert Jenkins imprint—on 22nd September 1966 under the title *Plum Pie.* And the Wodehouse/*Playboy* publicity didn't do anyone any harm.

On 16th February 1967 the BBC, encouraged by the success of *The World of Wooster,* screened the first episode of a new Wodehouse series. This one was called *Blandings Castle,* and it starred Sir Ralph Richardson and his wife Meriel Forbes as Lord Emsworth and sister Constance, with Stanley Holloway as Beach. And the success of this series led to yet another, called *Ukridge,* with Anton Rodgers in the title role and Julian Holloway as Corky.

Plum's book for this year was called *The Purloined Paperweight* when it was published by Simon & Schuster on 12th May 1967 and *Company for Henry* when it came out under the Herbert Jenkins imprint on. 26th October 1967. Too hastily put together, it contained a good deal of material that had been used in various earlier novels.

Still under pressure to provide a book a year, Plum spent part of 1967 dashing off a novel called *Do Butlers Burgle Banks?* but much of his time was devoted to his other great love, animals. In November 1967 he officially opened a hundred-kennel shelter for cats and dogs at Westhampton, Long Island. It was under the auspices of the Bide-A-Wee Home Association, to whom he had earlier donated $35,000 for its construction, and it was named the P. G. Wodehouse Shelter. Ethel was to be very active in the running of it now that Nella, Armine's widow, had taken up permanent residence at Basket Neck Lane and was helping to run the household.

Do Butlers Burgle Banks? was published on 5th August 1968, by which time Plum was working on what was to be the last Blandings Castle novel. He had himself been feeling rather like Lord Emsworth of late, and he wanted to give the vague but amiable peer a happy ending. It seemed that the only way to do this was to rid him of his dreaded sister Constance for good and all. Shrinking from the thought of violence, Plum decided that he could achieve his purpose by marrying her off. Thus in *A Pelican at Blandings,* which was published on 19th September 1969, Lord Emsworth is left to potter in peace about his domain.

Throughout 1969 Plum was busy on his book for the following year. But its theme was not entirely new to him since he had first started thinking about it in 1951. After making some preliminary notes, however, he had abandoned it and given it no more thought until 1953 when, having toyed with the basic plot, he again put it aside. It wasn't until 1956 that he dredged it up once more to make further notes; but it still didn't seem right and he put it away again until 1958, when little progress was made and it was again dropped. In 1966 he made another attempt, this time settling on a story line and a list of characters; but somehow the book was never written. Nevertheless, the time spent on it had not been wasted. When he returned to the idea in 1969 everything seemed to fall into place and he knew precisely what he intended to do. The book was called *The Girl in Blue,* and it was published on 29th October 1970 under the imprint of Barrie & Jenkins—Barrie & Rockcliff having finally merged their name with that of Herbert Jenkins to make one company.

Plum was now engrossed with the novel he hoped to have published on his ninetieth birthday. It was a Wooster-Jeeves story he had been working on since the end of 1969, summoning every ounce of concentration in order to get it finished in time. When it was submitted to his publishers on both sides of the Atlantic early in 1971, it was received with equal amounts of enthusiasm and relief, for it had been a matter of great importance to both publishing houses to be able to bring out a new Wodehouse book on this particular birthday of their remarkable author.

And so it was that on 15th October 1971 Barrie & Jenkins and Simon & Schuster simultaneously published Plum's ninety-third volume: but even for this auspicious occasion they had been unable to agree on its title. The British firm called it *Much Obliged, Jeeves* and the Americans called it *Jeeves and the Tie that Binds.* But under either title its publication was a fitting tribute to the man whose ninetieth birthday was being heralded in newspapers and magazines and on radio and television throughout the world.

Barrie & Jenkins had hoped that Plum would make the long-overdue trip to London to celebrate the day, and for a time the correspondence and transatlantic telephone calls had been promising. But the travelling days of the man who had once nipped to and fro between England and America whenever the fancy took him were over. He didn't want to leave the safe seclusion of Remsenburg for the whirl and frenzy of publicity from which he had so gratefully been able to escape years ago. And who could blame him? At ninety he had surely earned the contentment he had found.

The pattern of Plum's life as he had described it on his eightieth birthday had scarcely changed in any detail over the intervening years. His exercises and walks were still important items in the day's proceedings; he still watched soap operas on television; he still read thrillers; and he still wrote. Virtually nothing had changed—except that Plum, who had never really thought of himself as growing older, was ninety. But at that great age there was no doubt that he was indeed England's grand old master of literature.

For whatever odd reason, the land of his birth has never seen fit to officially honour Plum for his exceptional services to literature or even for his services to mankind generally as a laugh-maker. One hesitates to think it could be because of those wartime broadcasts . . . not when the ruler of a former enemy country is received in state and decorated. Perhaps it is just that those who decide these things are saving it for the hundredth birthday celebrations.

Be that as it may, the work continues. Plum's book for 1973 was called *Bachelors Anonymous,* and there is no knowing how many novels will follow. But one thing is certain: as long as books continue to be printed, there can be no end to the story of Pelham Grenville Wodehouse.

GENERAL
BIBLIOGRAPHY

BOOKS

Burlingame, Roger. *Of Making Many Books.* New York: Scribner's, 1946.

Deane, Mary. *The Book of Dene, Deane, Adeane.* London: Elliot Stock, 1899.

Donaldson, Frances. *Freddy.* New York: Lippincott, 1957.

Doran, George H. *Chronicles of Barabbas.* New York: Harcourt, Brace, 1935.

Drewry, John E. *Some Magazines and Magazine Makers.* Boston: Stratford Press, 1924, pp. 165–6.

Elwin, Verrier. *Motley.* Calcutta: Orient Longmans Ltd., 1954.

Ewen, David. *A Journey to Greatness.* New York: Henry Holt, 1956.

——— *The World of Jerome Kern.* New York: Henry Holt, 1960.

Fairlie, Gerard. *With Prejudice.* London: Hodder and Stoughton, 1952.

French, R.B.D. *P. G. Wodehouse.* Edinburgh and London: Oliver and Boyd, 1966.

Grossmith, George. *G. G.* London: Hutchinson, 1933.

Hall, Robert A., Jr., *Comic Style of P. G. Wodehouse.* Hamden, Conn.: Archon, 1974.

Hamilton, Cosmo. *People Worth Talking About.* New York: McBride, 1933, pp. 79–85.

Hart-Davis, Rupert. *Hugh Walpole.* New York: Macmillan, 1952.

Henson, Leslie. *My Laugh Story.* London: Hodder and Stoughton, 1926.

Homage to P. G. Wodehouse. Thelma Cazalet-Keir, ed. London: Barrie & Jenkins, 1973.

Howard, Leslie Ruth. *A Quite Remarkable Father.* New York: Harcourt, Brace, 1959.

Jaggard, Geoffrey. *Wooster's World.* London: Macdonald, 1967.

——— *Blandings the Blest.* London: Macdonald, 1968.

Jasen, David A. *A Bibliography and Reader's Guide to the First Editions of P. G. Wodehouse.* Hamden, Conn.: Archon, 1970.

Kaye-Smith, Sheila. *All The Books of My Life.* New York: Harper & Brothers, 1956.

Kingsmill, Hugh. *The Progress of a Biographer.* London: Methuen, 1949.

Kipling, Rudyard. *Maugham's Choice of Kipling's Best.* Intro. by Somerset Maugham. New York: Doubleday, 1953.

The Letters of Alexander Woollcott. Beatrice Kaufman and Joseph Hennessey, eds. New York: The Viking Press, 1944.

Mackail, Denis. *The Story of J.M.B.* London: Peter Davies, 1941.

——— *Life With Topsy.* London: Heinemann, 1942.

Marbury, Elisabeth. *My Crystal Ball.* New York: Boni and Liveright, 1923.

Middleton, George. *These Things Are Mine.* New York: Macmillan, 1947.

Mikes, George. *Eight Humorists.* London: Wingate, 1954, pp. 153–175.

Newman, Ernest. *From the World of Music.* London: Calder, 1956, pp. 181–184.

Nichols, Beverly. *Are They the Same at Home?* London: Cape, 1927.

Oppenheim, E. Phillips. *Pool of Memory.* Boston: Little, Brown, 1942.

Orwell, George. *Dickens, Dali and Others.* London: Secker and Warburg, 1946.

Overton, Grant M. *When Winter Comes to Main Street.* New York: Doran, 1922, pp. 99–101.

Pound, Reginald. *Arnold Bennett.* London: Heinemann, 1952, p. 342.

——— *The Strand Magazine.* London: Heinemann, 1966.

Swinnerton, Frank. *The Georgian Literary Scene.* London: Heinemann, 1935.

Tebbel, John. *George Horace Lorimer and the Saturday Evening Post.* New York: Doubleday, 1948.

Terriss, Ellaline. *Just a Little Bit of String.* London: Hutchinson, 1955, p. 181.

Usborne, Richard. *Wodehouse at Work.* London: Herbert Jenkins, 1961.

Voorhees, Richard J. *P. G. Wodehouse.* New York: Twayne, 1966.

ARTICLES

Aldridge, John W. "P. G. Wodehouse: The Lesson of the Young Master." *New World Writing* No. 13., New York: New American Library, 1958.

Avakian, George. "Bix Beiderbecke." *The Art of Jazz.* Ed. Martin T. Williams. New York: Grove Press, 1960, p. 67.

Belloc, Hilaire. Introduction to *Week-End Wodehouse.* London: Herbert Jenkins, 1939, pp. 5–9.

Cole, Hubert. "I've Been a Silly Ass." *Illustrated,* London VIII (December 7, 1946), pp. 7–9.

Cooke, Alistair. "The Hermit of Remsenburg." *The Guardian,* London (October 13, 1961), p. 5.

Hall, Robert A. Jr. "P. G. Wodehouse and the English Language." *Anuali,* Instituto Orientale di Napoli (December, 1964).

Hayward, John. "P. G. Wodehouse." *The Saturday Book,* Ed. Leonard Russell. London: Hutchinson, 1941, pp. 372–389.

Forbes, John D. "A Concordance of Wodehouse." *New York Times,* New York (August 8, 1948).

Jaggard, Geoffrey. "P. G. Wodehouse and the Immortals." *The Listener,* London (May 30, 1963), pp. 909–10.

Jasen, David A. "The Mysterious Wodehouse." *The Armchair Detective,* Minnesota 3 (October, 1969), pp. 38–39.

Joseph, Michael. "P. G. Wodehouse." *Bookman,* London LXXVI (June, 1929), pp. 150–2.

Le Carre, John. "Well Played, Wodehouse." *The Sunday Times,* London (October 10, 1971).

MacInnes, Colin. "The Girl in Blue." *The New York Times Book Review,* New York (February 28, 1971), pp. 1, 32.

McQuilland, Louis J. "P. G. Wodehouse." *Bookman,* London LXVIII (April, 1925), pp. 19–20.

Muggeridge, Malcolm. "The Wodehouse Affair." *The New Statesman,* 62 (August 4, 1961), p. 50.

Muir, Augustus. "The Popularity of P. G. Wodehouse." *Strand,* London (February, 1927), pp. 128–136.

Norman, Philip. "Thank You, Plum." *The Sunday Times Magazine,* London (July 20, 1969), pp. 8–15.

Sheridan, T. "Foremost English Humorist of Our Time." *Outlook,* Hong Kong III (May, 1954), pp. 13–15, 28.

Stevenson, Lionel. "The Antecedents of P. G. Wodehouse." *Arizona Quarterly* V (Autumn, 1949), pp. 226–234.

Thompson, C. Patrick. "Master Laugh Maker." *This Week,* New York (March 17, 1935), pp. 5, 15, 29.

Usborne, Richard. "P. G. Wodehouse is Ninety This Week." *Punch,* London (October 13, 1971), p. 504.

———— "P. G. Wodehouse." *The Guardian,* London (August 11, 1971).

Waugh, Evelyn. "An Act of Homage and Reparation to P. G. Wodehouse." *The Sunday Times Magazine,* London (July 16, 1961), pp. 21, 23.

Wind, Herbert Warren. "Chap With a Good Story To Tell." *The New Yorker,* New York (May 15, 1971).

Wodehouse, Leonora. "P. G. Wodehouse at Home." *Strand,* London (January, 1929), pp. 20–25.

———— "What His Daughter Thinks of P. G. Wodehouse." *The American Magazine,* New York (October, 1931), pp. 77, 78, 122.

"P. G. Wodehouse." *Strand,* London (December, 1921), pp. 506–7.

"Portrait." *Bookman,* London (October, 1924), p. 3.

"Plummie." *The New Yorker,* New York (October 15, 1960), pp. 36–37.

APPENDIX I
BIBLIOGRAPHY OF
PUBLISHED VOLUMES
BY P. G. WODEHOUSE

(UK–Great Britain; US–United States. Dates: Year–Month–Day)
1. The Pothunters / 02–9–18 / A. & C. Black / UK
2. A Prefect's Uncle / 03–9–11 / A. & C. Black / UK
3. Tales of St. Austin's / 03–11–10 / A. & C. Black / UK
4. The Gold Bat / 04–9–13 / A. & C. Black / UK
5. William Tell Told Again / 04–11–11 / A. & C. Black / UK
6. The Head of Kay's / 05–10–5 / A. & C. Black / UK
7. Love Among the Chickens / 06–6 / George Newnes / UK
7a. Love Among the Chickens / 09–5–11 / Circle / US
7b. Love Among the Chickens / 21–5 / Jenkins / UK
8. The White Feather / 07–10–9 / A. & C. Black / UK
9. Not George Washington / 07–10–18 / Cassell / UK
10. The Globe by the Way Book / 08–6 / Globe / UK
11. The Swoop / 09–4–16 / Alston Rivers / UK
12. Mike / 09–9–15 / A. & C. Black / UK
13. The Intrusion of Jimmy / 10–5–11 / W. J. Watt / US
13a. A Gentleman of Leisure / 10–11–15 / Alston Rivers / UK
14. Psmith in the City / 10–9–23 / A. & C. Black / UK
15. The Prince and Betty / 12–2–14 / W. J. Watt / US
15a. Psmith Journalist / 15–9–29 / A. & C. Black / UK
16. The Prince and Betty / 12–5–1 / Mills & Boon / UK
17. The Little Nugget / 13–8–28 / Methuen / UK
17a. The Little Nugget / 14–1–10 / W. J. Watt / US
18. The Man Upstairs / 14–1–23 / Methuen / UK
19. Something New / 15–9–3 / D. Appleton / US
19a. Something Fresh / 15–9–16 / Methuen / UK
20. Uneasy Money / 16–3–17 / D. Appleton / US
20a. Uneasy Money / 17–10–4 / Methuen / UK
21. Piccadilly Jim / 17–2–24 / Dodd, Mead / US
21a. Piccadilly Jim / 18–5 / Jenkins / UK
22. The Man With Two Left Feet / 17–3–8 / Methuen / UK
22a. The Man With Two Left Feet / 33– / A. L. Burt / US
23. My Man Jeeves / 19–5 / George Newnes / UK
24. Their Mutual Child / 19– / Boni & Liveright / US
24a. The Coming of Bill / 20–7–1 / Jenkins / UK
25. A Damsel in Distress / 19–10–4 / Doran / US
25a. A Damsel in Distress / 19–10–17 / Jenkins / UK
26. The Little Warrior / 20–10–11 / Doran / US
26a. Jill the Reckless / 21–7–4 / Jenkins / UK
27. Indiscretions of Archie / 21–2–14 / Jenkins / UK
27a. Indiscretions of Archie / 21–7–15 / Doran / US
28. The Clicking of Cuthbert / 22–2–3 / Jenkins / UK
28a. Golf Without Tears / 24–5–28 / Doran /US
29. Three Men and a Maid / 22–4–26 / Doran / US
29a. The Girl on the Boat / 22–6–15 / Jenkins / UK
30. The Adventures of Sally / 22–10–17 / Jenkins / UK

30a. Mostly Sally / 23–3–23 / Doran / US
31. The Inimitable Jeeves / 23–5–17 / Jenkins / UK
31a. Jeeves / 23–9–28 / Doran / US
32. Leave it to Psmith / 23–11–30 / Jenkins / UK
32a. Leave it to Psmith / 24–3–14 / Doran / US
33. Ukridge / 24–6–3 / Jenkins / UK
33a. He Rather Enjoyed It / 26–3–19 / Doran / US
34. Bill the Conqueror / 24–11–14 / Methuen / UK
34a. Bill the Conqueror / 25–2–20 / Doran / US
35. Carry On, Jeeves / 25–10–9 / Jenkins / UK
35a. Carry On, Jeeves / 27–10–7 / Doran / US
36. Sam the Sudden / 25–10–15 / Methuen / UK
36a. Sam in the Suburbs / 25–11–6 / Doran / US
37. The Heart of a Goof / 26–4–15 / Jenkins / UK
37a. Divots / 27–3–4 / Doran / US
38. The Small Bachelor / 27–4–28 / Methuen / UK
38a. The Small Bachelor / 27–6–17 / Doran / US
39. Meet Mr. Mulliner / 27–9–27 / Jenkins / UK
39a. Meet Mr. Mulliner / 28–3–2 / Doubleday Doran / US
40. Money for Nothing / 28–7–27 / Jenkins / UK
40a. Money for Nothing / 28–9–28 / Doubleday Doran / US
41. Mr. Mulliner Speaking / 29–4–30 / Jenkins / UK
41a. Mr. Mulliner Speaking / 30–2–21 / Doubleday Doran / US
42. Fish Preferred / 29–7–1 / Doubleday Doran / US
42a. Summer Lightning / 29–7–19 / Jenkins / UK
43. Very Good, Jeeves / 30–6–20 / Doubleday Doran / US
43a. Very Good, Jeeves / 30–7–4 / Jenkins / UK
44. Big Money / 31–1–30 / Doubleday Doran / US
44a. Big Money / 31–3–20 / Jenkins / UK
45. If I Were You / 31–9–3 / Doubleday Doran / US
45a. If I Were You / 31–9–25 / Jenkins / UK
46. Louder and Funnier / 32–3–10 / Faber & Faber / UK
47. Doctor Sally / 32–4–7 / Methuen / UK
48. Hot Water / 32–8–17 / Jenkins/Doubleday Doran / UK/US
49. Mulliner Nights / 33–1–17 / Jenkins / UK
49a. Mulliner Nights / 33–2–15 / Doubleday Doran / US
50. Heavy Weather / 33–7–28 / Little, Brown / US
50a. Heavy Weather / 33–8–10 / Jenkins / UK
51. Thank You, Jeeves / 34–3–16 / Jenkins / UK
51a. Thank You, Jeeves / 34–4–23 / Little, Brown / US
52. Right Ho, Jeeves / 34–10–5 / Jenkins / UK
52a. Brinkley Manor / 34–10–15 / Little, Brown / US
53. Blandings Castle / 35–4–12 / Jenkins / UK
53a. Blandings Castle / 35–9–20 / Doubleday Doran / US
54. The Luck of the Bodkins / 35–10–11 / Jenkins / UK
54a. The Luck of the Bodkins / 36–1–3 / Little, Brown / US

55. Young Men in Spats / 36–4–3 / Jenkins / UK
55a. Young Men in Spats / 36–7–24 / Doubleday Doran / US
56. Laughing Gas / 36–9–25 / Jenkins / UK
56a. Laughing Gas / 36–12–4 / Doubleday Doran / US
57. Lord Emsworth & Others / 37–3–19 / Jenkins / UK
57a. Crime Wave at Blandings / 37–6–25 / Doubleday Doran / US
58. Summer Moonshine / 37–10–8 / Doubleday Doran / US
58a. Summer Moonshine / 38–2–11 / Jenkins / UK
59. The Code of the Woosters / 38–10–7 / Jenkins/Doubleday Doran / UK/US
60. Uncle Fred in the Springtime / 39–8–18 / Doubleday Doran / US
60a. Uncle Fred in the Springtime / 39–8–25 / Jenkins / UK
61. Eggs, Beans & Crumpets / 40–4–26 / Jenkins / UK
61a. Eggs, Beans & Crumpets / 40–5–10 / Doubleday Doran / US
62. Quick Service / 40–10–4 / Jenkins / UK
62a. Quick Service / 40–11–11 / Doubleday Doran / US
63. Money in the Bank / 42–1–19 / Doubleday Doran / US
63a. Money in the Bank / 46–5–27 / Jenkins / UK
64. Joy in the Morning / 46–8–22 / Doubleday / US
64a. Joy in the Morning / 47–6–2 / Jenkins / UK
65. Full Moon / 47–5–22 / Doubleday / US
65a. Full Moon / 47–10–17 / Jenkins / UK
66. Spring Fever / 48–5–20 / Jenkins/Doubleday / UK/US
67. Uncle Dynamite / 48–10–22 / Jenkins / UK
67a. Uncle Dynamite / 48–12–3 / Didier / US
68. The Mating Season / 49–9–9 / Jenkins / UK
68a. The Mating Season / 49–11–29 / Didier / US
69. Nothing Serious / 50–7–21 / Jenkins / UK
69a. Nothing Serious / 51–5–24 / Doubleday / US
70. The Old Reliable / 51–4–18 / Jenkins / UK
70a. The Old Reliable / 51–10–11 / Doubleday / US
71. Barmy in Wonderland / 52–4–21 / Jenkins / UK
71a. Angel Cake / 52–5–8 / Doubleday / US
72. Pigs Have Wings / 52–10–16 / Doubleday / US
72a. Pigs Have Wings / 52–10–31 / Jenkins / UK
73. Ring for Jeeves / 53–4–22 / Jenkins / UK
73a. The Return of Jeeves / 54–4–15 / Simon & Schuster / US
74. Bring on the Girls / 53–10–5 / Simon & Schuster / US
74a. Bring on the Girls / 54–5–21 / Jenkins / UK
75. Performing Flea / 53–10–9 / Jenkins / UK
75a. Performing Flea / 61– / Penguin / US
75b. Author! Author! / 62–6–20 / Simon & Schuster / US
76. Jeeves & The Feudal Spirit / 54–10–15 / Jenkins / UK
76a. Bertie Wooster Sees It Through / 55–2–23 / Simon & Schuster / US
77. French Leave / 56–1–20 / Jenkins / UK
77a. French Leave / 59–9–28 / Simon & Schuster / US
78. America, I Like You / 56–5–3 / Simon & Schuster / US

APPENDIX II
BIBLIOGRAPHY OF
PUBLISHED SHORT STORIES
BY P. G. WODEHOUSE

Note: Only those stories issued in collections are listed with their original magazine appearances. The collection's number is listed in the last volume (see Appendix I). Dates follow the sequence Year-Month-Day. UK denotes English publication; US denotes American publication. Titles in parentheses indicate that the original title, listed above, has been changed by either the American or British publisher.

01–7	The Prize Poem / Public School Mag. / UK / 3
01–8	L'Affaire Uncle John / Public School Mag. / UK / 3
01–10	Author / Public School Mag. / UK / 3
02–2	The Tabby Terror / Public School Mag. / UK / 3
02–2	The Babe and the Dragon / Captain / UK / 3
02–7	Bradshaw's Little Story / Captain / UK / 3
02–8	The Odd Trick / Captain / UK / 3
02–10	How Paine Bucked Up / Captain / UK / 3
03–1	Harrison's Slight Error / Captain / UK / 3
03–5	How Pillingshot Scored / Captain / UK / 3
03–8/9	The Manoeuvres of Charteris / Captain / UK / 3
03	A Shocking Affair / ——— / 3
09–9	Out of School / Ainslee's / US / 18
10–10	Out of School / Strand / UK
10–2	The Good Angel / Strand / UK / 18
10–2	(Matrimonial Sweepstakes) / Cosmopolitan / US
10–3	The Man Upstairs / Strand/Cosmopolitan / UK/US / 18
10–3–19	Archibald's Benefit / Colliers / US / 18
10–4	Rough-Hew Them How We Will / Strand / UK / 18
10–8	Rough-Hew Them How We Will / Cosmopolitan / US
10–5–28	Deep Waters / Colliers / US / 18
10–6	Deep Waters / Strand / UK
10–6	The Man, The Maid and The Miasma / Cosmopolitan / US / 18
10–7	By Advise of Council / Strand / UK / 18
10–9–24	(The Pitcher and the Plutocrat) / Colliers / US
12–1	The Goal-Keeper and the Plutocrat / Strand / UK / 18
10–12	When Doctors Disagree / Strand / UK / 18
11–1–28	Ahead of Schedule / Colliers / US / 18
11–3	Absent Treatment / Strand / UK / 22a, 23
11–8–26	Absent Treatment / Colliers / US
11–8	Three From Dunsterville / Strand / UK / 18
11–9	Helping Freddie / Strand / UK / 23
26	(Fixing It For Freddie) / 35, 35a
11–12	Pots O' Money / Strand / UK / 18
11–12	In Alcala / London Magazine / UK / 18
12–5	The Man Who Disliked Cats / Strand / UK / 18
16–1	(Fatal Kink in Algernon) / Ladies Home Journal / US
12–6–29	Sir Agravaine / Colliers / US / 18
12–12	Sir Agravaine / Pearsons / UK
12–7	Ruth in Exile / Strand / UK / 18
12–10	The Tuppenny Millionaire / Strand / UK / 18

20–5	Dear Old Squiffy / Strand / UK / 27, 27a
20–7	Dear Old Squiffy / Cosmopolitan / US
20–6	A Mixed Threesome / McClure's / US / 28, 28a
21–3	A Mixed Threesome / Strand / UK
20–6	Doing Father a Bit of Good / Strand / UK / 27, 27a
20–8	Doing Father a Bit of Good / Cosmopolitan / US
20–7	Paving the Way for Mabel / Strand / UK / 27, 27a
20–9	Paving the Way for Mabel / Cosmopolitan / US
20–8	Washy Makes His Presence Felt / Strand / UK / 27, 27a
20–10	Washy Makes His Presence Felt / Cosmopolitan / US
20–9	A Room at the Hermitage / Strand / UK / 27, 27a
20–11	A Room at the Hermitage / Cosmopolitan / US
20–10	First Aid For Looney Biddle / Strand / UK / 27, 27a
20–12	First Aid For Looney Biddle / Cosmopolitan / US
20–10–10	The Rough Stuff / Chicago Tribune / US / 28, 28a
21–4	The Rough Stuff / Strand / UK
20–11	Mother's Knee / Strand / UK / 27, 27a
21–1	Mother's Knee / Cosmopolitan / US
20–12	Sundered Hearts / Strand/McClure's / UK/US / 28, 28a
21–1	Strange Experience of an Artist's Model / Strand / UK / 27, 27a
21–2	The Wigmore Venus / Strand/Cosmopolitan / UK/US / 27, 27a
21–5	The Coming of Gowf / Strand / UK / 28, 28a
21–6/7	The Coming of Gowf / McClure's / US
21–6	The Salvation of George Mackintosh / Strand / UK / 28, 28a
21–9	The Salvation of George Mackintosh / McClure's / US
21–8	The Long Hole / Strand / UK / 28, 28a
22–3	The Long Hole / McClure's / US
21–10	The Unexpected Clicking of Cuthbert / Strand / UK / 28, 28a
22–7	The Unexpected Clicking of Cuthbert / Elk's Magazine / US
21–11	The Heel of Achilles / Strand / UK / 28, 28a
22–6–11	The Heel of Achilles / Chicago Tribune / US
21–12	Jeeves in the Springtime / Strand/Cosmopolitan UK/US / 31, 31a
22–2	Scoring Off Jeeves / Strand / UK / 31, 31a
22–3	(Bertie Gets Even) / Cosmopolitan / US
22–3	Sir Roderick Comes to Lunch / Strand / UK / 31, 31a
22–4	(Jeeves and the Blighter) / Cosmopolitan / US
22–4	Aunt Agatha Takes the Count / Strand / UK / 31, 31a
22–10	(Aunt Agatha Makes a Bloomer) / Cosmopolitan / US
22–5	Comrade Bingo / Strand/Cosmopolitan / UK/US / 31, 31a
22–6	The Great Sermon Handicap / Strand/Cosmopolitan / UK/US / 31, 31a
22–7	The Purity of the Turf / Strand/Cosmopolitan / UK/US / 31, 31a
22–8	Bertie Changes His Mind / Strand/Cosmopolitan / UK/US / 35, 35a
22–9	The Metropolitan Touch / Strand/Cosmopolitan / UK/US / 31, 31a
22–11	Bingo and the Little Woman / Strand / UK / 31, 31a
22–12	Bingo and the Little Woman / Cosmopolitan / US
22–11	The Exit of Claude & Eustace / Cosmopolitan / US / 31, 31a
22–12	The Magic Plus Fours / Strand / UK / 37, 37a

29–9	Jeeves & the Song of Songs / Strand/Cosmopolitan / UK/US / 43, 43a
29–10	Jeeves & the Dog McIntosh / Strand/Cosmopolitan / UK/US / 43, 43a
29–11	Jeeves & the Love That Purifies / Strand/Cosmopolitan / UK/US / 43, 43a
29–12	Jeeves & the Spot of Art / Strand/Cosmopolitan / UK/US / 43, 43a
30–1	Jeeves & the Kid Clementina / Strand/Cosmopolitan / UK/US / 43, 43a
30–2	Jeeves & the Old School Chum / Strand/Cosmopolitan / UK/US / 43, 43a
30–3	Indian Summer of an Uncle / Strand/Cosmopolitan / UK/US / 43, 43a
30–4	Tuppy Changes His Mind / Strand/Cosmopolitan / UK/US / 43
30–5	Gala Night / Cosmopolitan / US / 49, 49a
30–6	Gala Night / Strand / UK
31–2	Ukridge & the Home From Home / Cosmopolitan / US / 57, 61a
31–6	Ukridge & the Home From Home / Strand / UK
31–3	(Sales Resistance) Go-Getter / Cosmopolitan / US / 53, 53a
31–8	(Sales Resistance) Go-Getter / Strand / UK
31–4	The Knightly Quest of Mervyn / Cosmopolitan / US / 49, 49a
31–7	(Quest) / Strand / UK
31–5	Fate / Strand/Cosmopolitan / UK/US / 55, 55a
31–7–4 & 31–8–1	The Medicine Girl / Colliers / US / 47, 57a
31–10	The Smile That Wins / American / US / 49, 49a
32–2	The Smile That Wins / Strand / UK
31–11	The Voice From the Past / American / US / 49, 49a
31–12	The Voice From the Past / Strand / UK
31–12	(The Missing Mystery) / American / US / 49, 49a
32–3	Strychnine in the Soup / Strand / UK
32–2	The Story of Webster / American / US / 49, 49a
32–5	(The Bishop's Cat) / Strand / UK
32–3	Cats Will Be Cats / American / US / 49, 49a
32–6	(The Bishop's Folly) / Strand / UK
32–4	Open House / American/Strand / US/UK / 49, 49a
32–12	Monkey Business (A Cagey Gorilla) / American/Strand / US/UK / 53, 53a
33–1	The Nodder (Love Birds) / American/Strand / US/UK / 53, 53a (The Yes Man)
33–2	The Juice of an Orange (Love on a Diet) / American/Strand / US/UK / 53, 53a
33–3	(A Star Is Born) / American / US / 53, 53a
33–4	The Rise of Minna Nordstrom / Strand / UK
33–6	The Castaways / Strand / UK / 53, 53a
33–8	The Amazing Hat Mystery / Cosmopolitan / US / 55, 55a
34–6	The Amazing Hat Mystery / Strand / UK
33–11	The Luck of the Stiffhams / Cosmopolitan / US / 55, 55a
34–3	The Luck of the Stiffhams / Strand / UK
34–9	Noblesse Oblige / Cosmopolitan / US / 55, 55a
34–11	Noblesse Oblige / Strand / UK
34–11	Good-Bye to All Cats / Cosmopolitan / US / 55, 55a
34–12	Good-Bye to All Cats / Strand / UK

34–12	The Fiery Wooing of Mordred / Cosmopolitan / US / 55, 55a
35–2	The Fiery Wooing of Mordred / Strand / UK
35–2	The Code of the Mulliners / Cosmopolitan / US / 55, 55a
35–4	The Code of the Mulliners / Strand / UK
35–5	Trouble Down at Tudsleigh / Strand / UK / 55, 61a
39–5	Trouble Down at Tudsleigh / Cosmopolitan / US
35–6	The Come-Back of Battling Billson / Cosmopolitan / US / 57, 61a
35–7	The Come-Back of Battling Billson / Strand / UK
35–7	Uncle Fred Flits By / Red Book / US / 55, 55a
35–12	Uncle Fred Flits By / Strand / UK
35–7–14	Farewell to Legs / This Week / US / 55a, 57
36–5	Farewell to Legs / Strand / UK
35–8	Archibald and the Masses / Cosmopolitan / US / 55, 55a
36–2	Archibald and the Masses / Strand / UK
35–10	Tried in the Furnace / Strand / UK / 55, 57a
39–3	Tried in the Furnace / Cosmopolitan / US
36–2	(A Triple Threat Man) / Red Book / US / 55a, 57
36–4	The Letter of the Law / Strand / UK
36–3	There's Always Golf! / Strand / UK / 55a, 57
36–4	(Not Out of Distance) / Red Book / US
36–9	Buried Treasure / Strand / UK / 57, 57a
36–9–27	(Hidden Treasure) / This Week / US
36–10–10/17	Crime Wave at Blandings / Sat. Eve. Post / US / 57, 57a
37–1	Crime Wave at Blandings / Strand / UK
36–11–28	(Reggie & the Greasy Bird) / Sat. Eve. Post / US / 57, 57a
36–12	The Masked Troubadour / Strand / UK
37–1–30	All's Well With Bingo / Sat. Eve. Post / US / 57a, 61
37–4	All's Well With Bingo / Strand / UK
37–2–20	Romance at Droitgate Spa / Sat. Eve. Post / US / 57a, 61
37–8	Romance at Droitgate Spa / Strand / UK
37–5–29	Bingo & The Peke Crisis / Sat. Eve. Post / US / 61, 61a
37–6	Bingo & The Peke Crisis / Strand / UK
37–7–3	Anselm Gets His Chance / Sat. Eve. Post / Strand / US/UK / 61, 61a
39–7–11	The Editor Regrets / Sat. Eve. Post / US / 61, 61a
39–9	The Editor Regrets / Strand / UK
39–9–2	Sonny Boy / Sat. Eve. Post / US / 61, 61a
39–12	Sonny Boy / Strand / UK
39–10–28	Bramley Is So Bracing / Sat. Eve. Post / US / 61a, 69, 69a
40–12	Bramley Is So Bracing / Strand / UK
40–1–20	Scratch Man / Sat. Eve. Post / US / 61a, 81, 81a
40–9	(Tee For Two) / Strand / UK
40–9–15	The Word in Season / Harper's Bazaar / US / 81, 81a
58–5–18	(Bingo Little's Wild Night Out) / This Week / US
47	Success Story / ——— / 69, 69a
47–10	(Joy Bells For Barmy) / Cosmopolitan / US / 81, 81a
59–1	The Right Approach / Playboy / US

APPENDIX III
BIBLIOGRAPHY OF
PUBLISHED PLAYS
BY P. G. WODEHOUSE

1. A GENTLEMAN OF LEISURE

Opening Night: August 24, 1911, The Playhouse, New York.
Total Performances: 76
Script: P. G. Wodehouse & John Stapleton
Retitled: *A Thief For A Night*
Opening Night: March 30, 1913, McVicker's Theatre, Chicago.

2. AFTER THE SHOW

Opening Night: 1911
Script: P. G. Wodehouse & Herbert Westbrook

3. BROTHER ALFRED

Opening Night: April 8, 1913, Savoy Theatre, London.
Total Performances: 14
Script: P. G. Wodehouse & Herbert Westbrook

4. THE PLAY'S THE THING

Opening Night: November 3, 1926, Henry Miller's Theatre, New York.
Total Performances: 326
Script: P. G. Wodehouse adaptation from Ferenc Molnar
English Opening Night: December 4, 1928, St. James's Theatre, London.
Revived: April 28, 1948, Booth Theatre, New York.
Total Performances: 244

5. HER CARDBOARD LOVER

Opening Night: March 21, 1927, Empire Theatre, New York.
Total Performances: 152
Script: P. G. Wodehouse & Valerie Wyngate
English Opening Night: August 21, 1928, Lyric Theatre, London.
Total Performances: 173

6. GOOD MORNING, BILL

Opening Night: November 28, 1927, Duke of York's Theatre, London.
Total Performances: 136
Script: P. G. Wodehouse adaptation from Ladislaus Fodor
Revived: March 20, 1934, Daly's Theatre, London.
Total Performances: 78

7. A DAMSEL IN DISTRESS

Opening Night: August 13, 1928, New Theatre, London.
Total Performances: 242
Script: P. G. Wodehouse & Ian Hay

8. BAA, BAA, BLACK SHEEP

Opening Night: April 22, 1929, New Theatre, London.
Total Performances: 115
Script: P. G. Wodehouse & Ian Hay

9. CANDLE-LIGHT

Opening Night: September 30, 1929, Empire Theatre, New York.
Total Performances: 128
Script: P. G. Wodehouse adaptation from Siegfried Geyer

10. LEAVE IT TO PSMITH

Opening Night: September 27, 1930, Shaftesbury Theatre, London.
Total Performances: 156
Script: P. G. Wodehouse & Ian Hay

11. WHO'S WHO

Opening Night: September 20, 1934, Duke of York's Theatre, London.
Total Performances: 19
Script: P. G. Wodehouse & Guy Bolton

12. THE INSIDE STAND

Opening Night: November 21, 1935, Saville Theatre, London.
Total Performances: 50
Script: P. G. Wodehouse

13. ARTHUR

Script: P. G. Wodehouse adaptation from Ferenc Molnar, 1947
Never produced but done on U.S. television.

14. GAME OF HEARTS

Script: P. G. Wodehouse adaptation from Ferenc Molnar, 1947
Never produced

15. DON'T LISTEN, LADIES

Opening Night: September 2, 1948, St. James's Theatre, London.
Total Performances: 219
Script: P. G. Wodehouse & Guy Bolton adaptation from Sacha Guitry

16. NOTHING SERIOUS
(SPRINGBOARD TO NOWHERE) (HOUSE ON A CLIFF)

Script: P. G. Wodehouse
No major production but done in U.S. in summer stock, 1950

17. PHIPPS (KILROY WAS HERE)

Script: P. G. Wodehouse & Guy Bolton, 1951
Never produced

18. COME ON, JEEVES

Script: P. G. Wodehouse & Guy Bolton, 1954
No major production but done in England in provinces

APPENDIX IV
BIBLIOGRAPHY OF
PUBLISHED MUSICALS AND SONG LYRICS
BY P. G. WODEHOUSE

1. SERGEANT BRUE

Opening Night: December 10, 1904, Strand Theatre, London.
Total Performances: 152
Book: Owen Hall
Lyrics: J. Hickory Wood & P. G. Wodehouse
Music: Liza Lehmann & Frederick Rosse
Song Lyrics by PGW:
"Put Me In My Little Cell"
U.S. Opening Night: April 24, 1905, Knickerbocker Theatre, New York.

2. THE BEAUTY OF BATH

Opening Night: March 19, 1906, Aldwich Theatre, London.
Total Performances: 287
Book: Seymour Hicks & Cosmo Hamilton
Lyrics: Chas. H. Taylor & P. G. Wodehouse
Music: Herbert E. Haines & Jerome Kern
Song Lyrics by PGW:
"Mister Chamberlain"

3. THE GAY GORDONS

Opening Night: September 11, 1907, Aldwich Theatre, London.
Book: Seymour Hicks
Lyrics: Arthur Wimperis, C. H. Bovill, Henry Hamilton & P. G. Wodehouse
Music: Guy Jones
Song Lyrics by PGW:
"Now That My Ship's Come Home" / "You, You, You"

4. THE BANDIT'S DAUGHTER

Opening Night: November 11, 1907, Bedford Music Hall, Camden Town, England.
Sketches: P. G. Wodehouse & Herbert Westbrook
Music: Ella King-Hall

5. NUTS AND WINE

Opening Night: January 4, 1914, Empire Theatre, London.
Sketches: P. G. Wodehouse & C. H. Bovill
Music: Frank Tours

6. POM POM

Opening Night: February 28, 1916, Cohan Theatre, New York.
Total Performances: 114
Book and Lyrics: Anne Caldwell & P. G. Wodehouse
Music: Hugo Felix

7. MISS SPRINGTIME

Opening Night: September 25, 1916, New Amsterdam Theatre, New York.
Total Performances: 227
Book: Guy Bolton
Lyrics: P. G. Wodehouse & Herbert Reynolds
Music: Emmerich Kalman & Jerome Kern

Song Lyrics by PGW:
"My Castle in the Air" / "Once Upon a Time"
"Saturday Night" / "This is the Existence" / "Throw Me a Rose"
"A Very Good Girl on Sunday" / "When You're Full of Talk"

8. HAVE A HEART

Opening Night: January 11, 1917, Liberty Theatre, New York.
Total Performances: 78
Book: Guy Bolton & P. G. Wodehouse
Lyrics: P. G. Wodehouse
Music: Jerome Kern
Song Lyrics by PGW:
"And I Am All Alone" / "Bright Lights" / "Daisy"
"Have a Heart" / "Honeymoon Inn" / "I See You There"
"I'm Here, Little Girl, I'm Here" / "I'm So Busy"
"Look in His Eyes" / "My Wife—My Man" / "Napoleon"
"Peter Pan" / "Polly Believed in Preparedness"
"The Road That Lies Before" / "Samarkand"
"Shop" / "They All Look Alike" / "You Said Something"

9. OH, BOY!

Opening Night: February 20, 1917, Princess Theatre, New York.
Total Performances: 475
Book: Guy Bolton & P. G. Wodehouse
Lyrics: P. G. Wodehouse
Music: Jerome Kern
Song Lyrics by PGW:
"Ain't It a Grand and Glorious Feeling"
"Be a Little Sunbeam" / "Every Day" / "The First Day of May"
"Flubby Dub, the Cave Man" / "Koo-La-Loo"
"Land Where the Good Songs Go" (also in #13)
"Let's Make a Night of It" / "Little Bit of Ribbon"
"Nesting Time in Flatbush" / "Oh, Daddy, Please" / "An Old Fashioned Wife"
"A Package of Seeds" / "A Pal Like You"
"Rolled Into One" / "Till the Clouds Roll By" / "We're Going To Be Pals"
"Words Are Not Needed" / "You Never Knew About Me"
English Opening Night: January 27, 1919, Kingsway Theatre, London.
Total Performances: 167
Retitled: OH, JOY!

10. LEAVE IT TO JANE

Opening Night: August 28, 1917, Longacre Theatre, New York.
Total Performances: 167
Book: Guy Bolton & P. G. Wodehouse
Lyrics: P. G. Wodehouse
Music: Jerome Kern
Song Lyrics by PGW:
"Cleopatterer" / "The Crickets Are Calling"
"I'm Going to Find a Girl" / "It's a Great Big Land"
"Just You Watch My Step" / "Leave It To Jane"
"A Peach of a Life" / "Poor Prune" / "Sir Galahad"
"The Siren's Song" / "The Sun Shines Brighter"
"There It Is Again" / "Wait Till Tomorrow"

"What I'm Longing to Say" / "Why?"
Revived: May 25, 1959, Sheridan Square Playhouse, New York.
Total Performances: 928

11. KITTY DARLIN'

Opening Night: September 19, 1917, Teck Theatre, Buffalo, New York.
Total Performances: 14
Book: Guy Bolton
Lyrics: P. G. Wodehouse
Music: Rudolf Friml
Song Lyrics by PGW:
"Am I To Blame?" / "The Blarney Stone" / "The Dawn of Love"
"Dear Bath" / "Dear Caracloe" / "Dear Old Dublin"
"I'd Do the Same" / "Just We Two"
"Kitty Darlin' " / "The Maid and the Valet"
"Noah" / "Peggy's Leg"
"Spread the News" / "Swing Song"
"The Sword of Thy Father" / "Tick, Tick, Tick"
"When She Gives Him a Shamrock Bloom" / "You'll See"

12. THE RIVIERA GIRL

Opening Night: September 24, 1917, New Amsterdam Theatre, New York.
Total Performances: 78
Book: Guy Bolton
Lyrics: P. G. Wodehouse
Music: Emmerich Kalman & Jerome Kern
Song Lyrics by PGW:
"The Fall of Man" / "Gypsy, Bring Your Fiddle" / "Half a Married Man"
"Just a Voice to Call Me, Dear"
"Let's Build a Little Bungalow in Quogue"
"Life's a Tale" / "The Lilt of a Gypsy Strain" / "Man, Man, Man"
"Sometimes I Feel Just Like Grandpa"
"There'll Never Be Another Girl Like Daisy"
"Will You Forget?" / "Why Don't They Hand It To Me?"

13. MISS 1917

Opening Night: November 5, 1917, Century Theatre, New York.
Total Performances: 48
Sketches: Guy Bolton & P. G. Wodehouse
Music: Jerome Kern & Victor Herbert
Song Lyrics by PGW:
"The Beauty Doctor" / "A Dancing Courtship" / "A Dancing M. D." / "Go, Little Boat"
"I'm The Old Man in the Moon" / "The Palm Beach Girl"
"The Land Where the Good Songs Go" (see also #9)
"Peaches" / "The Picture I Want To See" (see also #14)
"The Society Farmerettes" / "Tell Me All Your Troubles, Cutie"
"We Want To Laugh" / "We're Crooks" / "Who's Zoo in Girl Land"
"You're the Little Girl I've Looked So Long For"

14. OH, LADY! LADY!

Opening Night: February 1, 1918, Princess Theatre, New York.
Total Performances: 219

Book: Guy Bolton & P. G. Wodehouse
Lyrics: P. G. Wodehouse
Music: Jerome Kern
Song Lyrics by PGW:
"Before I Met You" / "Bill" (see also #30) / "Dear Old Prison Days" / "Do It Now"
"Do Look At Him" / "Greenwich Village" / "I'm To Be Married Today"
"It's a Hard, Hard World for a Man"
"Little Ships Come Sailing Home"
"Moon Song" / "Not Yet" / "Oh, Lady! Lady!" / "Our Little Nest"
"A Picture I Want to See" / "Some Little Girl"
"The Sun Starts to Shine Again"
"Waiting Round the Corner" / "Wheatless Days"
"You Found Me And I Found You"

15. SEE YOU LATER

Opening Night: April 15, 1918, Academy of Music, Baltimore, Maryland.
Book: Guy Bolton & P. G. Wodehouse
Lyrics: P. G. Wodehouse
Music: Jean Schwartz & Joseph Szulc
Song Lyrics by PGW:
"Anytime is Dancing Time" / "Desert Island"
"Honeymoon Island" / "I Never Knew" / "I'm Going to Settle Down"
"In Our Little Paradise" / "Isn't It Wonderful"
"It Doesn't Matter" / "Love's a Funny Thing" / "Lover's Quarrels"
"Mother Paris" / "Nerves!" / "See You Later, Girls" / "See You Later Shimmy"
"The Train That Leaves for Town"
"You Whispered It" / "Young Man"

16. THE GIRL BEHIND THE GUN

Opening Night: September 16, 1918, New Amsterdam Theatre, New York.
Total Performances: 160
Book: Guy Bolton & P. G. Wodehouse
Lyrics: P. G. Wodehouse
Music: Ivan Caryll
Song Lyrics by PGW:
"Back to the Dear Old Trenches" / "Flags of the Allies"
"The Girl Behind the Gun" / "Godsons and Godmothers"
"A Happy Family" / "I Like It, I Like It" / "I'm True To Them All"
"I've a System" / "Oh, How Warm It Is Today" / "Some Day Waiting Will End"
"That Ticking Taxi's Waiting at the Door"
"There's a Light in Your Eyes"
"There's Life in the Old Dog Yet"
"Woman Hasn't Any Mercy On a Man"
English Opening Night: May 20, 1919, Winter Garden Theatre, London.
Total Performances: 430
Retitled: *Kissing Time*

17. THE CANARY

Opening Night: November 4, 1918, Globe Theatre, New York.
Total Performances: 152
Book: George Barr & Louis Verneuill
Lyrics: Anne Caldwell & P. G. Wodehouse
Music: Ivan Caryll

Song Lyric by PGW:
"Thousands of Years Ago"

18. OH, MY DEAR!

Opening Night: November 27, 1918, Princess Theatre, New York.
Total Performances: 189
Book: Guy Bolton & P. G. Wodehouse
Lyrics: P. G. Wodehouse
Music: Louis Hirsch
Retitled: ASK DAD
Song Lyrics by PGW:
"Ask Dad" / "Boat Song" (see also #13) / "Childhood Days" / "City of Dreams"
"Come Where Nature Calls" / "I Love a Musical Comedy Show"
"I Shall Be All Right Now" / "I Wonder Whether I've Loved You All My Life"
"I'd Ask No More" / "If They Ever Parted Me From You"
"It Sorta Makes a Fellow Stop and Think"
"The Land Where Journeys End and Dreams Come True"
"Now and Then But Not All the Time"
"Phoebe Snow" / "Try Again" / "You Never Know"

19. THE ROSE OF CHINA

Opening Night: November 25, 1919, Lyric Theatre, New York.
Total Performances: 47
Book: Guy Bolton
Lyrics: P. G. Wodehouse
Music: Armand Vecsey
Song Lyrics by PGW:
"Bunny Dear" / "College Spirit"
"Down on the Banks of the Subway"
"The Legend of the Tea Tree"
"Love is a Wonderful Feeling"
"Lovely Ladies" / "Never More" / "Our Chinese Bungalow"
"Proposals" / "Romeo and Juliet" / "Spirit of the Drum" / "Tao Loved His Li"
"When You Are In China" / "Yale" / "Yesterday"

20. SALLY

Opening Night: December 21, 1920, New Amsterdam Theatre, New York.
Total Performances: 570
Book: Guy Bolton
Lyrics: Clifford Grey & P. G. Wodehouse
Music: Jerome Kern
Song Lyrics by PGW:
"The Church Round the Corner"
"You Can't Keep a Good Girl Down" (Joan of Arc)
English Opening Night: September 10, 1921, Winter Garden Theatre, London.
Total Performances: 383

21. THE BLUE MAZURKA

Written: 1921, never produced.
Book: Guy Bolton & P. G. Wodehouse
Lyrics: P. G. Wodehouse

Music: Franz Lehar & Jerome Kern
Song Lyrics by PGW:
"The Hickey Doo" / "If You've Nothing Else To Do"

22. THE GOLDEN MOTH

Opening Night: October 5, 1921, Adelphi Theatre, London.
Total Performances: 281
Book: Fred Thompson & P. G. Wodehouse
Lyrics: P. G. Wodehouse
Music: Ivor Novello
Song Lyrics by PGW:
"Dartmoor Days" / "Dear Eyes That Shine" / "Fairy Prince"
"Give Me a Thought Now and Then"
"If I Ever Lost You" / "Lonely Soldier" / "My Girl"
"Nuts in May" / "Romance is Calling" / "We've Had a Busy Day"

23. PAT (THE GIBSON GIRL)

Written: 1922, never produced.
Book: Guy Bolton & P. G. Wodehouse
Lyrics: P. G. Wodehouse & Billy Rose
Music: Vincent Youmans

24. THE CABARET GIRL

Opening Night: September 19, 1922, Winter Garden Theatre, London.
Total Performances: 462
Book: George Grossmith & P. G. Wodehouse
Lyrics: P. G. Wodehouse
Music: Jerome Kern
Song Lyrics by PGW:
"First Rose of Summer" / "Journey's End"
"London, Dear Old London" / "Looking All Over For You"
"Mr. Gravvins—Mr. Gripps" / "Nerves" (see also #15)
"Oriental Dreams" / "The Pergola Patrol" / "Shimmy With Me"
"Those Days Are Gone Forever" / "Whoop-De-Oodle-Do"
"You Want the Best Seats, We Have 'Em"

♦ 25. THE BEAUTY PRIZE

Opening Night: September 5, 1923, Winter Garden Theatre, London.
Total Performances: 214
Book: George Grossmith & P. G. Wodehouse
Lyrics: P. G. Wodehouse
Music: Jerome Kern
Song Lyrics by PGW:
"Cottage in Kent" / "Honeymoon Isle" / "I'm a Prize"
"It's a Long Long Day" / "Joy Bells"
"Meet Me Down on Main Street" / "Moon Love" / "Non-Stop Dancing"
"You Can't Make Love By Wireless"

26. SITTING PRETTY

Opening Night: April 8, 1924, Fulton Theatre, New York.

Total Performances: 95
Book: Guy Bolton & P. G. Wodehouse
Lyrics: P. G. Wodehouse
Music: Jerome Kern
Song Lyrics by PGW:
"All You Need Is a Girl" / "Bongo on the Congo"
"Days Gone By" / "Dear Old Fashioned Prison of Mine"
"A Desert Island" / "The Enchanted Train" / "Is This Not a Lovely Spot?"
"Mr. & Mrs. Rorer" / "The Polka Dot" / "Shadow of the Moon"
"Shufflin Sam" / "Sitting Pretty" / "There Isn't One Girl"
"Tulip Time in Sing Sing" / "Worries" / "A Year From Today"

27. HEARTS AND DIAMONDS

Opening Night: June 1, 1926, Strand Theatre, London.
Total Performances: 46
Book: Graham John & P. G. Wodehouse
Lyrics: P. G. Wodehouse & Graham John
Music: Bruno Granichstaedten

28. OH, KAY!

Opening Night: November 8, 1926, Imperial Theatre, New York.
Total Performances: 256
Book: Guy Bolton & P. G. Wodehouse
Lyrics: Ira Gershwin
Music: George Gershwin
English Opening Night: September 21, 1927, His Majesty's Theatre, London.
Total Performances: 213

29. THE NIGHTINGALE

Opening Night: January 3, 1927, Jolson Theatre, New York.
Total Performances: 96
Book: Guy Bolton & P. G. Wodehouse
Lyrics: P. G. Wodehouse
Music: Armand Vecsey
Song Lyrics by PGW:
"Breakfast in Bed" / "May Moon" / "Two Little Ships"

30. SHOW BOAT

Opening Night: December 27, 1927, Ziegfeld Theatre, New York.
Total Performances: 572
Book: Oscar Hammerstein 2nd
Lyrics: Oscar Hammerstein 2nd & P. G. Wodehouse
Music: Jerome Kern
English Opening Night: May 3, 1928, Drury Lane Theatre, London.
Total Performances: 350
Song Lyric by PGW:
"Bill" (see also #14)

31. ROSALIE

Opening Night: January 10, 1928, New Amsterdam Theatre, New York.
Total Performances: 335

Book: Guy Bolton & Bill McGuire
Lyrics: Ira Gershwin & P. G. Wodehouse
Music: George Gershwin & Sigmund Romberg
Song Lyrics by PGW:
"Hussars March" / "Oh Gee! Oh Joy!" / "Say So"
"West Point Song" / "Why Must We Always Be Dreaming?"

32. THE THREE MUSKETEERS

Opening Night: March 13, 1928, Lyric Theatre, New York.
Total Performances: 318
Book: Bill McGuire
Lyrics: P. G. Wodehouse & Clifford Grey
Music: Rudolf Friml
Song Lyrics by PGW:
"March of the Musketeers" / "Your Eyes"
English Opening Night: March 28, 1930, Drury Lane Theatre, London
Total Performances: 242

33. ANYTHING GOES

Opening Night: November 21, 1934, Alvin Theatre, New York.
Total Performances: 420
Book: Guy Bolton & P. G. Wodehouse
Lyrics: Cole Porter
Music: Cole Porter
English Opening Night: June 14, 1935, Palace Theatre, London.
Total Performances: 250

INDEX